COLLABORATION FOR IMPACT

LESSONS FROM THE FIELD

COLLABORATION FOR IMPACT

LESSONS FROM THE FIELD

JOHN R. BUTCHER AND
DAVID J. GILCHRIST

Australian
National
University

PRESS

Published by ANU Press
The Australian National University
Acton ACT 2601, Australia
Email: anupress@anu.edu.au

Available to download for free at press.anu.edu.au

ISBN (print): 9781760463960
ISBN (online): 9781760463977

WorldCat (print): 1197587584
WorldCat (online): 1197587322

DOI: 10.22459/CFI.2020

Cover design and layout by ANU Press

CONTENTS

ABBREVIATIONS

ACN	Anglesea Community Network
AIFS	Australian Institute for Family Studies
ANROWS	Australia's National Research Organisation for Women's Safety
ANZSOG	Australia and New Zealand School of Government
APSC	Australian Public Service Commission
BAU	business as usual
CAP	Children's Action Plan
CBEM	Community-Based Emergency Management
CGR	collaborative governance regime
CQ	collaborative intelligence
DHHS	Department of Health and Human Services
EMV	Emergency Management Victoria
GOC	Global Obesity Centre
GSC Change	Great South Coast Change
ICC	interagency collaborative capacity
IPSP	independent public services provider
MOU	memorandum of understanding
NAO	network administrative organisation
NHMRC	National Health and Medical Research Council
NPM	new public management
PCP	Primary Care Partnership

SLO   social licence to operate
TOR   terms of reference
WHO STOPS   Whole of Systems Trial of Prevention Strategies
                for Childhood Obesity

BOXES AND TABLES

ACKNOWLEDGEMENTS

The origins of this project go back to a one-day workshop in 2015 jointly convened by the Australia and New Zealand School of Government (ANZSOG) and the Curtin Not-for-profit Initiative and held at The Australian National University (ANU), where a wide range of invited speakers probed the challenges of working across sectoral boundaries. The presentations given that day were collected in the edited book *The Three Sector Solution*, which was published in 2016 by ANU Press.

That book was the work of many hands, as is the present volume.

First, we would like to thank ANZSOG and the John Curtin Institute of Public Policy (JCIPP) at Curtin University for funding the research on which this book is based, following the establishment of this project by the Curtin Not-for-profit Initiative. Special mention goes to Professor John Phillimore for taking on the role of principal investigator and providing critical administrative support for the project, and to Dr Sophie Yates, currently a Postdoctoral Fellow at UNSW Canberra, who provided a consistent and reliable point of liaison with ANZSOG. Special thanks also go to Professor John Wanna, who, in his role as the Sir John Bunting Chair of Public Administration at ANU and as an associate investigator on this project, gave moral, intellectual and material support when it mattered most.

We are grateful to the members of the informal reference group established to provide advice and feedback during the development, implementation and analysis phases of this project, and to those who attended a one-day executive workshop at the ANU to discuss our preliminary findings. Our thanks go to Professor Robyn Keast, Melina Morrison, Gillian McFee, Helen McDevitt, Tessa Boyd-Caine, Jane Clifton-Bassett, Tim Crosier, Viviene Twyford, Associate Professor

Gemma Carey, Jade Hart, Catherine Althaus and Lachlan McKenzie. Isi Unikowski deserves special mention for his thoughtful contributions on the day and for producing a comprehensive record of the discussion.

We offer our thanks to a number of others without whose vital assistance this project might have faltered. These include Leza Duplock (JCIPP), who provided vital administrative support; Sam Vincent (ANZSOG/ANU), who acted as liaison with ANU Press; Grace Rosario (Not-for-profits UWA) for her work on earlier drafts; Carolyn Williams, who did a fantastic job transcribing the interviews; and Jan Borrie, who professionally and capably copyedited the manuscript. If we have missed anyone, we apologise.

Finally, we are grateful to everyone who participated in interviews and facilitated introductions to collaboration leaders here in Australia and in New Zealand. It was a privilege to engage in stimulating discussions with such intelligent, enthusiastic, committed and capable professionals and community leaders. This book draws heavily on their wisdom and experience. We only hope this book does them justice.

John R. Butcher
David J. Gilchrist
September 2020

FOREWORD

This book provides readers with an in-depth and comprehensive examination of the myriad issues surrounding collaboration undertaken in the pursuit of public purposes. John Butcher and David Gilchrist provide a wealth of information and insightful commentary on the voluminous literature on collaboration. Refreshingly, they also present direct commentary from organisational and community practitioners in five original case studies involving collaboration, reflecting on their experiences and the challenges facing them at both an interorganisational and an interpersonal level.

The book allows the reader to take a deep dive into this fascinating subject; but if you prefer a quick dip, you can do that, too, by turning to the 'practice considerations' that are presented at the end of each chapter. These should prove to be invaluable aids to individuals and organisations wishing to do collaboration better in future.

I am writing this foreword under the conditions of social distancing in a time of global pandemic. The COVID-19 crisis is driving home the fact that relationships are important and that the quality of cooperation, coordination and collaboration between nation-states, corporations, non-governmental organisations, institutions and citizens will be critical in meeting the social, health and economic challenges confronting us.

In some respects, social distancing might be regarded as antithetical to the kinds of collaborative practice described in this book. After all, one of the things emphasised by the research is the importance of the interpersonal dimension of collaboration. The many interviews conducted with practitioners in Australia and New Zealand reinforced the fact that collaborations embody relationships between people rather than between organisations. Although organisations provide the authorisation and resources that enable collaboration to occur, collaborations are dependent on the values, aptitudes, skills and motivations of people.

Superficially, one might expect the strict application of social distancing to cause collaborative efforts to grind to a halt. Internationally, there are worrying signs of a resurgence of national self-sufficiency and a retreat from international cooperation.

However, in other respects, we may find that the COVID-19 crisis was a positive disruptor. People are finding ways to enable collaboration to occur. At work and at home, they are increasingly turning to digital technologies to collaborate via virtual conferencing platforms—and even enjoying it.

A key observation that runs through this book is that collaboration is often pursued almost as a last-ditch effort to find solutions to wicked problems. In other words, when traditional programmatic, siloed, bureaucratic frameworks either fail or cease to be effective, collaboration is invoked as a means to harness the capabilities of multiple actors. Collaboration is seen as an answer to incoherence and fragmentation.

Sometimes, collaboration swims against the tide of prevailing norms, institutional legacies and habits of mind. Recently in Australia, for example, Commonwealth and state political leaders have formed a national cabinet to collaborate and make significant policy decisions at breakneck speed. A conservative federal government has reached out to trade unions to find agreed solutions to social and economic problems exposed by the coronavirus.

We see the competition regulator working with the supermarket duopoly to ensure continuation of the supply of basic goods and the equitable distribution of life's essentials. Private businesses and corporations have agreed to share information, intellectual property, technology and resources to deliver such things as personal protective equipment and medical treatments. Citizens and community organisations are coalescing to deliver solutions for people who are particularly vulnerable to the effects of this crisis. All these efforts evoke the spirit of collaborative purpose.

Of course, collaboration for public purposes was a mantra in public administration long before the COVID-19 crisis. The research on which this book is based was carried out in a pre-COVID-19 era. That does not, however, invalidate its findings and recommendations. Rather, the current global pandemic demonstrates the importance of collaborative approaches. Indeed, the necessity of collaboration—which spans the boundaries between institutions, programs, systems and communities—is amply demonstrated.

In a pre-COVID-19 era, collaborative approaches might have been urged on frontline practitioners without any clear guidance as to how to go about it, and with only rhetorical justification to embrace it. The pandemic has, or should have, cemented in the consciousness of public policy practitioners the absolute necessity for collaboration.

In my opinion, John Butcher and David Gilchrist have forensically examined the key elements of effective collaborative practice and have provided clear, comprehensible and, most importantly, actionable guidance for anyone contemplating collaborative endeavour for public purposes. I would also draw to the reader's attention that, although the cases selected for study were drawn from what might be broadly termed the social policy domain and involve collaborations that are led by the public sector, most—if not all—of the observations and practical guidance are highly transferrable to other policy domains and sectors.

I am pleased to have had the opportunity, in my role as Executive Director of the John Curtin Institute of Public Policy (JCIPP), to support the research on which this book is based. The JCIPP hosted the project and matched funding provided by ANZSOG. This was entirely consistent with Curtin University being the face of ANZSOG in Western Australia. We welcome and thank ANZSOG for its support.

While Butcher and Gilchrist will readily concede that this book does not represent the 'last word' on collaboration, reading it will certainly be of great value to policy practitioners in any sector seeking informed practical guidance and insight into the whys and wherefores of collaboration. I thoroughly recommend it to you.

John Phillimore
April 2020

1

INTRODUCTION

What is collaboration?

Collaboration has become a word du jour in public policy circles in recent years—one that has become well embedded in the policy rhetoric and organisational narratives of the public and not-for-profit sectors. We are by now well accustomed to hearing policymakers and policy practitioners of all stripes talking about 'wicked problems' and invoking the need to marshal the capabilities of diverse individuals, organisations and sectors. And, indeed, sometimes this happens, and sometimes it leads to amazing results. Often, however, it does not happen or it happens but cannot be sustained.

'Collaboration' refers to any joint activity by two or more parties for the purpose of linking or sharing information, resources, activities and capabilities to achieve aims that no single party could have achieved separately (Bryson et al. 2006: 44; Bardach 1998: 8). Collaboration can occur in any domain and at any scale. For the purposes of this book, we are specifically concerned with collaborations for public purposes— in other words, collaborations designed to achieve public policy ends, particularly in relation to social problems.

It is our contention that collaboration—appropriately conceived, designed, implemented and governed—offers a means to break down organisational, policy and sectoral 'silos' that impede the effective treatment of problems. However, there are multiple impediments to collaborative action in public policy spaces dominated by large, hierarchical and bureaucratic organisations with distinct institutional and administrative histories.

In the following chapters, we introduce readers to a range of activities that underpin collaborative action and the personal skills and attributes exhibited by effective collaborators. Although these are important—and even vital—factors for effective collaboration, it is equally, if not more, important to consider the *collaborative capacity* of the organisations, entities or systems party to collaborative action. This is what Eugene Bardach refers to as 'interagency collaborative capacity' or ICC.

According to Bardach (1998: 20–21), ICC has *objective* and *subjective* components. The *objective* components of interagency action include formal agreements, personnel, budgetary and other resources, whereas the *subjective* components are mainly factors such as belief in the legitimacy and the desirability of collaborative action, the readiness to act on this belief and trust in those whose cooperation is essential for success (Bardach 1998: 22–23). For Bardach (1998: 22), the subjective components of collaboration are even more important than the objective components in that they serve to reinforce a collaborative *ethos* without which collaborative capacity is significantly compromised.

Although it is easy to *talk* about collaboration—and public sector managers in Australia and elsewhere *have* been talking about it for at least two decades—it is hard to *do*. There is a tendency in some settings for policymakers and decision-makers to enjoin frontline workers to 'go forth and collaborate' while paying scant attention to the collaborative capacity inherent in their organisations and operational systems. It is our aim to shed light on the objective *and* subjective components of collaboration by closely studying a number of initiatives in Australia and New Zealand that claim to place collaborative capacity at their heart. It is our hope that lessons drawn from the real-world experiences and personal observations of people serving on the collaboration front line will provide guidance and inspiration for those who are contemplating collaborative action.

Why collaborate?

As observed by John Bryson and his colleagues at the Humphrey School of Public Affairs at the University of Minnesota, 'collaboration is not an easy answer to hard problems but a hard answer to hard problems' (Bryson et al. 2009: 14). Even so, enthusiasm for collaboration has not dimmed in contemporary policy discourses despite its inherent difficulty. The ideal—or, as Australian policy scholar Janine O'Flynn (2008) has suggested, the 'aspirational ideal'—of collaboration retains an almost talismanic quality, evoking notions of reciprocity, social capital, network governance, shared value and collective impact.

It is widely accepted that collaboration across portfolio, organisational, programmatic and sectoral boundaries allows the capacities and capabilities of multiple stakeholders to be brought to bear on complex social problems (McInerney 2015: 295). Policymakers, policy thinkers, commentators and policy practitioners of all kinds extol the virtues of collaboration and avow its transformative potential. This is particularly true in social policy domains where it is widely accepted that many socioeconomic problems facing policymakers cannot be addressed by any one sector or organisation (Austin and Seitanidi 2012: 727).

However, the application of complex multiparty solutions to social problems also means placing greater priority on understanding and improving interorganisational and cross-sectoral relationships and taking more cooperative or participatory approaches (Suárez 2011: 308). For many organisations, this represents a departure from past practice. Acting collaboratively does not come easily or naturally, especially in the public sector, where longstanding incentives reinforce siloed behaviours (O'Leary 2014: 19).

The collaboration challenge

Collaboration depends less on bureaucratic mechanisms based on control, hierarchy and chains of command and more on relational mechanisms such as trust, shared values, implicit standards and consultation (Favoreu et al. 2016: 440). Unfortunately, cultural barriers and longstanding organisational routines often present significant obstacles to making the kinds of adaptive changes necessary to forge more collaborative ways of working (Favoreu et al. 2016: 449; Keast and Brown 2006: 51–52).

A 2012 report by the Australian Public Service Commission characterised collaboration as 'a win–win view of' problem-solving and 'collaborative strategies' as 'the best approach to tackling wicked problems which require behavioural change as part of their solution' (APSC 2012: 10). At its best, the report said, collaboration can lead to 'higher stakeholder commitment, more comprehensive and effective solutions, and fewer resources having to be used by any one stakeholder'. In the worst cases, however, 'collaboration can end poorly—dialogue can turn into conflict, hardened positions and stalemate' (APSC 2012: 10).

While advocating that public sector organisations foster a culture that encourages collaboration and engagement, the Commission's report offered the following cautionary note:

> It is clear that existing public sector institutions and structures were, by and large, not designed with a primary goal of supporting collaborative inter-organisational work. It can be challenging enough to implement governance arrangements and foster cultures that facilitate collaboration across internal organisational boundaries within hierarchical, vertically structured organisations. (APSC 2012: 17)

This observation rests on an implicit recognition that the Australian policy landscape is one in which governmental, organisational, programmatic and sectoral silos have proved to be remarkably persistent. This is a legacy that presents formidable barriers to sustainable collaboration.

'Are we there yet?'

Over a decade ago, Janine O'Flynn (2008) pondered whether we were witnessing a 'collaborative turn' in public policy or merely 'the latest fad to penetrate the Public Service'? Interrogating the 'rhetoric and reality' of collaboration discourses in Australian public policy, O'Flynn (2008: 184) proposed:

> Collaboration has become so central to our conversations about public policy that few see the need to either define it or unpack what it means: collaboration has truly become part of the Zeitgeist.

She went on to conclude that, at best, 'we could be at the beginning of some evolutionary process that will propel us, in time, towards more genuinely collaborative approaches' (O'Flynn 2008: 191).

Seven years later, Australian policy scholar Helen Dickinson (2016) concluded that, while there *is* evidence of a shift away from *transactional* governance towards *relational* governance, we have yet to fully understand the implications for the kinds of skills and abilities that public servants will need to operate within more *hybridised* forms of public sector governance.

Organisational, programmatic and jurisdictional silos represent major barriers to the dissemination of knowledge and good practices. In the public sector, the reactive nature of public policy often stands in the way of investigating better practices, properly documenting the development and implementation of programs and services or sharing learnings among organisations or between jurisdictions.

At the same time, competitive pressures inherent in transaction-based service delivery impede the diffusion of learnings in the not-for-profit and private sectors because such information is regarded as commercially sensitive. In addition, traditional control strategies used to govern intra-organisational information systems often fall short of the requirements of cross-boundary efforts (Pardo et al. 2006) owing to barriers to information-sharing such as legislative restrictions, the absence of a specific legal framework or protocols and/or the lack of technical interoperability (Lips et al. 2011).

The language of collaboration

It is commonplace for policy practitioners in both the public and the not-for-profit sectors to use the word 'collaboration' in a generic sense to denote a range of practices such as cooperation, coordination, partnership, networking, co-design, coproduction and information exchange. And, while one might reasonably expect each of these practices to be present to some degree in any collaboration, they do not necessarily amount to collaboration in and of themselves.

When it comes to collaboration, clarity of language is important because different understandings and expectations can lead to confusion and frustration, and potentially to dysfunctional or suboptimal outcomes (Keast 2016a: 39–40). It is useful, therefore, to clearly distinguish between three categories of interorganisational relationships:

1. *Cooperative relationships* that involve only a sharing of information and/or expertise, and in which each participant remains independent and interacts only when necessary to harmonise their efforts.
2. *Coordinative relationships* in which parties interact and plan with each other to better align what they are already doing while remaining independent and continuing to operate in their usual manner.
3. *Collaborative relationships* based on a recognition of interdependence and accompanied by a mutual commitment to working in new ways with the other members of the network to effect systems changes (Mandell et al. 2017: 329; Keast 2016a: 31).

Fewer silos, more listening and better skills

When asked to speculate about what the public sector might look like in 10 years, the head of the Victorian Department of Premier and Cabinet, Chris Eccles, said he expects to see a public sector that is focused on outcomes, less siloed and portfolio-driven and more reliant on collaboration, cooperation and co-design (Eccles 2016). A key reason it has proved so difficult to break down public sector agency and programmatic silos after a decade or more of talking about 'joined-up' government has to do with the way programs and services are funded through government budget processes (Chief Minister, Treasury and Economic Development Directorate 2015).

Governments increasingly accept that complex social problems require a spectrum of responses. Collaboration can provide spaces in which top-down and bottom-up approaches can meet, new adaptive solutions can be tested and risks can be equitably shared.

Meaningful engagement with communities of interest needs to be normalised as an integral element of the authorising environment and, where possible, steeped in principles of coproduction and co-design. This will require a process of transformative change in public sector culture, accompanied by the embedding of concrete, tangible disciplines within a reconceived authorising environment that supports, incentivises and rewards engagement, collaboration, innovation and experimentation.

Contemporary public policy implicitly and explicitly acknowledges the interests of multiple stakeholders. It is incumbent on public managers to listen to service users and community groups, to mobilise collective resources and knowledge in the public interest and to nurture coproductive behaviours (Sicilia et al. 2016). Unfortunately, the collaborative design and delivery of public services face fundamental challenges, such as an insistence on approaches that mimic 'the architectures and practices of private sector organisations framed by business cases, target-based measurement and return on investment tools' (Wilson et al. 2016: 3).

Praxis leads policy?

There is abundant circumstantial evidence that collaborative practice is often the child of necessity—informed more by the pragmatic decisions of people exercising their initiative at the coalface and colluding across organisational boundaries by creatively exploiting the blind spots in their authorising environments than by adherence to policy edicts. As Wilson et al. (2016: 2) observe: 'In the messy reality of public management, the practices of collaboration have often run ahead of the policies of collaboration, leading to challenging relational issues between erstwhile partners.'

Such a view is reinforced by Keast (2016b), who examines the various markers of successful (and unsuccessful) collaboration between government agencies and not-for-profit organisations. She points out that, while 'authentic' collaboration is unfamiliar territory to many, far from being a 'black box', there is ample knowledge on which we might draw to deliver successful collaborations. According to Keast (2016b: 172), 'successful collaboration relies heavily on good processes and their implementation'. She identifies a number of key processes that are essential to build on existing relationships and nurture new ones, establish trust, agree on what to work on together and *how* to work together, build new leadership capacities and manage conflicts (Keast 2016b: 172).

Keast (2016b: 169) notes that collaborative work is an inherently complex and dynamic endeavour that defies 'prescriptive recipes for implementation' and embodies diverse macro-level processes in the form of administrative structures and procedures, as well as what she refers to as 'micro-relational processes' in the form of 'small, but powerful actions' that help to 'generate the space for reciprocity and mutual gain to emerge' (p. 170). Importantly, Keast (2016b: 172) says that the implementation of the processes 'has to be authentic and follow the intent of the collaboration itself'.

It is crucial to bring appropriate forms of leadership to collaborative endeavours in multi-stakeholder settings. As Crosby and Bryson (2005: 184) observe:

> A central challenge for leaders is to bring diverse stakeholders together in shared-power arrangements in which they can pool information, other resources and activities around a common purpose. The focus should be on key stakeholders—those most affected by a social need or public problem or who have important resources for meeting the need.

A flawed service delivery architecture

In many respects, the current level of interest in collaboration is not just a response to problem complexity, but also a reaction to increasing *system* complexity. In 2016, reports to the Commonwealth Government by the Productivity Commission and the consultancy firm KPMG drew attention to systemic barriers to collaboration that are, to some extent, hardwired into Australia's service delivery architectures.

The Productivity Commission made some sobering observations about the shortcomings of Australia's service delivery systems. These are neatly encapsulated in the following quote:

> Governments seldom take advantage of providers' experience and expertise in program delivery when designing systems of service provision. Instead, programs are designed by government agencies that are often remote from the realities of 'what works'. Often what looks good on paper does not translate to the real world, and contracts specify approaches to service delivery that are inconsistent with achieving high quality services, equity or efficiency. (Productivity Commission 2016: 31–32)

Separately, a report provided by KPMG to the Commonwealth Attorney-General's Department suggested that—despite the potential to use competition to influence cost, quality and productivity and get better value for money—a purely market-based model might lead to fragmented services, reduced accountability, impaired coordination and disincentives for collaboration (KPMG 2016).

Repeated efforts to reform the bureaucratic, administrative state throughout the twentieth century have largely focused on making government bureaucracy more effective and efficient in its operations (Forrer et al. 2014: 214–15). In the 1980s, new public management (NPM) promoted greater creativity, flexibility and innovation in approaches to the delivery of public goods and services. NPM sought to 'reinvent' government by reducing or redefining the role of the state, encouraging privatisation and competition, using private sector expertise, becoming more customer-focused, decentralising authority, becoming more outcome-oriented and creating more transparency and accountability for results (Forrer et al. 2014: 217). What NPM did *not* do was challenge the basic presumptions of the bureaucratic model (Forrer et al. 2014: 216).

It is important to acknowledge that the bureaucratic model of public sector leadership and management has served well in providing standardised public services to large numbers of people (Forrer et al. 2014). However, the bureaucratic model may be unable to deal with complex problems in public policy that present the following characteristics:

- They are multijurisdictional, crossing local, state and even international borders.
- They are multi-programmatic, often involving several types of government programs and agencies.
- They do not lend themselves to command-and-control types of solutions.
- Citizens primarily interact with private or not-for-profit organisations and only indirectly with government.
- Leadership is diffused and must be coordinated to achieve best results.
- Roles are determined by knowledge and ability, not by positional authority in a hierarchy (Forrer et al. 2014: 209–10).

Collaboration is hard work

An important reason collaborative practice is not 'settled' is that it is very hard to do. Collaboration is a complex and resource-intensive exercise and many attempts at collaboration never get off the ground. A number of key success factors can be distilled from a survey of the collaboration literature. In general, collaborations succeed where the following characteristics are present:

1. There are prior structural relationships between partners.
2. There are clear objectives and partners agree about the problem they are trying to solve.
3. There is a supportive authorising environment and formal authority is conferred by powerful sponsors.
4. The collaboration has skilled, committed leaders who use formal and informal authority to resolve imbalances of power and influence and establish mutual understanding, respect and trust.
5. There are effective governance structures with final authority for decision-making.
6. The collaboration follows a detailed implementation plan and adheres to agreed rules of operation.

7. Accountability and evaluation processes are built in and adapted to the specific needs of the collaboration.

8. The collaboration has a public profile and celebrates its accomplishments.

Significantly, collaboration requires an authorising environment that encourages ICC (Bardach 1998). Conversely, if particular models of collaboration are mandated and prescribed from the top down, there is a risk that the collaboration will become just another requirement that needs to be acquitted and reported (Pell 2016).

Which model of collaboration?

Collaboration entails choices about the model of collaboration to be employed and the kinds of instruments and governance frameworks that best serve the needs of the collaboration and the partner agencies. Although many collaborations involve some type of formal agreement— for example, a contract or memorandum of understanding (MOU)—the achievement of shared purposes requires levels of cooperation and trust that cannot be enforced through a legal document alone (Forrer et al. 2014: 276). Trust exists where there are clear expectations and confidence that what has been committed to will be done. However, organisational, interpersonal and political complexities present potential obstacles to building trust across sectoral, jurisdictional, organisational and domain boundaries and, although trust can take a long time to build up, it can be quickly lost (Edwards et al. 2012).

As a starting point, it is important to understand that in cross-sector collaborations, public managers have considerably less control over their partners than in purely transactional contracting (Forrer et al. 2014: 276). While cross-sector collaborations require flexibility on the part of public managers, flexibility does not mean that standards are not set, expectations are not established or outcomes are not monitored (Forrer et al. 2014: 259).

Forrer et al. (2014) describe four types of *cross-sector* collaboration:

1. *Collaborative contracting*: Collaborative contracts are a complex form of contracting that generally exhibits one or more of the following characteristics: incomplete specifications of expectations; they are relational and involve aspects of governance that extend beyond the formal or written terms of agreements; and they are generally long term in nature, with repeated interactions (Forrer et al. 2014: 59).

2. *Partnerships*: In which public officials engage a private sector or not-for-profit organisation in the joint production of public goods or services and certain aspects of production and service delivery are shared, such as planning, design specifications, risk and financing.

3. *Networks*: In which public managers use formal and informal structures to allow governmental and non-governmental actors to work interdependently.

4. *Independent public services providers (IPSPs)*: An emergent type of collaboration involving the creation of self-directed entities comprising businesses, non-profit organisations and governmental units that collaborate in the production or delivery of public goods or services but operate outside the sphere of government control and oversight (Forrer et al. 2014: 18–19).

It should be noted that typologies such as the one presented above are not uncontested. McGregor-Lowndes and Turnour (2003), for example, have critiqued governments' use of 'partnership rhetoric', noting that 'partnership' has specific meanings in commercial law—especially in terms of the fiduciary relationship between partners—that are not necessarily reflected in instruments such as service provision agreements between governments and not-for-profit service providers.

Origins of this book

The research on which this book is based grew out of a one-day workshop held at The Australian National University in 2015. Entitled 'Cross-Sector Working for Complex Problems: Beyond the Rhetoric', the workshop's aim was to promote understanding of cross-sector approaches to complex policy problems at a practice level. The workshop brought together policy practitioners in the public and not-for-profit sectors and academic researchers to elucidate the promise and challenges of collaboration across sectoral boundaries and resulted in the book *The Three Sector Solution: Delivering public policy in collaboration with not-for-profits and business*, published by ANU Press and the Australia and New Zealand School of Government (ANZSOG).

A clear message from the workshop was that collaboration is 'easier said than done'—a conclusion emphatically supported by the research literature. Following the publication of *The Three Sector Solution*, it was decided to develop a grounded research project to identify the core elements of good collaborative practice. Our research adds empirical weight to an emerging Australian literature on collaboration for public purposes (Keast 2016b; Alford and O'Flynn 2012; Alford 2009) and provides an evidential base for the adaptations required of public officials, executives of not-for-profits and their boards of management.

The cases

The research employed a collective case study approach. Data collection occurred principally through semi-structured interviews with key actors involved in the inception, design and implementation of the collaborative initiatives under study.

The five cases selected for study exhibit considerable diversity. They operate in different jurisdictions, involve different levels of government and operate at different geographical scales; they each have distinct institutional histories and span a number of policy domains; and they are governed with differing degrees of formality. Their aims and purposes include:

1. the development of a comprehensive national practice framework for the prevention of violence against women and their children
2. facilitating community-led emergency management planning and resilience
3. supporting the reintegration of offenders into the community on release from a custodial sentence
4. community-led strategies to reduce and prevent childhood obesity
5. coordinating pre-emptive multidisciplinary intervention for children at risk of formal notification.

Each of the individuals selected for interview played a significant part in the initiation, design and/or implementation of the collaborative initiative. They included senior executives, officials, frontline implementers, thought leaders and the members of backbone/governance groups.

Organisation of the book

Chapter 2: A new business as usual

In Chapter 2, we consider collaboration as a potential precursor to a new 'business as usual' (BAU). In essence, collaborative strategies are often pursued once it has been recognised that traditional programmatic approaches have demonstrably failed. The logic of collaboration hinges on a recognition that no single organisation or sector acting on its own has the capacity or capability to solve complex policy problems. Complex, or wicked, problems occur at the interstices of policy domains and formal accountabilities. This is particularly true for each of the cases investigated for this book. While collaboration makes intuitive sense, it is often 'countercultural' insofar as its success rests on a set of skills, behaviours and processes that represent a departure from accepted 'legacy' practices (Hanleybrown et al. 2014: 2).

Collaboration often entails an agenda for change—change in the nature of relationships, networks, governance, accountability and ways of working. Leading and sustaining change processes are difficult, even when the logic of change is broadly accepted. There is a tendency for government and social-purpose organisations to employ the language, or rhetoric, of collaboration without demonstrating a commitment to the cultural and operational adjustments required to collaborate.

Collaborative approaches can sometimes meet internal resistance in partner agencies, especially when the practices and behaviours required for collaboration are perceived to transgress operational rules and protocols or are seen as a threat to organisational or personal authority and influence. In part, internal resistance to collaboration derives from scepticism or apprehension about the impact of collaboration: 'What if it fails?'

Chapter 3: Designing impactful collaboration

A core purpose of collaboration is to bring diverse capabilities to bear on complex problems that are beyond the ability of any single organisation to solve on its own. Clarity about the expected impact of collaboration is critical. However, collaborative approaches sometimes represent a major departure from traditional, siloed, programmatic service delivery architectures. For this reason, and because collaboration operates outside the usual incentive structures that apply in primary operating spaces, collaborative strategies are sometimes subject to enhanced scrutiny. Collaborations, therefore, might operate with a heightened sense of urgency concerning tangible demonstrations of impact. Clear pathways to impact are essential to initiating collaboration and a strong evidential base is important for sustaining the confidence and ongoing support of partners and other stakeholders.

In Chapter 3, we profile the experience of one of our cases, the Whole of Systems Trial of Prevention Strategies for Childhood Obesity (WHO STOPS), which has explicitly modelled its approach on the collective impact model. Demonstrations of impact, however, are often beset by problems of definition and measurement, as well as practical problems, such as overcoming the lack of interoperability of business systems or the reluctance of data custodians to share information. In addition, the executives of partner organisations can sometimes be impatient for results; however, collaborations typically take two to three years to mature. Sometimes, too, impact is narrowly defined to exclude important indicators of important, and necessary, organisational and behavioural adaptations.

Chapter 4: Collaborative intelligence and organisational intelligence

In Chapter 4, we describe the nature and importance of collaborative intelligence (CQ), which refers to the mindset necessary for collaboration to flourish and embodies a set of values, behaviours and processes that are fundamentally 'relational' in nature, rather than 'transactional'. CQ implicitly accepts the centrality of relationships as providing the foundation for collaborative action. Moreover, CQ is based on an implicit recognition that *people* collaborate and, therefore, interpersonal relationships are important building blocks of collaborative action. Therefore, it is essential that those tasked with making collaboration happen bring appropriate aptitudes and skills to the table. These include a preparedness to listen and consider diverse views, a willingness to compromise and engage in shared decision-making and an understanding of systems and the environment in which collaboration occurs.

Although individuals might bring CQ to collaboration, whether or not CQ is rewarded or reinforced is dependent on *organisational intelligence*, which determines the nature of the authorising environment (Yolles 2005). Thus, it is not sufficient to reflect solely on the qualities individual actors bring to collaboration; it is essential to also consider the characteristics of authorising environments in which they work so we might assess what *authority* they have to collaborate.

Chapter 5: Designing the collaboration and its operational framework

It is important to ensure that the collaboration model is fit for purpose. That said, collaboration is not always the answer and can sometimes look very much like a solution in search of a problem.

In Chapter 5, we discuss the key elements of collaboration design. In many respects, all collaborations are unique. They are highly context dependent; collaboration partners bring different institutional and administrative histories to the table; the presenting problems they seek to address are multifactorial in nature; and stakeholders have diverse perspectives and interests. Collaborative strategies need to be built on a comprehensive understanding of the presenting problem(s) and the social, political and policy ecologies in which they arise.

It is important to identify the things on which collaboration partners agree *and* the things on which they disagree. Where there is disagreement, it might be possible to establish protocols to guide discussion and so avoid conflict and fallout. Independent collaboration 'brokers' can play a positive role by helping to bridge gaps in nomenclature and understanding.

Collaborations work best when there is clarity about aims, strategy, process, communication and conduct. However, respectful, cordial communication can sometimes be difficult, especially when strong personalities are involved and/or parties bring divergent views to the table (Kahane 2017). It is essential, therefore, that collaborations forge a shared understanding—based on a common language—of the collaboration's purpose, objectives, rationale, strategic direction and proposed actions.

Chapter 6: Authorisation, governance and assurance

The provision of assurance to authorisers is important for sustaining confidence in, and the internal legitimacy of, collaborative strategies, and depends on a robust governance framework. In Chapter 6, we address the importance of unambiguous executive management support for collaboration. It is essential to establish strong management pathways to enable formal authority to cascade down to the collaboration and assurance to flow up to executive management. Formal pathways for authority and assurance can also be enhanced by the appointment of senior collaboration champions. Direction and oversight of collaborative initiatives can be provided by a governance group or 'backbone organisation' whose members—collaboration leads and partners—provide an essential conduit for the flow of assurance to authorisers and other stakeholders.

Collaboration frequently occurs in what Kotter (2012) refers to as 'secondary operating spaces'. These secondary spaces are informal or semiformal operating environments that are less tightly bound by the normal requirements of the dominant primary operating spaces. Secondary operating spaces allow partners to establish operational norms and ways of working that meet the needs of collaboration *and* provide assurance to authorisers. These collaborative spaces might be formalised via instruments such as MOUs, relational contracts or other mechanisms.

Chapter 7: Leading collaboration

In Chapter 7, we discuss the attributes of effective collaboration leaders. Collaborative leadership is a critical factor in the success of any collaborative initiative. Collaborations often experience difficulties in sustaining their founding purpose and maintaining the necessary levels of personal and organisational commitment over the longer term. In addition, collaborative initiatives sometimes meet with institutional and stakeholder resistance.

Effective collaboration leaders exhibit high levels of CQ, including exemplary interpersonal and communications skills, the ability to instil trust and act with authenticity, and strong facilitative and catalytic capacities. They need to be able to utilise formal and informal processes to engage their fellow collaborators, share responsibility and ensure that all partners feel they are an important part of the process. In the complex environments characteristic of collaboration, contradictions and tensions sometimes arise between the collaboration leadership and the prevailing values and norms in partner organisations. Collaboration leaders need to be able to protect the collaborative process politically and adapt to an ever-changing environment while keeping collaborative objectives in sight.

Chapter 8: Engagement

In Chapter 8, we examine how each of the cases has confronted the need for constructive engagement with both internal and external stakeholders to reduce institutional and stakeholder resistance, ensure adequate resourcing and maintain the support of authorisers.

Collaboration typically involves multiple organisations and sectors, each with their own administrative history, mission, organisational culture and operating systems. Success depends, in part, on the resources, people, management systems and authorising structures provided by partner organisations. It also depends on earning the confidence and support of external stakeholders, including the people and/or communities affected by a new BAU.

Collaboration sometimes meets with internal resistance from middle managers because the incentive structures under which they operate tend to reward fidelity to operational protocols rather than risk-taking. To the extent that engagement around collaboration tends to be focused externally, internal stakeholders can be overlooked. Collaboration 'champions' (within partner organisations) and 'influencers' (within affected communities) can play an important role in leveraging internal and external support for collaboration.

Chapter 9: Enabling place-based solutions

Importantly, collaboration is about 'doing with' not 'doing for' or 'doing to'. One of the strengths of collaboration is the potential for developing bespoke solutions that reflect local circumstances and preferences. Whereas bureaucracies traditionally favour standardised systems for service delivery in which treatments of social problems are constrained by organisational, portfolio and/or programmatic silos, collaboration can create opportunities to involve a set of diverse actors in processes of defining problems and agreeing on strategies. It needs to be borne in mind that collaboration is sometimes offered as a solution when 'traditional' approaches have demonstrably failed or as a remedy for resource scarcity.

Understandably, past failures predispose some stakeholders to scepticism and collaborative approaches can reveal tensions within and between partner organisations and within communities. In Chapter 9, we examine the case of the Community-Based Emergency Management (CBEM) initiative in Victoria, which has embraced a community-led approach to disaster readiness and community resilience. We also reflect on the inherent difficulties of mandating a standardised format for collaboration. In this regard, we consider the experience of New Zealand's Children's Action Plan, where attempts to impose a standardised operating framework met resistance from community stakeholders.

Chapter 10: Earning trust, credibility and legitimacy

Successful collaboration requires stakeholders to give up power and control, to take risks and to operate outside accepted frameworks. In Chapter 10, we explore how collaboration leaders can earn and retain the trust of stakeholders—both internal and external—to maintain legitimacy and credibility. We consider the example of Change the Story, a collaborative initiative whose aim was the development of a comprehensive national framework for the prevention of violence against women and their children. From the outset, Change the Story confronted the challenge of forging broad agreement in a diverse and sometimes fractious policy space. Observations from other cases are also drawn on.

We also consider the utility of social licence to operate (SLO) as a means for framing demonstrations of stakeholders' trust in collaborative processes (Butcher 2018). Originally pioneered as a mechanism for enterprises to gain the permission of affected communities for mining operations—particularly indigenous communities—SLO has now spread to other resource industry sectors, such as forestry and renewable energy, and is also being applied in the international aid and development space. A key feature of SLO is that it most often applies when enterprises are 'operating out of place', often in postcolonial settings, and is centrally concerned with obtaining the 'permission' or 'licence' from communities for activities that affect them. The relevance of SLO to collaboration will be discussed in the context of the establishment of Children's Teams in New Zealand communities in which Māori form a significant share of the local population.

Chapter 11: Conclusion: Are we collaborating yet?

In Chapter 11, we review the major learnings drawn from our case studies. We distil the major elements of successful collaboration with a view to providing practical guidance to policymakers and frontline practitioners. We identify the new skill sets needed, the key elements of a collaboration-friendly authorising environment and develop a value proposition that supports the authentic pursuit of collaborative processes in the solution of significant problems. We discuss the need to embrace experimentation when pursuing collaborative responses to wicked social problems, arguing that collaboration can only thrive in a 'safe to fail' authorising environment that accepts measured risk-taking.

Appendix

In the appendix, we collate the 'practice considerations' presented at the end of Chapters 2 to 10. Our purpose is to present in one place our suggestions about how practitioners might go about systematically untying the Gordian knot called *collaboration*.

References

Alford, John. 2009. *Public value from co-production by clients*. ANZSOG Working Paper. Canberra: Australia and New Zealand School of Government.

Alford, John L., and Janine O'Flynn. 2012. *Rethinking Public Service Delivery: Managing with external providers*. Basingstoke, UK: Palgrave Macmillan.

Austin, James E., and M. May Seitanidi. 2012. 'Collaborative value creation: A review of partnering between nonprofits and businesses. Part I—Value creation spectrum and collaboration stages.' *Nonprofit and Voluntary Sector Quarterly* 41(5): 726–58. doi.org/10.1177/0899764012450777.

Australian Public Service Commission (APSC). 2012. *Tackling Wicked Problems: A public policy perspective*. Canberra: APSC.

Bardach, Eugene. 1998. *Getting Agencies to Work Together: The practice and theory of managerial craftsmanship*. Washington, DC: Brookings Institution Press.

Bryson, John M., Barbara C. Crosby, and Melissa M. Stone. 2006. 'The design and implementation of cross-sector collaborations: Propositions from the literature.' *Public Administration Review* 66(s1): 44–55. doi.org/10.1111/j.1540-6210.2006.00665.x.

Bryson, John M., Barbara C. Crosby, Melissa M. Stone, and Emily O. Saunoi-Sandgren. 2009. *Designing and managing cross-sector collaboration: A case study in reducing traffic congestion*. Collaboration: Networks and Partnerships Series Report. Washington, DC: IBM Center for The Business of Government.

Butcher, John R. 2018. '"Social licence to operate" and the human services: A pathway to smarter commissioning?' *Australian Journal of Public Administration* 78(1): 113–22. doi.org/10.1111/1467-8500.12340.

Butcher, John R., and David J. Gilchrist. 2016. *The Three Sector Solution: Delivering public policy in collaboration with not-for-profits and business.* Canberra: ANU Press. doi.org/10.22459/TSS.07.2016.

Chief Minister, Treasury and Economic Development Directorate. 2015. *Connected Community, Connected Government: Opportunities for e-services delivery in the ACT.* Canberra: ACT Government.

Crosby, Barbara C., and John M. Bryson. 2005. 'A leadership framework for cross-sector collaboration.' *Public Management Review* 7(2): 177–201. doi.org/10.1080/14719030500090519.

Dickinson, Helen. 2016. 'From new public management to new public governance: The implications for a "new public service".' In *The Three Sector Solution: Delivering public policy in collaboration with not-for-profits and business*, eds John Butcher and David Gilchrist, pp. 41–60. Canberra: ANU Press. doi.org/10.22459/TSS.07.2016.03.

Eccles, Chris. 2016. 'Chris Eccles: What will the public sector look like in ten years?' *The Mandarin*, 30 June.

Edwards, Meredith, John Halligan, Bryan Horrigan, and Geoffrey Nicoll. 2012. *Public Sector Governance in Australia.* Canberra: ANU E Press. doi.org/10.22459/PSGA.07.2012.

Favoreu, Christophe, David Carassus, and Christophe Maurel. 2016. 'Strategic management in the public sector: A rational, political or collaborative approach?' *International Review of Administrative Sciences* 82(3): 435–53. doi.org/10.1177/0020852315578410.

Forrer, John, James Jed Kee, and Eric Boyer. 2014. *Governing Cross-Sector Collaboration.* Bryson Series in Public and Nonprofit Management. Hoboken, NJ: John Wiley & Sons.

Hanleybrown, Fay, John Kania, and Jennifer Splansky Juster. 2014. 'Essential mindset shifts for collective impact.' *Stanford Social Innovation Review* 12(4).

Kahane, Adam. 2017. *Collaborating with the Enemy: How to work with people you don't agree with or like or trust.* Oakland, CA: Berrett-Koehler Publishers.

Keast, Robyn. 2016a. 'Integration terms: Same or different?' In *Grassroots to Government: Creating joined-up working in Australia*, ed. Gemma Carey, pp. 25–46. Melbourne: Melbourne University Press.

Keast, Robyn. 2016b. 'Shining a light on the black box of collaboration: Mapping the prerequisites for cross-sector working.' In *The Three Sector Solution: Delivering public policy in collaboration with not-for-profits and business*, eds John Butcher and David Gilchrist, pp. 157–78. Canberra: ANU Press. doi.org/10.22459/TSS.07.2016.08.

Keast, Robyn, and Kerry Brown. 2006. 'Adjusting to new ways of working: Experiments with service delivery in the public sector.' *Australian Journal of Public Administration* 65(4): 41–53. doi.org/10.1111/j.1467-8500.2006.00503a.x.

Kotter, John. 2012. 'Accelerate!' *Harvard Business Review*, 1 November.

KPMG. 2016. *Future Focus of the Family Law Services: Final report*. Canberra: KPMG.

Lips, A. Miriam B., Rose R. O'Neill, and Elizabeth A. Eppel. 2011. 'Cross-agency collaboration in New Zealand: An empirical study of information sharing practices, enablers and barriers in managing for shared social outcomes.' *International Journal of Public Administration* 34(4): 255–66. doi.org/10.1080/01900692.2010.533571.

McGregor-Lowndes, Myles, and Matthew Turnour. 2003. 'Recent developments in government community service relations: Are you really my partner?' *The Journal of Contemporary Issues in Business and Governance* 9(1): 31–42.

McInerney, Paul-Brian. 2015. 'Walking a fine line: How organizations respond to the institutional pluralism of intersectoral collaboration.' *Social Currents* 2(3): 280–301. doi.org/10.1177/2329496515589849.

Mandell, Myrna, Robyn Keast, and Dan Chamberlain. 2017. 'Collaborative networks and the need for a new management language.' *Public Management Review* 19(3): 326–41. doi.org/10.1080/14719037.2016.1209232.

O'Flynn, Janine. 2008. 'Elusive appeal or aspirational ideal? The rhetoric and reality of the "collaborative turn" in public policy.' In *Collaborative Governance: A new era of public policy in Australia?* Eds Janine O'Flynn and John Wanna, pp. 181–95. Canberra: ANU E Press. doi.org/10.22459/CG.12.2008.17.

O'Leary, Rosemary. 2014. *Collaborative Governance in New Zealand: Important choices ahead*. Wellington: Fulbright New Zealand.

Pardo, Theresa A., Anthony M. Cresswell, Fiona Thompson, and Jing Zhang. 2006. 'Knowledge sharing in cross-boundary information system development in the public sector.' *Information Technology and Management* 7(4): 293–313. doi.org/10.1007/s10799-006-0278-6.

Pell, Charlotte. 2016. 'Debate: Against collaboration.' *Public Money & Management* 36(1): 4–5. doi.org/10.1080/09540962.2016.1103410.

Productivity Commission. 2016. *Introducing Competition and Informed User Choice into Human Services: Identifying sectors for reform.* Canberra: Productivity Commission.

Sicilia, Mariafrancesca, Enrico Guarini, Alessandro Sancino, Martino Andreani, and Renato Ruffini. 2016. 'Public services management and co-production in multi-level governance settings.' *International Review of Administrative Sciences* 82(1): 8–27. doi.org/10.1177/0020852314566008.

Suárez, David F. 2011. 'Collaboration and professionalization: The contours of public sector funding for nonprofit organizations.' *Journal of Public Administration Research and Theory* 21(2): 307–26. doi.org/10.1093/jpart/muq049.

Wilson, Rob, Paul Jackson, and Martin Ferguson. 2016. 'Editorial: Science or alchemy in collaborative public service? Challenges and future directions for the management and organization of joined-up government.' *Public Money & Management* 36(1): 1–4. doi.org/10.1080/09540962.2016.1103408.

Yolles, Maurice. 2005. 'Organisational intelligence.' *Journal of Workplace Learning* 17(1–2): 99–114. doi.org/10.1108/13665620510574496.

2

A NEW BUSINESS AS USUAL

Introduction

'Business as usual'—often shortened to the acronym BAU—is not always a bad thing, especially when it refers to proven, effective and productive business systems that help organisations achieve their aims. In recent times, however, BAU has received a bad rap and today is used more often as shorthand for institutions, programs, systems and ways of doing things that are ineffectual, and even dysfunctional.

BAU can also imply executive and organisational resistance to change, as well as a maladaptive attachment to legacy systems, protocols and operational policies. Doing things in a particular way 'because that is how they have always been done' is not a virtue, especially when business systems and processes act as an impediment to productive activity. That said, organisations sometimes demonstrate a maladaptive attachment to ineffective—and even anachronistic—ways of doing business. And those within organisations responsible for enforcing compliance with those systems sometimes play a gatekeeping role by discouraging alternative approaches (see Chapter 8, this volume).

Collaborative strategies are often pursued once it has been accepted that traditional programmatic approaches have failed and are sometimes portrayed as pathways to the creation of a new, or renewed, BAU. This implies a broad acceptance that pre-existing ways of doing business have not achieved the desired policy aims or delivered the expected social outcomes. It also implies a willingness to shake the tree and find new ways of working.

An answer to complexity

The logic of collaboration hinges on the recognition that no single organisation or sector acting on its own has the capacity or capability to solve complex policy problems. Complex, or wicked, problems occur in spaces where policy domains and formal accountabilities intersect. This is particularly true for each of the five cases investigated for this book.

Consider for a moment the policy domains in which our cases operate and the variety of agencies, not-for-profit organisations and professions that, in one way or another, play a role in meeting individual, family and community needs (Table 2.1).

Table 2.1 Policy domains and agencies of case studies

Policy domain	Agencies and actors
Vulnerable children Violence against women and families	Police Courts Individual/family/community support Housing Primary health care and hospitals Schools and early childcare services Drug and alcohol services Income support Women's and family refuges Mental health services
Emergency services	Volunteer rural fire brigades State emergency services First responders (police, ambulance) Energy providers Telecommunications Community services and local community groups/organisations Schools and school authorities Local businesses and landowners Financial institutions Income support Hospitals Mental health providers Land management authorities (state forests, national parks, and so on)

Policy domain	Agencies and actors
Reintegration of offenders	Corrections and parole Housing providers Individual/family/community support Primary health care Drug and alcohol support Income support Mental health support Labour market support
Childhood obesity	Primary health and dental care Community health care Schools Local councils Local retailers Sporting organisations Youth outreach Health education

In each of these policy domains, achieving outcomes for individual clients, families and communities is highly dependent on different organisations, disciplines, public sector agencies, levels of government and community sector organisations working together—or, at least, not working *against* one another. No matter how much frontline workers want to have a positive impact on the lives of the people they serve, their natural tendency is to adhere to the formal policies and protocols prescribed by their employing organisations. Furthermore, because these same policies and protocols have also been designed to meet the needs of internal governance and assurance, they do not necessarily lend themselves to collaboration across organisational or sectoral lines.

Barriers to changing BAU

Institutional and systemic barriers to collaboration are, to some extent, hardwired into Australia's service delivery architectures. Repeated efforts to reform the bureaucratic, administrative state throughout the twentieth century largely focused on making government bureaucracy more effective and efficient in its operations (Forrer et al. 2014: 214–15).

New public management (NPM) was an earlier attempt to derive a new BAU. The reforms of the 1990s sought to remedy the inefficiency and inflexibility of state monopoly systems by encouraging creativity, flexibility and innovation in the delivery of public goods and services, introducing greater competition and becoming more customer-focused, decentralising authority, focusing on outcomes and fostering greater transparency and accountability for results (Forrer et al. 2014: 217).

The older bureaucratic model of public sector leadership and management that had served well in providing standardised public services to large numbers of people proved itself unable to deal with the challenges presented by complex problems—problems sharing the following characteristics:

- They are multijurisdictional, crossing local, state and even international borders.
- They are multi-programmatic, often involving several types of government programs and agencies.
- They do not lend themselves to command-and-control types of solutions.
- Citizens often interact indirectly with government; their chief contacts are with private or not-for-profit organisations.
- Leadership is diffused and must be coordinated to achieve best results.
- Although rules and procedures can provide a framework, the key to success is flexibility.
- Roles are determined by knowledge and ability, not by positional authority in a hierarchy (Forrer et al. 2014: 209–10).

These are precisely the kinds of problems that collaboration is intended to address. However, despite more than a decade of thinking about 'whole-of-government' or 'joined-up' approaches, collaboration across programmatic, organisational, portfolio and sectoral boundaries remains difficult and problematic (Carey et al. 2015).

Countercultural, not counterintuitive

There is a tendency for government and social-purpose organisations to employ the *language* of collaboration without demonstrating a commitment to making the cultural and operational adjustments required to collaborate. Clearly, collaboration is easier to talk about than it is to *do*. The status quo endures, even when it no longer delivers results.

According to Canadian thought leader and associate of the Tamarack Institute Mark Cabaj, collaboration is *not* counterintuitive, but it *is* countercultural.[1] Successful collaboration rests on a set of skills, behaviours and processes that represent a departure from accepted 'legacy' practices (Hanleybrown et al. 2014: 2) and often entails an agenda for

---

1   Mark Cabaj's presentation on cross-sector social impact networking was given in Canberra on 26 April 2018 and was co-sponsored by the Commonwealth departments of Social Services and Education and Training.

change—change in the nature of relationships, networks, governance, accountability and ways of working. Leading and sustaining the kinds of change necessary for collaboration to occur are difficult, even when the logic of collaboration is broadly accepted.

Collaboration as 'transgressive' practice

The transgressive quality of collaboration derives from the fact that it usually involves the violation of accepted conventions, norms, rules and boundaries. Although some might think that describing collaboration as *transgressive* exaggerates the degree to which it violates organisational norms, many of the people interviewed for this study clearly perceive themselves to be working in ways that operate outside usually accepted bureaucratic conventions. Several interviewees invoked the aphorism 'collaboration is like designing and building an aeroplane while flying it'. They are operating in environments in which BAU no longer applies, boundaries are malleable, the limits of authority are untested, practical guidance is scarce and scrutiny is intense.

For the most part, collaboration occurs in a secondary operating space (see Chapter 6) in which many of the conventions of the primary operating space do not apply in quite the same way. Furthermore, the operational and behavioural norms that will apply in this secondary operating space are to a large extent undefined—at least at the outset—and need to be co-designed and coproduced by participants. For most participants, this means *unlearning* old norms and attitudes while creating and signing up to new ones. Moreover, these new norms might only apply within the collaboration space and thus require participants to become, effectively, 'bicultural' as they transition back and forth across a shifting boundary between the primary and secondary operating spaces.

Collaboration is also transgressive in the sense that participants (collaboration leads, in particular) often find themselves in the position of forcing operational or cultural change in the face of institutional or organisational resistance. The collaboration leads interviewed for our cases often speak about the need to judiciously test boundaries, to exercise (and then back up) their own judgement and to 'act first and seek forgiveness later'.

In this light, when people are asked to 'go forth and collaborate', they are, in effect, being asked to be disruptive, in the best sense of the word. Authorisers (ministers and executives) need to understand this; they need to be cognisant of the risk that attempts to encourage collaboration might generate pushback, territoriality and complaints—and they need to be prepared to provide executive cover for their collaboration leads. It is also incumbent on collaboration leads to keep their executive apprised of any potential repercussions and to provide them with timely briefings and assurances (see Chapter 6).

Collaboration is transgressive to the extent that it entails contradictions of and challenges to institutional rules, traditional practices, functional demarcations and programmatic systems. Sometimes described as 'creative rule-breaking', collaboration depends on a set of skills and aptitudes that do not entirely conform to those traditionally used in public sector recruitment (see Chapter 4).

For example, where public sector recruitment favours formal qualifications, functional skills and relevant work experience—all framed within particular institutional, organisational and programmatic settings—collaboration requires intellectual nimbleness, creativity, empathic communication, tenacity and a preparedness to 'work outside the square'. This might make collaboration a hard sell within Australia's public sectors, steeped as they are in hierarchical, rule-based and siloed cultures.

Pushing organisational boundaries

Collaboration is neither new nor an emerging theme in public policy and governance discourses. Even so, in terms of its framing and practice, collaboration is in reality often more 'aspirational' than 'actual'. Partnership-based approaches to public sector governance are based, ideally, on relational mechanisms such as trust, shared values, implicit standards, collaboration and consultation (as opposed to bureaucratic mechanisms based on control, hierarchy and chains of command) (Favoreu et al. 2016: 440). However, as Favoreu et al. (2016: 449) point out, the implementation of such approaches faces considerable obstacles in the form of 'cultural barriers and organisational routines that are difficult to overcome, such as partitioning, or the prevalence of the hierarchical logic, which tends to be contrary to the collaborative logic'. In the Australian context, Keast and Brown (2006: 51–52) observe that deliberative endeavours to forge more collaborative ways of working via network-based service delivery models can be jeopardised by failures to make adaptive changes to behaviours, expectations and processes.

Moreover, this is a trans-Tasman phenomenon. In New Zealand, an expert panel established by the Minister for Social Development offered the following observations in relation to that country's approach to protecting vulnerable children:

> Traditional delivery and purchase models have failed to provide a range of effective services and approaches or to be sufficiently child-centred. Stakeholders have described a siloed system with insufficient partnership and collaboration around children's needs. Current funding approaches are restrictive and do not permit innovation or the creation of sustainable services to meet changing needs.
>
> The current system, with diffuse accountabilities across various agencies, has been ineffective in ensuring vulnerable children and families get the services they need, when and where they need them. A 'negotiation and best efforts' approach has failed, particularly with respect to government agencies. (Ministry of Social Development 2015: 64–65)

Risk, disruption and innovation

In a keynote address to a workshop on cross-sector working held at The Australian National University in 2015, a former Secretary of the Department of the Prime Minister and Cabinet, Peter Shergold, advocated new forms of governance to enable public sector agencies, not-for-profits and businesses to work collaboratively in the pursuit of agreed social aims.

Shergold (2016: 26) believes 'cross-sectoral working in the public interest could act to reinvigorate the participatory nature of democratic governance'. Forging new adaptive models for more collaborative governance would require a greater appetite on the part of policymakers for risk-taking within an authorising environment that embraces experimentation and accepts the possibility of failure. Addressing complex problems in public policy requires innovation, and innovation cannot occur in the absence of risk. Nor can government expect to pass all the risk on to nonstate actors—at least not if it wants to reap the rewards of risk-taking.

This appears to be well understood by another former head of the Department of the Prime Minister and Cabinet, Martin Parkinson, who in 2016 told the Committee for the Economic Development of Australia:

> Innovation is not certain to be successful. It often involves failure, sometimes a lot of it—innovation is, after all, inherently risky. Yet often we impose too many costs on the efforts of those who fail. (Martin 2016)

He went on to say that the public sector has to become more innovative, adding:

> It's got to be okay to fail. If the incentive structure, whether in the private sector or in the public sector, doesn't allow you to fail and fail fast, and then if you've learned something, try and try again, then I think you actually might find it really hard to foster that culture of innovation that we all want to see. (Martin 2016)

Sørensen and Torfing (2012: 2) point out that many public organisations offer a stable operational platform for the exploration and exploitation of new ideas and solutions. The sheer size of the public sector enables it to absorb the costs of innovation failures, especially if they fail 'fast and cheap' (Sørensen and Torfing 2012: 2). Sørensen and Torfing (2012: 5) also observe that innovation in the public sector is enhanced by multi-actor collaboration in that it 'draws upon and brings into play all relevant innovation assets in terms of knowledge, imagination, creativity, courage, resources, transformative capacities and political authority'—something market competition and bureaucratic steering fail to do.

Both innovation *and* collaboration can be stifled in the embrace of a rules-bound governance framework. If collaborative, adaptive and iterative approaches to policy formulation and delivery are to become second nature in both the public and the not-for-profit sectors, it will be necessary to surmount the obstacles posed by 'the organisational hand-brake of path-dependent legacies in government, business, and the not-for-profit sector' (Butcher 2015: 253).

Collaboration can provide the intellectual stimulus and incentives for risk-sharing required for finding new solutions to emerging problems.

Instilling a collaborative mindset

Over the coming decade, the public sector will need to be increasingly focused on outcomes, less siloed and portfolio-driven, and more reliant on collaboration, cooperation and co-design (Eccles 2016). Instilling a collaboration mindset, however, requires public sector agencies in particular to swim against the current of a system that incentivises rigid top-down steering and public sector silos in favour of interconnected networks of actors (Aagaard 2012: 4–5).

Collaboration has both formal and informal dimensions. Collaboration often occurs 'under the radar', engaged in by public entrepreneurs with a deep sense of public service, acting without executive mandate and following nonstandard procedures (O'Leary 2014: 17).

Actors in any sector might elect to collaborate informally with colleagues in other business units, organisations or sectors as part of their normal modus operandi for problem-solving. In so doing, they might be working within accepted, but undocumented, terms of engagement with the implicit sanction of their employing organisation. Alternatively, they might simply be operating within the dictates of their own sense of professional propriety and might not perceive any need to obtain formal sanction. Others, however, might choose not to engage in collaborative behaviours in the absence of an explicit directive or sanction.

In a case study of the Danish Crime Prevention Council, Aagaard (2012: 10–11) observed that, despite concerted attempts to establish a coordinated multi-stakeholder approach to crime prevention, participants in the collaboration remained 'primarily embedded in the institutional universe of their own organisation, and do not see themselves in any significant interdependent relation to other members'—in part because 'members are uncertain of what sort of backing they have from their own organisations in concrete matters'. Aagaard (2012: 14) concludes that 'there is still a lot of path dependency in the public sector' and further observes that path dependency serves to constrain and slow innovation.

Rosemary O'Leary (2014: 54) concludes that public sector managers would benefit from training aimed at instilling a 'collaborative mindset', encompassing:

- personal attributes (being open-minded, patient, change-oriented, flexible, unselfish, persistent, diplomatic, honest, trustworthy, respectful, empathetic, goal-oriented, decisive, friendly and having a sense of humour)
- interpersonal skills (such as good communication, the ability to listen and to work with people)

- group process skills (including facilitation, interest-based negotiation, collaborative problem-solving, skill in understanding group dynamics, culture and personalities, compromise, conflict resolution and mediation).

O'Leary (2014: 55) offers the following recommendations to agency heads wishing to create a more collaborative environment:

- Accept ideas from people and places you would never think of.
- Learn from others.
- Bring in thought leaders who might create a spark of an idea in your employees.
- Seek people with strong public service motivation, dedicated to the overall wellbeing of citizens.
- Seek people who will think widely about options.
- Seek people willing 'to play outside their comfort zone'.
- Seek people comfortable with acting 'transformationally' rather than staying in an old 'transactional' mode.
- Seek people who can see collaborative advantage.
- Seek people with exemplary collaborative skills such as negotiation, conflict resolution, collaborative problem-solving, facilitation and strategy. If your employees do not have these skills, obtain training for them.
- Provide an enabling environment to buffer short-term factors that undermine the collaborative impulse.
- Empower network members to enable participation.
- Frame problems and solutions to create the space needed for collaborators to find productive ways to work together.
- Educate employees about the importance of the strategic use of individual attributes, interpersonal skills and group process skills while collaborating.
- Incentivise and reward collaboration among individuals and organisations.
- Embed collaboration in performance evaluation and core competencies.
- Document and share how collaborations are working so managers can learn from successful and failed experiences.

- Reshape management and leadership education to include intensive self-assessment and emotional intelligence development.
- Address challenges to data sharing and incompatible technologies that block interagency and intra-agency collaborative work.
- Address structural barriers to interagency work.

In common with the majority of thought leaders in the 'collaboration space', Forrer et al. (2014) assert that leading organisations in cross-sector collaboration requires a fundamentally different skill set to that required by the traditional bureaucratic model of public administration. They contend that cross-sector collaborations require leaders with the ability to forge common purpose among actors who have their own organisational agendas. Also critical is the ability to see the larger system beyond their own organisational niche because collaboration allows a variety of viewpoints and approaches to solving a particular public problem. Forrer et al. (2014: 234) suggest that four general areas of leadership are the most critical when addressing complex problems in a cross-sector environment:

1. Generating support from other actors.
2. Leading outside of one's formal role.
3. Understanding the wider system.
4. Building trust.

Of course, trust plays an essential role in the success of all collaborative endeavours, much more so than would be the case with a traditional program run by a single public agency or not-for-profit organisation (Forrer et al. 2014: 229).

What the cases tell us

Collaboration is posited as a remedy for the jurisdictional, organisational, programmatic and sectoral siloing that create and reinforce the fragmentation of service delivery. And for these reasons, collaborative approaches are most often applied to problems that are longstanding and have already proved resistant to attempts at resolution.

Thus, in a real sense, the task of remedying the ineffectiveness of existing interventions becomes an important focus of collaboration. As one of our interviewees from New Zealand said:

> We didn't need to be told it wasn't working; we'd known for many years it wasn't working. I worked with a workforce that worked their fingers to the bone and it still wasn't working. So, the desperation to give effect to things that were more effective for *whānau* [families]—that had to change. (Children's Action Plan)

Collaborations can also coalesce around informal initiatives or 'pilots' that have achieved local salience or prominence. That said, it is also clear from our interviews that there is a palpable weariness with pilot schemes, which tend to be time-limited, have finite resourcing, are tightly bounded in operational terms and are unable to gain traction or demonstrate sustainability.

The need for a new BAU was a consistent organising theme across each of our cases. Implicit in the call for a new BAU is the fact that pre-existing arrangements—often based on programmatic funding, highly specified contracts and multiple eligibility requirements, triage systems and authorising environments—are not working. In each of our five case studies, the push towards collaboration was fuelled by frustration with a status quo that:

1. constrained the ability of organisations and workers to efficiently and effectively mobilise resources and assets to respond to complex problems
2. created bureaucratic, operational and organisational barriers for individuals, families and communities seeking assistance with complex problems.

However, while people might regard the existing modus operandi as problematic, changing established practices and expectations is far from easy, as attested by one New Zealand interviewee:

> I think everyone's first response is, 'This is asking more of me. I'm required to do more. I'm required to do what I already have to do in my paid job, and you're asking more of me now.' So, the change strategy has got to be about how you redefine BAU more so that it's actually BAU; this is the new way of working. That is, if you adopt this model you don't need to do the BAU any more; you're actually doing a new BAU. That's the hardest thing for people to get their heads around and understand. (Children's Action Plan)

Another interviewee pointed out the tendency to resolve the perceived inconsistencies between the status quo and proposed new ways of working by resorting to 'compartmentalisation':

> They are still maintaining a separation, I think, in terms of the perspective where people think: 'This is children's teamwork and then this is my BAU. As an agency, we give this much time to Children's Team and this much time to business as usual.' And we're saying: 'But actually all your resources should be working collaboratively, sharing information and coming up with one plan.' But they compartmentalise the work, so that perpetuates a kind of 'it's different to what we normally do', whereas we are saying: 'Actually, it is what you do.' (Children's Action Plan)

Collaborative approaches are sometimes represented as 'transformational'; however, any such claims must be treated carefully and likely fall into the realm of wishful thinking. Indeed, many of the people interviewed for this study have made such claims. Others, however, have offered a contrary view, suggesting that the impact of collaborative approaches on the dominant operating culture of organisations is slight and brief.

Also, collaborative approaches can sometimes meet internal resistance within partner agencies, especially when the practices and behaviours required for collaboration are perceived as transgressing operational rules and protocols or threatening organisational or personal authority and influence. In part, internal resistance to collaboration derives from scepticism or apprehension about the impact of collaboration: 'What if it fails?'

Final observations

The collaboration literature gives a lot of attention to the need to devise and navigate new ways of working—to overturn BAU and establish a new normal. However, collaboration is built on an implicit assumption that the environment is complex and dynamic and, therefore, in a state of continual flux. The informal or semiformal nature of collaboration suggests impermanence. Although collaborative approaches should aim to reframe BAU, there is a risk that the new ways of working will become rigid and codified and just as maladaptive as the ones they replaced.

Practice considerations

1. Is there a collaborative mindset in your organisation? Does collaboration figure as an organising theme of your organisation's way of working, and does collaboration occur in practice?

2. Are people within your organisation free to engage collaboratively across programmatic, organisational or sectoral boundaries?

3. What opportunities exist in your organisation for employees to add to their collaboration skill set?

4. Does your organisation have any collaboration 'protocols' to guide and regulate collaborative processes?

5. What aspects of your organisation's/sector's BAU potentially acts to constrain or inhibit collaboration?

6. What would have to happen to allow for change to occur?

7. Is it presently possible in your organisation for people to 'lead from below'— to exercise creativity and initiative in ways that are conducive to the revision of current practices or the adoption of new ones?

8. Are there people who occupy positions of influence within your organisation who might be prepared to champion or lead a process involving the review of, and reflection on, those aspects of BAU that are not conducive to collaboration?

9. Can you identify people in your organisation, or in your partner organisations, who might be enlisted as 'collaboration champions'?

References

Aagaard, P. 2012. 'Drivers and barriers of public innovation in crime prevention.' *The Innovation Journal* 17(1): 2–17.

Butcher, John R. 2015. 'Squaring the virtuous circle: Exploring the potential of the "five Cs".' *Australian Journal of Public Administration* 74(2): 249–56. doi.org/10.1111/1467-8500.12121.

Carey, Gemma, Pauline McLoughlin, and Brad Crammond. 2015. 'Implementing joined-up government: Lessons from the Australian social inclusion agenda.' *Australian Journal of Public Administration* 74(2): 176–86. doi.org/10.1111/1467-8500.12096.

Eccles, Chris. 2016. 'Chris Eccles: What will the public sector look like in ten years?' *The Mandarin*, 30 June.

Favoreu, Christophe, David Carassus, and Christophe Maurel. 2016. 'Strategic management in the public sector: A rational, political or collaborative approach?' *International Review of Administrative Sciences* 82(3): 435–53. doi.org/10.1177/0020852315578410.

Forrer, John, James Jed Kee, and Eric Boyer. 2014. *Governing Cross-Sector Collaboration*. Bryson Series in Public and Nonprofit Management. Hoboken, NJ: John Wiley & Sons.

Hanleybrown, Fay, John Kania, and Jennifer Splansky Juster. 2014. 'Essential mindset shifts for collective impact.' *Stanford Social Innovation Review* 12(4).

Keast, Robyn, and Kerry Brown. 2006. 'Adjusting to new ways of working: Experiments with service delivery in the public sector.' *Australian Journal of Public Administration* 65(4): 41–53. doi.org/10.1111/j.1467-8500.2006. 00503a.x.

Martin, Peter. 2016. 'Martin Parkinson tells CEDA Australian managers below par.' *Sydney Morning Herald*, 10 October.

Ministry of Social Development. 2015. *Investing in New Zealand's Children and their Families: Expert panel final report*. Wellington: New Zealand Ministry of Social Development.

O'Leary, Rosemary. 2014. *Collaborative Governance in New Zealand: Important choices ahead*. Wellington: Fulbright New Zealand.

Shergold, Peter. 2016. 'Three sectors, one public purpose.' In *The Three Sector Solution: Delivering public policy in collaboration with not-for-profits and business*, eds John Butcher and David Gilchrist, pp. 23–34. Canberra: ANU Press. doi.org/10.22459/TSS.07.2016.02.

Sørensen, Eva, and Jacob Torfing. 2012. 'Introduction: Collaborative innovation in the public sector.' *Innovation Journal* 17(1): 1–14.

3

DESIGNING IMPACTFUL COLLABORATION

Introduction

A core purpose of collaboration is to bring diverse capabilities to bear on complex problems that are beyond the ability of any single organisation to solve on its own. However, collaborative approaches often represent a major departure from traditional, siloed, programmatic service delivery architectures. For this reason, and because collaboration operates outside the usual incentive structures that apply in primary operating spaces, collaborative strategies are sometimes subject to enhanced scrutiny.

Collaborations operate with a heightened sense of urgency concerning tangible demonstrations of impact. Clarity about the expected impact of collaboration is critical, and clear pathways to impact are essential. In addition, a strong evidential base is important for sustaining the confidence and ongoing support of partners and other stakeholders.

In this chapter, we consider the challenges of demonstrating the impact of collaboration. These include:

- a lack of clarity or agreement about desired or expected outcomes
- problems of definition and measurement
- a reluctance to share information
- impatience for results on the part of authorisers.

With regard to the last point, it is important to bear in mind that collaborations typically take two to three years to mature. Sometimes, too, 'impact' is narrowly defined so as to exclude significant indicators of important, and necessary, organisational and behavioural adaptations.

We give particular attention to the experience of one of our cases, the Whole of Systems Trial of Prevention Strategies for Childhood Obesity (WHO STOPS Childhood Obesity, also known as WHO STOPS), which has modelled its approach on the 'collective impact framework' pioneered by Kania and Kramer (2011).

Collective impact framework

The collective impact framework works on the premise that social change cannot be created by individual entities operating in isolation. Rather, enduring change requires the collective efforts of multiple actors all working towards similar and/or complementary goals. Such collective efforts—which entail improved coordination, cooperation and collaboration—provide a foundation for 'collective impact'. As defined by Kania and Kramer (2011: 39), collective impact is a form of collaborative initiative that involves:

> long-term commitments by a group of important actors from different sectors to a common agenda for solving a specific social problem. Their actions are supported by a shared measurement system, mutually reinforcing activities, and ongoing communication, and are staffed by an independent backbone organisation.

This type of collaboration focuses on supporting diverse stakeholders—drawn from civil society, not-for-profit organisations, the public sector and the business community—to work collectively, focusing on 'a single set of goals, measured in the same way' (Kania and Kramer 2011: 36). The collective impact model seeks shared solutions for complex social problems that are beyond the capacity or capability of any single entity to address alone (Kania and Kramer 2011).

Collective impact is framed around five principles. These are set out in Table 3.1.

Table 3.1 The collective impact framework

Framework elements	Practice considerations
1. Common agenda	It is essential for all participants to agree on the primary goals for the collective impact initiative.
2. Shared measurement systems	Identify a short list of indicators for which data can be collected consistently at the community level and across all participating organisations. This ensures that all efforts remain aligned and enables the participants to hold each other accountable and learn from each other's successes and failures.
3. Mutually reinforcing activities	Each stakeholder's efforts should fit into an overarching plan within which their differentiated activities are coordinated and mutually reinforced.
4. Continuous communication	Collective impact depends on continuous and frank communication between partners and stakeholders. Communication is an essential component of providing assurance to participants, some of whom might come to the table with incompatible priorities and operational norms. It might require several years of regular meetings for participants to overcome doubt, cultivate constructive relationships and recognise the common motivation behind their respective efforts. Participants need assurance that their own interests will be treated fairly, that decisions will be made on the basis of objective evidence and the best possible solution to the problem and the priorities of one organisation will not be favoured over those of another.
5. Backbone support organisation	Establishing a backbone support organisation is critical to the creation and management of any collective impact initiative. The backbone organisation provides the supporting infrastructure for collaboration. It should have a discrete identity that distinguishes it from any of the partner organisations and it should comprise people who have skills in adaptive leadership: the ability to focus people's attention and create a sense of urgency, the ability to apply pressure to stakeholders without overwhelming them, the competence to frame issues in a way that presents opportunities as well as difficulties and the strength to mediate conflict among stakeholders.

Source: Kania and Kramer (2011).

Performance measures

The capacity for collaboration to deliver results is not universally accepted. Pell (2016), for example, offers a pessimistic view of collaboration, which, she suggests, is often uncritically promoted as being an inherently 'good thing' that is pursued as an end in its own right without demonstrable benefit. In Pell's view, collaboration as a policy goal does not resolve the inherent functional limitations of programs designed to deliver standardised transactional services. Pell suggests that no one knows whether collaboration 'works' because the 'impact from the citizen's point of view is not studied empirically'; the ultimate arbiter of effectiveness 'is always the funder, the government agency or those collaborating' (Pell 2016: 5). Pell's reservations about collaboration reflect a realistic concern about the potential for collaboration to be subverted by partner organisations and made into a 'tick a box' exercise that has little genuine impact.

In their investigation of the impact of sectoral partnerships, Andrews and Entwistle (2010) found a positive association between public–public partnerships and public service effectiveness, efficiency and equity. They also found that public–private partnership is negatively associated with effectiveness and equity. However, they found

> no statistically significant relationship between partnering with the nonprofit sector and performance. These findings held true even when controlling for past performance, service expenditure, and organisational environments. (Andrews and Entwistle 2010: 693).

Despite this, government and not-for-profit groups continue to work together. Andrews and Entwistle (2010: 689–90) postulated that, as not-for-profits often specialise in the 'delivery of bespoke or very personalized services, it may be that improvements in effectiveness do not show up in the "hard" performance indicators collected by central government'.

In other research, Babiak and Thibault (2009) contend that multiple cross-sector partnerships involving public, non-profit and commercial sectors have not been well canvassed in the literature. They suggest that multisector partnerships formed across multiple boundaries involve the union of different—and potentially incompatible—missions, goals and values (Babiak and Thibault 2009). They also contend that 'feelings of ambiguity, resentment, uncertainty, and suspicion' can result from 'perceived power imbalances' arising from resource inequities and political backing (Babiak and Thibault 2009: 137).

Drawing on the work of Carter (1989), Power (1994) and de Bruijn (2007), Koppenjan (2008: 704) points out the principal disadvantages and risks of using performance measures in a collaboration context:

- In many cases, it is impossible to agree upon performance measures; since policy making is in essence a political bargaining game and parties have an interest in safeguarding their discretionary powers and keeping objectives vague.

- Policy outcomes are complex and multidimensional. Not all outcomes can be defined and quantified. Focusing on hard, quantified outcomes may result in neglecting softer, more abstract values, often related to quality, resulting in the neglect of important (public) values and poor quality of performance.

- Since the causality between policies and outcome tends to be unknown, the risk of using performance indicators is that the focus on activities (outputs), which are relatively easy to specify, will drive out the attention for outcomes.

- Since policy making is complex, involving many objectives and regulations that may be conflicting and that have to be implemented in different cases and situations, operational decisions are assigned to professionals who make trade-offs on the basis of their professional values and expertise, aligning policies with concrete situations. Ex ante formulated outcomes reduce their possibilities of doing so.

- Collaboration implies that actors are dependent on the efforts of others in order to perform. Furthermore, policy outcomes are influenced by autonomous developments in the environment. Holding parties accountable for outcomes of policies may therefore be unfair.

- Using performance indicators may tempt monitoring actors to use hierarchical interventions and micromanagement. Collaborating parties may be tempted to 'toy the numbers' in order to create an image of effectiveness.

- The use of performance measures may create disincentives for actors to engage in experiments, to invest in innovations or to be responsive to new demands and unexpected developments.

The elusive ideal of tangible impact

All collaborations set out to deliver tangible impacts. By 'tangible', we mean that the effects of collaboration are observable, potentially measurable and positive (insofar as they contribute to the realisation of the goals of the collaboration). Collaborations commonly take a long time to establish. As will be discussed in Chapters 5, 8 and 10, designing the collaboration, engaging with stakeholders, building trust and establishing legitimacy and credibility require significant investments of time and energy. It is, therefore, unrealistic to expect demonstrations of tangible impact in the early stages of collaboration. Despite this, it is often in the nature of authorisers—who are sometimes blinkered by short-termism—to be impatient for 'results'.

What the cases tell us

Collaboration partners sometimes come under a lot of pressure to demonstrate tangible impact early in the life of the collaboration. Conversely, 'intangible' impacts—such as new ways of working, cultural or process change and revitalised stakeholder relationships—are not always accorded the importance they deserve. Furthermore, a number of interviewees pointed out that authorisers often do not understand that collaborations require intensive—and complex—processes of relationship-building, establishing legitimacy and trust, collectively framing the problem and agreeing on ways of working.

Demonstrating impact

A recurring theme in each of our cases is the importance, and problematic nature, of 'evidence of impact'. There is often institutional impatience around evaluation and impact measurement. As suggested by one interviewee:

> I get annoyed sometimes about, 'Can you evaluate it? Can you tell us what's happening?' These things take time in terms of how you manage them. And it takes away the human context.

It takes time to establish a different way of working and it is not always possible to immediately attribute observable changes to this or that element of the new system, assuming there *are* observable changes in the short to medium term. The reality is, with regard to longstanding entrenched social problems, a long-term perspective is required.

Path to impact

For each of the cases investigated for this study, the object of collaboration was to achieve beneficial outcomes at the individual and community levels that could not be realised by organisations or sectors acting on their own and working within the bounds of prevailing institutional and programmatic structures. Participants in each of the collaborations displayed an acute awareness of the importance of 'evidence of impact' and each confronted the challenge of demonstrating impact to the satisfaction of authorisers and stakeholders.

The 'path to impact' for each of the collaborations is briefly summarised below.

Throughcare

Throughcare arose from the recognition that, without coordinated support, offenders returning to the community following release from a custodial sentence were at high risk of violating parole conditions or reoffending, resulting in a return to prison. Offenders might have multiple complex needs pertaining to housing, income, employment, education, drug and alcohol dependence, family violence and mental health. Throughcare aimed to assist offenders to navigate the complex maze of supports and services and so re-establish positive connections with their families and the community. Key indicators of impact would include greater success in accessing relevant services, compliance with parole conditions and reduced rates of recidivism. Understandably, it might take a number of years for a coherent picture to emerge from the data.

Change the Story

Change the Story came about because of a recognition that Australia lacked a coherent and consistent practice framework for the prevention of violence against women and their children. The aim of the collaboration was to articulate an evidence-based practice framework and win support for the framework among diverse stakeholders, including state and territory governments, epistemic communities (academic researchers and practitioners), advocacy groups and community sector organisations. Measures of success included the results of exhaustive expert peer review of the framework, support for the framework from advocacy groups, clinical practitioners and not-for-profit organisations supporting women and their children and the adoption of the framework by state and territory governments.

Community-Based Emergency Management

Community-Based Emergency Management (CBEM) came about as a response to intensive government and community soul-searching in the wake of natural disasters that resulted in significant loss of life and livelihood; widespread individual, family and community trauma; and extensive damage to property and infrastructure. CBEM seeks to support communities to become more resilient and to more effectively mobilise a range of community assets when confronted by, or recovering from, extreme events. Because CBEM takes a 'bespoke' approach that encourages community actors to frame their own needs and responses, it is difficult to identify direct and comparable measures of impact. For the most part, evidence of impact resides in the subjective judgement of key actors and communities.

Children's Teams

The establishment of multidisciplinary Children's Teams in 10 New Zealand communities was a key plank of a national response to perceived failures to protect vulnerable at-risk children. Children's Teams were intended to provide improved coherence and coordination in a fragmented and siloed service delivery system. The aim was to establish a more accessible, responsive and culturally appropriate gateway to the services and supports offered by multiple statutory and community services and so improve service outcomes for vulnerable children and their families. Guided by the maxim 'nationally supported, locally led', Children's Teams were encouraged to take into account the needs, preferences and characteristics of local communities. Children's Teams came under pressure to provide early evidence of impact even though the reality is that it might take a number of years for clear trends to emerge. Concrete measures of impact are varied and will be difficult to attribute.

WHO STOPS

The acronym 'WHO STOPS' refers to the Whole of Systems Trial of Prevention Strategies for Childhood Obesity and provides the framework for the oversight of two community initiatives in Victoria: SEA Change, based in Portland and established in 2014,[1] and GenR8 Change, based in Hamilton and established in 2015.[2] WHO STOPS was established as a partnership between Deakin University and the Victorian Department of Health and Human Services (DHHS) with the aim of identifying the incidence of, contributors to and possible solutions for childhood obesity. Key partners include the Western District Health Service Primary Care Partnership (PCP), local councils and community health services. The WHO STOPS model offers a prime example of collaboration informed by research and the application of a robust evidential base. We expand on the WHO STOPS experience in the following sections.

---

1   See seachangeportland.com.au.
2   See www.genr8change.com.

WHO STOPS: Research-led design

WHO STOPS is a community-based initiative that enables local community leaders and members to work together to address complex local drivers of childhood obesity. WHO STOPS proceeds from the understanding that any attempt to address the systemic determinants of noncommunicable disease at a population level requires the strengthening of existing community capacity and conferring community ownership of efforts to apply system thinking to community-wide childhood obesity prevention.

WHO STOPS stands out among the five cases we investigated for the intellectual rigour of its design and implementation. The local initiatives in Portland and Hamilton embody 'systems thinking' based on understandings of community agency and local 'ownership' of priorities and approaches. Researchers from the Global Obesity Centre (GOC) at Deakin University have played a significant role with respect to design, facilitating community consultation, measurement and evaluation.

WHO STOPS is a quasi-experimental interventional study—funded by the National Health and Medical Research Council (NHMRC)—intended to assess whether the adoption of 'systems change interventions' increases the capacity of communities to apply evidence-informed action across community systems and consequently affect the prevalence of childhood obesity (Allender et al. 2016).[3] The study will test whether it is possible to:

1. strengthen community action for childhood obesity prevention
2. measure the impact of increased action on risk factors for childhood obesity.

The research project will test the proposition that permanent reductions in childhood obesity are possible if the complex and dynamic causes of obesity are well understood and addressed through increased community ownership and responsibility. It is hypothesised that a systems intervention for childhood obesity will be:

- effective in its impact
- efficient in its implementation
- scalable in its delivery
- sustainable in its longevity.[4]

---

3   Also see ANZCTR (2016).
4   See ibid.

The WHO STOPS approach was described in lay terms by one of the lead researchers:

> We think that multiple-setting, multiple-strategy interventions are what the literature suggests are best-practice approaches for childhood obesity prevention. We are also of the view that communities themselves need to be empowered to act on issues like childhood obesity because of their complexity. That raises another perspective—and this is really what we're testing with the grant: that we have a systems thinking approach that we believe helps communities manage complexity and changes in causation over time. So, what the grant is really trying to measure is whether this approach to understanding and visualising that complexity allows communities to own the issue, to take action more rapidly, more effectively and in a more sustainable way.

Establishing a common agenda for change

The key to getting the WHO STOPS initiatives off the ground was demonstrating that childhood obesity was a problem that needs to be addressed. One of the researchers from the GOC encapsulated the importance of establishing the nature and extent of the problem:

> Around an issue like obesity … there needs to be some awareness of the size of the problem and who it's relevant to and that it's something that we should be doing something about. So that requires data.

> … We have accurate data that show children are overweight in this region. We have ideas for how we might be able to fix that. So, I guess at that point there's an invitation from the community: 'We want to hear more about this process.' And leaders within the community … will say, 'Yes, this is a priority for us, for our health service, for our PCP'—whoever it is.

Drawing on the baseline data—and assisted by researchers from the GOC—SEA Change and GenR8 Change employed a facilitated community engagement process to create a shared understanding of the problem and identify the range of potential actions available to the community. It has been particularly important to explain and make sense of the problem in a localised context to bring people in. As a member of the Great South Coast Change backbone group observed:

It's not just the data, it's actually the analysis, it's making meaning of the data. I think that's been really important. So, that initial connection around it being local data, so you're telling people about their own community and it's being interpreted by someone who's respected [the GOC] and in a way that makes sense. I think that that ability to tell that story in a local way is really important.

Utilising a 'systems change intervention' approach, members of the community (parents and children), local stakeholders (schools, sporting groups, the local council, health services), leaders (councillors, principals) and influencers (people who 'get things done') were brought together to:

- create an agreed systems map of childhood obesity causes for a community
- identify intervention opportunities through leveraging the dynamic aspects of the system
- convert these understandings into community-built, systems-oriented action plans.

The following excerpts from the websites of the local backbone groups, SEA Change and GenR8 Change, provide some insight into their rationale and approach.

Box 3.1 Excerpt from the SEA Change website

Our community is working together through the SEA Change initiative to make healthy eating and physical activity the easiest choice for a healthier community.

Unhealthy weight effects two thirds of the adult Australian population (and 1 in 4 children) and that figure is rising. Children who are at an unhealthy weight have a 70% chance of being so as adults and over time this can lead to chronic health conditions.

Unhealthy weight is known to take 10+ years off a person's life expectancy. It also has a huge impact on the quality of life.

Bringing it home ...

Weight, height and behavioural data collected in June 2016 shows us that an alarming 40% of Portland primary school–aged children are classified at unhealthy weight. 30 years ago, less than 10% of the population had unhealthy weight.

So where does SEA Change Portland come into this?

SEA Change Portland has started working towards a better future for our families. Our community has been making some big changes so that the healthy choice is becoming the easiest choice, especially for our children.

What have we done so far?

Community workshops in 2014 & 2016 have involved people from schools, families, businesses, clubs and the general community, in identifying many factors influencing unhealthy lifestyles. Actions to address these issues as a community began.

Where are we at right now?

Individuals and groups are making sustainable changes in all areas of the community. People are telling their stories and sharing healthy lifestyle news through SEA Change.

Where to from here?

What can you do as a community member?

- promote the vision
- encourage other people to get involved and
- participate or help in any way you can to support community actions.

Source: seachangeportland.com.au.

Box 3.2 Excerpt from the GenR8 Change website

How did GenR8 change begin?

Prompted by local childhood obesity data collected in 2015, the partnership between Southern Grampians and Glenelg Primary Care Partnership, Deakin University, Southern Grampians Shire Council and Western District Health Service continued to evolve as a community led intervention was built according to best available evidence.

Taking some key learnings from SEA Change Portland and the evidence available, GenR8 Change—Making the Healthy Choice the Easy Choice—was developed under the following guiding principles:

- **Children centered:** Evidence indicated the only successful community led interventions have been those centered on addressing obesity in children.

- **Multi-strategy, multi-level approach:** One single program and idea is not going to create sustainable change. We need multiple people and organisations making changes within different environments to embed sustainable change.

- **Whole of System thinking:** GenR8 Change involves the whole community, and considers all factors influencing our food and physical activity choices. It isn't about trying to change individual behaviours; it's about creating an environment that supports healthy choices to be easy choices.

- **Not a project and not funded:** GenR8 Change does not have an end point. This isn't a project so it is not funded, and it won't just stop. It's all about utilising existing community and agency capacity under a collective impact framework to create and embed sustainable change.

Source: www.genr8change.com/history.

Having established the aims of the collaboration and identified the range of possible actions, it is also important for collaboration partners to undertake a 'collaborative health check':

> In our current action plan, a lot of it is actually how do you make the collaboration work better? That was looking at issues against a checklist of what a good, healthy collaborative group would look like. We actively work at it, too; it doesn't just happen. But everything from looking at the diversity of the skill sets that we bring and even our thinking styles and those type of things through to communication internally, our different organisations, our different organisations' expectations. (Member, SEA Change backbone group)

Various backbone group members acknowledged the challenges of adapting to new ways of working that lie outside traditional or familiar control frameworks. The challenge was summed up by a member of the SEA Change backbone group:

> One of the things that I find a challenge with that is it's a lot of talking … I'm probably used to working with a male industry background and someone makes a decision and then we go off. But this is where we kind of have these conversations and make sure everyone does have the buy-in, and I think the result at the end is good … I come with a marketing background … so I want to put a logo and a brand on everything. But if it's driven from the community, there's a shift in my head … to constantly remind me that, 'Stop, we don't need to brand this', 'Is the community actually driving that', or to remember that it's a community-driven project, so don't own it—let the kids go.

Shared measurement systems

In early 2015, researchers from the GOC at Deakin University, with the cooperation of local agencies, undertook a comprehensive data collection exercise across the five Victorian shires of Corangamite, Glenelg, Moyne, Southern Grampians and the City of Warrnambool. The purpose of the data collection was to obtain an accurate breakdown of the weight and health status of children and so provide a reliable baseline against which any future changes might be assessed.

That said, actions taken to date in Portland and Hamilton do not readily lend themselves to the linear logics of *problem* + *solution* + *treatment* = *impact*. The systems-change approach taken by WHO STOPS commences from the fundamental premise that childhood obesity is a multifactorial phenomenon. While it is possible to measure the incidence of childhood obesity at a population level and compare data over time, there are many contributing factors; the precise relationships between those factors are not fully understood, and the effects upon the incidence of obesity of changes to any part of the system cannot be predicted with precision. Of necessity, the approach taken by WHO STOPS is long term and exploratory, which might fit uncomfortably with some authorisers. As a member of one of the backbone groups observed:

> The starting point was the pressure was on us right at the get-go to get some sort of movement happening, and there was a funding pressure through Portland District Health. They had health promotion funding and they'd appointed staff and they were sitting there saying, 'All right, we need to get some movement and get some runs on the board to keep the department happy.' The issue ... here is that this approach is very, very different in the sense that there's not outcomes and measures that we can specifically aim for. It's like, 'Well, listen, the community and the movement will take it where it needs to go'.

A similar observation was made by a member of another backbone group:

> You've got a board of management that oversees a reasonably new executive that has their ideas and what they want to see. And then the Department of Health as well—that you're answering to—that are saying, 'Outputs, outputs, outputs'. And we now know that it is about 'outcomes', and we have to have an outcomes-based approach.

Fortunately, a long-term approach is reinforced by an overarching backbone group, Great South Coast (GSC) Change (see below). GSC Change's backing enables the local backbone groups in Portland and Hamilton to 'stay the course', and the involvement of the GOC in data collection and community engagement provides powerful validation for moving away from project-centric thinking to an enabling approach centred on sustainable actions.

Ultimately, it is expected that these initiatives will be able to demonstrate impact over the longer term, as attested by a member of the GSC Change:

> We've gone beyond just reporting process; we're actually going to be reporting on impact and outcome. So, there's much more robust data that's coming out of this project.

> ... The data has enough in it to be able to say whether or not this has an effect at a population level. And there's very few projects that can really say that with any degree of confidence.

Mutually reinforcing activities

The starting premise of WHO STOPS is that the incidence and prevalence of childhood obesity are a consequence of multiple, mutually reinforcing factors. Allender et al. (2016), referring to the 2015 *Lancet* obesity series (Swinburn et al. 2015; Gortmaker et al. 2011), cite the challenge for community-based childhood obesity prevention initiatives as 'the creation of sustained, large-scale interventions that work at multiple levels'.

Allender et al. (2016) point to evidence suggesting that population-level interventions depend on

> fostering a shared understanding of the systemic determinants of non-communicable disease and asking how existing systems can be strengthened or new systems created to better promote health and prevent disease.

The approach adopted by WHO STOPS seeks to build capacity within communities to bring 'systems thinking' to bear on identifying 'the most important cause and effect relationships within a specific system boundary that create feedback and so amplify or stabilise change across a system' (Allender et al. 2016). Allender et al. (2016) point out that, whereas more 'traditional' interventions have focused on 'linear cause-and-effect relationships', systems interventions

> focus on non-linear relationships (e.g., tipping points), feedback where a 'causal' variable might in turn be impacted by an 'outcome variable', and complexity in the multilevel factors involved, as well as multiplex relationships among these factors.

Strong partnerships between researchers and community leaders in the Great South Coast region of Victoria have enabled the following:

1. The establishment in 2015 of a sustainable childhood obesity monitoring system across six local government areas using locally sourced competitive funding to conduct training, manage data collection, conduct analysis and support an in-kind contribution from health services, local government and schools to conduct data collection with commitments from partners to 'provide in-kind support to collect these data again in 2017 and 2019' (Allender et al. 2016).

2. The development and piloting of a range of 'systems action tools and techniques' for the purposes of building 'community capacity and ownership of efforts to apply system thinking to community-wide childhood obesity prevention' (Allender et al. 2016).

Building collaborative relationships with multiple stakeholders around broad goals enables a wide variety of organisations, groups and individuals to get involved in creating change. SEA Change and GenR8 Change each focus on supporting the local community to embrace common goals and to support local actors to take ownership of actions to reduce childhood obesity. As one interviewee said:

> Traditionally, I've gone to schools, offered programs, be it accreditation programs or things like that. But you always felt like you were selling it to them. But with the freedom of [WHO STOPS], it's, 'What would you like to do in this space? Where are the gaps? I'm here to support you.'

Accordingly, community members were able to identify multiple systems that impact childhood obesity and possible design interventions such as:

- improvements in individual health literacy
- changes to school food and physical environments
- banning of sugar-sweetened beverages within institutions
- local government regulation for better health (Allender et al. 2016).

Working under the WHO STOPS umbrella, the backbone groups for both SEA Change and GenR8 Change have endeavoured to style their efforts as a community-based 'movement' in which ideas from all quarters are welcomed, rather than as a 'program' bounded by policy prescriptions and operational rules.

Continuous communication

Effective collaboration requires a high standard of communication, both among partners and immediate stakeholders and with the communities in which the collaboration seeks to be embedded. In the case of WHO STOPS, for which the express aim has been to instil an enduring sense of collective community ownership, this has entailed efforts to make the fundamental shift from 'doing to' (which members of the SEA Change backbone group typified as the traditional health system approach) to 'doing for'. And, as one member of the SEA Change backbone group remarked: 'It takes a different skill set to be able to "do with" as opposed to "do for".'

'Doing with' often runs counter to the expectations of communities, accustomed as they are to the typical 'fund and deliver' approach so often employed by governments. 'Doing with' depends on trust, goodwill and reciprocity; it depends on building relationships and establishing connections. And, as another member of the SEA Change backbone group noted: 'If there's a connection, it's been much easier to start a conversation and perhaps easier to sustain a relationship.' Importantly, 'doing with' is about communities participating actively in setting aims, articulating strategies and taking actions within an authorising environment in which government and service providers act as enablers by helping to curate spaces where collaboration can be supported and sustained. As a member of GSC Change said:

> Then what happens is the community self-identifies, so through the process they actually see the maps and they actually work out, 'Well, hey, I can actually make the change here, and I'm actually part of the solution.' So, then you take them through that solution process and they actually self-nominate where they have an influence or a passion to actually make change. Within a community, that can be agencies, different agencies, through to passionate parents—anyone who wants to sign up and then act in that area. They prioritise those themselves about what they want to work on, and it really just snowballs from there.

Central to the communication task in both Portland and Hamilton are collaboration champions or ambassadors. These are people who 'hold key influence, just influence and pull within the community' (Gen R8 Change, backbone group member), who can leverage their position and standing in the community to build community support and build a sense of community ownership of the agenda for change:

> They very much influence people that they're connected to. We don't have, in a sense, a lot of power and control—and we shouldn't—over what and how information is disseminated. But the champions do because they're out in the community. And they're respected by the community, and they're seen to be doing things that others would like to follow. So, by, in a sense, using them to start whatever it is—an action—they then work out how that will work in their community, how that will look, whether that's going to work or be left … The champions seem to have the capacity to run with the idea, to see something be successful or fail. (SEA Change, backbone group member)

Champions are instrumental in building relationships, creating trust and sustaining the impetus for change:

> It's about the relationships and developing the relationships and developing that trust. That's a positive that comes out of a small community—the collaboration and the things that can happen very quickly when people have aligned their objectives can be very quick and very positive and there can be really long, sustainable change if you've got that individual motivation from the champions. (SEA Change, backbone group member)

However, as one SEA Change backbone group member observed:

> Constantly building relationships takes time. In a small community, everyone wears a multitude of different hats and most of the people that are in these spaces tend to be in multi-hat spaces.

Continuous communication requires continuous effort; people's attention shifts and memories fade and new players come on board. It is challenging to sustain the communication effort, continually craft the message, maintain consistency and thus ensure that key information pathways (such as social media, websites, electronic bulletins, and so on) are kept up to date. A member of the GenR8 Change backbone group acknowledged the need to continually bring the community back on-message:

> There has been a bit of a project-centric mindset that appears every now and again and we'll subtly—through the Facebook page and the blog posts and the articles that are shared—try and gently realign the thoughts to system-level thinking as opposed to project or even individual behavioural change.

Backbone support organisations

WHO STOPS embodies a set of shared aims and these are given local effect by three 'backbone' groups that act as catalysts for action, forums for sharing knowledge and spaces within which collaboration can occur.

The overarching backbone group, GSC Change, was established to 'reduce the levels of childhood obesity across the Great South Coast by facilitating community change', by bringing 'communities and local service providers together, to address multiple complex factors that influence children's weight'.[5] GSC Change comprises representatives from the Victorian DHHS, the Southern Grampians and Glenelg PCP and researchers from the GOC, based in the Centre for Population Health Research at Deakin University. Its role is to:

- act as the backbone to GSC Change at a regional scale, including:
  - setting an agreed regional agenda
  - setting indicators and monitoring against agreed regional measures
  - continually communicating regional progress.
- establishing and supporting the Change Ambassadors Group, and forums, to drive actions for higher-level systems change
- harmonise the change with other regional priorities, approaches and activities to maximise multiple outcomes for community health and wellbeing within the region
- build and evolve regional support structures and capacity to support ongoing obesity prevention work beyond the life of the NHMRC grant.[6]

In addition to GSC Change, local backbone groups have been established to guide SEA Change and GenR8 Change. A member of GSC Change who is also employed by the Southern Grampians and Glenelg PCP attends both groups and so provides continuity (of purpose) as well as acting as a conduit for the exchange of information.

In the communities of Portland and Hamilton, the backbone groups encourage and support community actions that contribute to reducing childhood obesity consistent with the collective impact principles of a clear and common agenda for change, a shared system of measurement, mutually reinforcing activities and continuous communication between community stakeholders.

Employing a *capacity-building* approach, researchers from the GOC assisted SEA Change and GenR8 Change to:

1. identify relevant stakeholders
2. recruit community leaders and 'influencers'
3. conduct public workshops for the purposes of identifying priorities and stimulating ideas.

---

5   'Great South Coast Change Backbone Group: Terms of reference', 2017, Unpublished primary source document.
6   ibid.

It is important that the backbone group is inclusive of the range of affected interests/stakeholders:

> We found the most effective backbone support is when we get representation from a number of key agencies. If we haven't had that key agency buy-in, if it's feeling like it's being owned or directed or driven by one key agency, it sort of stalls a little bit. (Member, GenR8 Change backbone group)

The same person went on to say:

> The first thing in setting up a backbone [group is] you need to have that leadership buy-in. Step one is you've got to have leadership buy-in. So, who are your key agencies, the key players in making sure that there's that commitment?

Final observations

Evidence of impact

A recurring theme in each of the cases is the importance—and problematic nature—of 'evidence of impact'. This is true in equal measure for the WHO STOPS initiatives and for the other collaborations investigated for our study.

It is generally acknowledged that the design of interventions should have a sound evidential base to persuade decision-makers, authorisers and stakeholders about the soundness of the approach. Once collaboration has commenced, authorisers and stakeholders expect the collaboration to produce evidence of impact. This can be problematic in that the relationship-building and trust-building phase of collaboration can take a long time and it can be difficult to reassure authorisers that progress is being made.

In these early stages, collaboration leads and partners are often obliged to rely on anecdotal evidence to make the case for continued support. Although collaboration leads and partners might be able to document systemic or process changes, or offer anecdotal accounts of improved relationships among stakeholders, these might not carry weight with authorisers looking for more conventional measures of impact such as the number of clients served or a reduced incidence of the problems targeted by the collaboration.

There is often institutional impatience around evaluation and impact measurement. Participants in each of the collaborations confirm the problematic nature of anecdotal evidence when seeking ongoing authorisation for continued collaborative action. In some cases, authorisers are impatient for more orthodox measures of impact—notwithstanding the often lengthy process of relationship-building (sometimes in the face of institutional resistance).

An important take-home message for authorisers is that it takes time to establish a different way of working and it is not always possible to immediately attribute observable changes to this or that element of the new system, assuming there *are* observable changes in the short to medium term. The reality is, with regard to longstanding entrenched social problems, a long-term perspective is required. For some social problems, observable, measurable impact might take years to become apparent. In the short term, other, more qualitative measures might need to suffice—measures that gauge the willingness of collaboration partners, street-level service providers and key stakeholders to stay the course (see Chapter 10).

Complexity

Everyone can agree that reducing childhood obesity is a 'good thing'. Indeed, superficially, it seems to be a simple, bounded problem. The WHO STOPS case reveals, however, that the contributors to childhood obesity are many and varied and range across multiple sectors and policy domains. There is no 'one-stop-shop' solution. It is important, therefore, that anyone involved in collaboration is aware of the complexity of the issues that are being confronted. For many social problems, the combined efforts of multiple actors are required to achieve change.

Understandably, authorisers working within traditional operating cultures that emphasise the achievement of fast, demonstrable results will want to 'claim' success. However, it can be difficult to attribute improvements to any one party when there are many actors working towards the same outcome. Authorisers, partners and stakeholders need to be prepared to live with ambiguity—and to share accountability—when it comes to the attribution of success or even occasional failures.

Resourcing

Long-term social change is often a journey of discovery. 'Solutions' are not always readily apparent, uncertainty is high and occasional U-turns are unavoidable. Many organisations operate within the constraints of budgetary, electoral or contractual cycles and this predisposes authorisers to favour initiatives that exhibit linear 'problem–treatment–impact' logics. It can be difficult, therefore, to establish secure ongoing resourcing for a long-term process of social change where it is neither possible to identify any particular solution in advance nor to nominate the time frame within which the problem is likely to be solved (Kania and Kramer 2011).

For collective impact, as for any collaboration, it is necessary that authorisers fully appreciate the time and effort required to establish collaborative ways of working and to sustain collective processes. In the case of WHO STOPS, there was a conscious effort to avoid the perception that the change initiatives in Portland and Hamilton represented a 'project' bounded by budgets, dedicated resourcing and time frames. Instead, the emphasis was on achieving 'systems change' by forging new relationships, fostering dialogue, reducing barriers and identifying opportunities to work and think differently. The key protagonists realised that project-based resourcing could not sustain the kind of change agenda they were aiming for; these initiatives needed to work within available resources and be self-sustaining:

> One thing that I think we were all very consistent on was that we were sick of short-term project-based funding. We were over it, and we were looking for an approach, a way of doing work, sustainably for the long term … And we were consciously saying: 'We don't want funding for this. We actually have to work out how to fund it ourselves sustainably.' (Member, SEA Change backbone group)

Managing expectations

Collaboration partners sometimes experience significant pressures to get things done to meet the expectations of authorisers and stakeholders. The levels of personal commitment brought to collaboration by those engaged in it, coupled with the demands of the authorising environment and the natural inclination of authorisers to want to see results, can inadvertently give rise to an unhealthy work environment that can leave people feeling depleted and exhausted.

Social change relies on making gradual improvements over time; it is not a quick fix, nor does it rely on a single breakthrough by a single organisation. According to Kania and Kramer (2011: 41): 'Systemic change, however, ultimately depends on a sustained campaign to increase the capacity and coordination of an entire field.' The whole-of-systems change to which the WHO STOPS initiatives aspire, for example, means being prepared to play the long game. It might take decades for population-level effects to become apparent, and tangible impacts—in terms of the prevalence of childhood obesity—will be difficult to conclusively demonstrate in the short term. A member of the SEA Change backbone group described the problem in the following terms:

> I think people like to see the change. They like to see it to be tangible. So, there's a leap of faith, and it's taken me two years to wrap my head around the fact that I'm not visually seeing a huge amount of people changing size or anything like that. And I think in the past that was the old model: you come in, you have a thing, here's your journey, this is the result you'll get, do your tests, measure it against this, bang, and you'd see that. So, whether it be figures or whatever, you'd sort of have something to compare against ... you had some tangible thing.

> This is asking people to take a leap of faith that change will happen by participating and that, if it doesn't, that's okay. And I think that's certainly what I find when we approach and start doing actions or outputs or different programs. You'll sit in a meeting and quite regularly what I hear is people going: 'But what am I doing? What am I going off to do?' 'Well, what do you want to go off to do? What is your contribution?'

Practice considerations

1. Establish a baseline against which the impact of collaboration will be assessed. Ask questions such as: a) What is the nature of the problem(s); b) What factors contribute to the persistence of the problem(s); c) What is the nature of the desired change(s); d) How will collaboration contribute to the change agenda; and e) What will a positive impact look like?

2. Identify relevant sources of baseline data as well as any gaps in information. Where there are gaps, investigate whether other indicators or surrogate measures might be used. Identify institutions or people with relevant knowledge and expertise to peer review existing data and advise on cost-effective means for the ongoing collection, interpretation and reporting of data.

3. Engage with relevant data custodians in each of the partner organisations to identify any issues or problems—and solutions. These might include privacy considerations, the de-identification of data, statutory restrictions, the interoperability of data platforms and so on.

4. Is it possible to enlist the assistance or participation of independent researchers or research organisations with demonstrated expertise in the problems being addressed? What sources of external validation are available to affirm the collaborative approach and strategic aims?

5. Identify and evaluate the applicability of all available and relevant tools for the measurement of impact. Investigate resources such as the Social Impact Toolbox developed by the University of Technology Sydney in partnership with Community Sector Banking[7] or Platform C—a platform created to offer support, learning and connections for people looking to achieve large-scale impact through collaboration.[8]

6. Devise an impact framework for sign-off by authorisers. Have direct and indirect measures of collaboration impact been peer reviewed by people with relevant expertise? Have all relevant internal and external stakeholders been consulted? Have the feasibility and sustainability of data collection been assessed?

7. As part of the impact framework, consider how the impact of collaboration will be reported. Ensure that any reporting of collaboration impact is subject to governance processes agreed by authorisers.

8. Spell out the 'path to impact' for authorisers and stakeholders. Keep in mind that collaborations take time to mature and it might be difficult to directly attribute impact to collaboration.

9. What interim indicators might be used to validate the collaboration? How might collaboration be a driver of cultural change, changed behaviour or practice or changes in operational and/or public policy?

---

7   See www.socialimpacttoolbox.com.
8   See platformc.org.

References

Allender, Steven, Lynne Millar, Peter Hovmand, Colin Bell, Marj Moodie, Rob Carter, Boyd Swinburn, Claudia Strugnell, Janette Lowe, and Kayla de la Haye. 2016. 'Whole of systems trial of prevention strategies for childhood obesity: WHO STOPS Childhood Obesity.' *International Journal of Environmental Research and Public Health* 13(11): 1143.

Andrews, Rhys, and Tom Entwistle. 2010. 'Does cross-sectoral partnership deliver? An empirical exploration of public service effectiveness, efficiency, and equity.' *Journal of Public Administration Research and Theory* 20(3): 679–701. doi.org/10.1093/jopart/mup045.

Australian New Zealand Clinical Trials Registry (ANZCTR). 2016. 'Whole of Systems Trial of Prevention Strategies for Childhood Obesity: WHO STOPS Childhood Obesity.' *Trial Review.* [Online]. Available from: anzctr.org.au/Trial/Registration/TrialReview.aspx?id=371109.

Babiak, Kathy, and Lucie Thibault. 2009. 'Challenges in multiple cross-sector partnerships.' *Nonprofit and Voluntary Sector Quarterly* 38(1): 117–143. doi.org/10.1177/0899764008316054.

Carter, Neil. 1989. 'Measuring government performance.' *The Political Quarterly* 59(3): 369–375. doi.org/10.1111/j.1467-923X.1988.tb02407.x.

de Bruijn, Hans. 2007. *Managing Performance in the Public Sector.* London: Routledge. doi.org/10.4324/9780203946336.

Gortmaker, Steven L., Boyd A. Swinburn, David Levy, Rob Carter, Patricia L. Mabry, Diane T. Finegood, Terry Huang, Tim Marsh, and Marjory L. Moodie. 2011. 'Changing the future of obesity: Science, policy, and action.' *The Lancet* 378(9793): 838–847. doi.org/10.1016/S0140-6736(11)60815-5.

Kania, John, and Mark R. Kramer. 2011. 'Collective impact.' *Stanford Social Innovation Review* 69(Winter): 36–41.

Koppenjan, Joop. 2008. 'Creating a playing field for assessing the effectiveness of network collaboration by performance measures.' *Public Management Review* 10(6): 699–714. doi.org/10.1080/14719030802423061.

Pell, Charlotte. 2016. 'Debate: Against collaboration.' *Public Money & Management* 36(1): 4–5. doi.org/10.1080/09540962.2016.1103410.

Power, Michael. 1994. *The Audit Explosion.* London: Demos.

Swinburn, Boyd, William Dietz, and Sabine Kleinert. 2015. 'A Lancet commission on obesity.' *The Lancet* 386(10005): 1716–1717. doi.org/10.1016/S0140-6736(15)00722-9.

4

COLLABORATIVE INTELLIGENCE AND ORGANISATIONAL INTELLIGENCE

Introduction

Successful collaboration requires a number of personal and organisational attributes to come together. Individuals involved in collaboration—especially collaboration leaders—must evince a set of personal characteristics and capacities that extend beyond traditional professional skills and education. We have termed this set of characteristics 'collaborative intelligence' or 'CQ'. CQ is a predisposition to thinking more generously than is usually necessary in more conventional operating environments and encompasses those difficult to determine distinctive traits possessed by individuals who excel at collaboration. CQ is a collective asset that can be developed, modelled and shared in collaborative spaces. It is based on an implicit recognition that *people* collaborate and, therefore, interpersonal relationships are important building blocks of collaborative action.

The organisations involved in a collaborative arrangement must also exhibit capacities and structures that support the collaborative activity outside the normal operating environment. Indeed, genuine collaboration is achieved when the collaborators are focused on the problem being solved and when the methods used are flexible and fit for purpose—even where this fitness may deviate from normal operating arrangements. The role of the organisations involved and their leaders is to provide permission and accept the risk related to such operating environments. This requires a level of *organisational intelligence* to support the collaboration effectively. Collaboration is not only a product of the individuals involved in collaboration; it is also a combination of the individuals and their authorising environments, or the CQ and the organisational intelligence of the entire collaborative effort.

In this chapter, we use CQ as a lens through which to examine the personal characteristics needed by those leading and acting in collaborations; we then examine the challenges associated with collaborations involving traditionally structured organisations and discuss how organisational intelligence affects the organisational licence to collaborate, or the stance that must be adopted by authorisers in these traditional structures for them to effectively support collaborations.

What is CQ?

Effective collaboration requires a special kind of emotional intelligence, which we will call 'collaborative intelligence' or 'CQ'. Collaboration makes demands of participants that take them outside their usual operational comfort zone. This can be challenging, especially for people whose dominant experience is of working in hierarchical, chain-of-command organisational cultures in which fidelity to process and protocol figures strongly. CQ is a set of values, behaviours and processes that are fundamentally 'relational' in nature, rather than 'transactional'. The CQ skill set allows individuals to build relationships with each other. This is important because it is people who collaborate, and those relationships are the foundation on which collaboration is built.

As one interviewee remarked on the nature of CQ:

> I think collaboration is often misunderstood as something that you just do. Or occasionally I hear the phrase 'barriers to collaboration', as if you've just got to break the dam and it will flow naturally. But, in my view, collaboration is a learned set of skills. It's hard; it's complex; it happens at various levels in various ways. It can happen a bit or it can happen in a very deep and enduring way. I think having a group of people that, if you like, learn on the job together how to collaborate was really critical to the success of this [project] both in development and implementation.

CQ is shorthand for describing the attributes of effective participants in collaborative environments. It encompasses a number of personal attributes, such as knowing when to take charge and when to let others lead, a willingness to listen and respond nimbly to changed circumstances or new information, a capacity for empathy and the ability to see things from other people's points of view, a deep appreciation of systems and how they intersect and interact, respect for the collaborative process itself and the ability to forge enduring relationships based on trust.

CQ also implicitly acknowledges that organisational cultures and hierarchies can inhibit collaboration; effective collaboration requires trust, transparency and the granting of opportunity for multiparty control—qualities that are difficult to realise in siloed, hierarchical systems.

CQ is also a product of maturity and experience and, where it is lacking, collaboration cannot be effective, as observed by another interviewee:

> We did have some pointy heads … who had no interpersonal skills … [T]hose are the sorts of people—and there's no other way to dress this up—that pissed people off. This supercilious, looking-down-your-nose arrogance. Some of these people were [in their] early twenties, 25, not terribly worldly … They'd never been in these sort of operational, real-world situations. We'd actually been out there and done stuff for 30 years; these guys come out of university with a degree.

There is broad agreement among those interviewed that successful collaboration relies on this kind of emotional intelligence. Without CQ, true collaboration cannot happen.

A CQ skill set

Everyone interviewed for the study was asked to nominate the essential skills or attributes that embody CQ and are necessary for effective collaboration. Although the responses varied somewhat in terms of expression, there was, overall, a high degree of consistency about the skills and attributes people considered important. Set out below is a list of personal attributes together with a list of hard and soft skills that should, ideally, be present in those charged with participating in collaboration.

Personal qualities

Interviewees for each of the cases emphasised the importance of the personal character attributes of effective collaborators. These are not typically the qualities one might expect to see in a selection criteria or a duty statement. In Table 4.1, we have listed the attributes identified by participants as essential to effective collaboration—the attributes associated with a strong CQ. Perhaps expectedly, maturity and commitment were high on the list of requirements, as were honesty, integrity and flexibility. However, so too were characteristics such as openness and humility, adaptability and generosity, while a willingness to share power and to credit success to others were also identified as critical.

Table 4.1 Attributes of a person with high CQ

Maturity and judgement (life experience)	A person with high CQ will demonstrate mature judgement based on their professional and lived experience. This has less to do with a person's chronological age and more to do with their ability to understand the needs and motivations of others and to work with that knowledge in honest and constructive ways.
Commitment and passion	Commitment to the collaboration 'mission' and an emotional, as well as intellectual, engagement with the problems at hand are essential; they provide the 'fuel' needed to sustain collaborative intent.
Honesty and integrity	Honest dealing is an essential foundation for building trust within collaborations (for example, between collaboration partners), trust between the collaboration and participating organisations (for example, assurance) and with external stakeholders.
Interpersonal skills	Collaborations bring together people, groups and organisations with diverse interests, motivations and preferred communication styles. The ability to connect with others, to see things from other points of view and to harness the capacity of others to focus on collaborative purpose is indispensable.
Charisma and the capacity to inspire	Of all the components of CQ, charisma is the most elusive simply because it cannot be taught. It can, however, be recruited for, and deployed to collaborative purposes. Charismatic personalities can bring people along on the collaboration journey. They are often best paired with someone who is more strategic and methodical in their approach—someone who acts as a stabilising force for the purpose of providing internal and external assurance.
Consistency and follow-through	'Say what you intend to do and do what you say': Trust in collaboration—particularly for external stakeholders—resides in accountability for action. This means acting in a manner consistent with the mission and values of the collaboration, as well as following through with commitments and obtaining internal and external support (or consent) for necessary changes in emphasis or approach.

Openness and humility	Share doubts, be honest about failure and error, do not overclaim, be upfront about underdelivery, listen to advice and accept criticism. These are strengths, not weaknesses. Importantly, these qualities have greater potency when they occur in a supportive authorising environment that recognises and accepts the risks inherent in collaborative working.
Willingness to share power and credit	Give credit where credit is due and, sometimes, be prepared to give credit even where it is not entirely due. Delegate authority whenever possible to those nearest the coalface, but without sacrificing accountability or performance. Build trust in, and commitment to, collaboration by letting others share in collaboration successes; this might predispose collaboration partners to accept shared accountability for occasional failures.
Generosity, patience and compassion	These qualities most embody the spirit of collaboration. The generous person exhibits mature judgement, but is not judgemental; the patient person accepts that collaboration is a 'long game' and understands that most people come to collaboration from quite different starting positions; the compassionate person cares about outcomes and strives to understand the positions of those who might not wholly embrace the collaboration and its aims.
Problem-solver and self-starter	Collaborative action does not always wait for 'permission'. Often, formal sanction for collaboration gains traction when individuals have been collaborating 'covertly', exercising creativity and exhibiting personal commitment by addressing problems that they—and those in their personal and professional networks— have a capacity to influence. Collaboration does not follow a predictable trajectory; collaboration partners need to be nimble and entrepreneurial.
Courage and emotional resilience	Collaboration needs courage—for example, to challenge the status quo and to respond constructively to stakeholder reticence, organisational inertia and executive indifference. Collaboration is hard work and requires large investments in relationship-building and communication. It can be tiring and dispiriting at times. Therefore, emotional resilience is very important, as are supporting strategies within the collaboration to relieve the strain on colleagues.
Flexibility and adaptability	An ability to 'roll with the punches', to identify and capitalise on opportunities and to change course is essential, as are being open to new ideas and receptive to signals in the operating environment and the community.
Creativity, lateral thinking and reflectiveness	Collaboration rests on creative thinking: considering problems from different perspectives and working towards a new synthesis or a 'new normal'. Creativity rests on 'thinking outside the box', taking time to reflect (and encouraging others to reflect) on the collaboration journey and, importantly, identifying the lessons learned along the way and weaving those lessons into your collaboration practice.

Hard and soft skills

There is also a set of hard and soft skills that complement and enhance collaborative processes. By and large, these skills can be learned but they are also moulded by the presence of the character attributes identified above. The hard skills relate to some of the more common capacities that are required to operate within a corporate environment, while others are very much focused on interpersonal skills and capacities. Clearly, the ability to work with others, communicate and build trust is absolutely crucial to collaborating effectively.

The personality attributes are what make it possible for individual collaborators to build trust between themselves, while the hard and soft skills give the individuals the knowledge to negotiate in an informed manner within the limits of their power to be able to act on collaborative ideas. As observed by the director of a Children's Team in New Zealand:

> I think you need to have people in those [relationship-building] roles who've got the ability to see the strategic angle of things so that they can understand the ecosystem and how the bits work and how those levers work, some of which are informal levers and some of which are formal levers. But they also have to be able to actually understand from a transactional level how to get things done and to make sure that happens.

It should be noted that the levels of collaboration skills represented around the table are often uneven; as such, for collaboration to be effective, it is a prime objective of the collaboration process to raise the CQ of all of those around the table, and this requires insightful, skilled leadership. The skill level of the whole group becomes greater than that of its parts. Collaboration is all about relationships, and those groups of individuals with the high levels of maturity and flexibility that we term CQ are able to create stronger relationships that allow them to use these skills and common language to build CQ within the team and create strong collaborative efforts.

The hard and soft skills that are useful to collaboration are listed in Table 4.2, and are paired with questions that are designed to help identify these skills in individuals.

Table 4.2 Hard and soft skills

Connectedness (within communities and communities of interest)	To what extent do the people involved in collaboration have existing relationships of trust within affected communities? Do they have the capacity to leverage trust in the objects of the collaboration via their standing within affected communities?
Corporate memory and knowledge	Do those involved in collaboration have a strong understanding of the history and culture of the communities, organisations and interests operating in the policy space or of the impact of the problems that are the focus of the collaboration? Are they aware of past initiatives and/or failures and able to weave learnings from those experiences into present challenges?
Systems knowledge and capacity to cultivate networks	To what extent do the people involved in collaboration understand the 'ecosystem' in which the collaboration is to occur?
Stakeholder relations	Do collaboration partners have a strong understanding of the various internal and external stakeholders affected by collaboration, including their respective interests, priorities, points of difference and the issues that unite them?
Negotiation, facilitation and conflict-resolution	Do they understand the possible sources of cynicism and doubt, as well as the sources of support, and do they have the skill and personal integrity to manage complexity and win trust? Are they able to offer themselves as honest brokers to encourage trust and manage differences of opinion among stakeholders?
Governance, assurance and risk management	Is there a strong understanding of, and commitment to, the application of effective governance, the identification and mitigation of risk and the importance of providing assurance to internal and external stakeholders to protect the integrity and core purposes of the collaboration?
Interpersonal communication and relationship-based practice	Do the individuals involved in a collaboration possess the ability to engage in respectful, constructive, non-conflictual communications with collaboration partners and external and internal stakeholders, including the executives of partner organisations?
Recognising when change is needed	Do individual collaboration partners understand what needs to change and why, and can they make a persuasive case for change and win support for necessary actions that give effect to sustainable change?
Outcomes focus and understanding of impact measurement	Do collaboration partners have a practical understanding of the desired/intended outcomes to be achieved and how they might be measured and supported? Do they accept the necessity and importance of impact measurement and the practical means for gathering and reporting evidence of impact?

What the cases tell us

The skills and characteristics associated with individuals who are successful and effective collaborators also serve to inform our sense of what collaborative arrangements should look like. However, collaboration—because it is problem-centric and involves diverse participants—is also a complex activity in terms of its structure and processes. In this section, we examine this phenomenon.

Many people have a preconception of what collaboration should look like. Often, this picture is one of formality: structure, authority and process are often thought to be clearly delineated within a documented modus operandi. Collaborative frameworks are also expected to be reciprocal, operate predominantly across public–not-for-profit sector boundaries and entail the clear articulation of aims and the means by which they will be pursued.

These primary expectations are also in line with the extensive academic literature on cross-sector collaboration. Therefore, in instigating this research, we were expecting to see evidence of the prioritisation of these structures in examples of effective collaborations. However, it quickly became apparent, both in the process of case selection and in the course of the investigation of the cases themselves, that the reality on the ground did not neatly align with this initial—and what we came to appreciate as somewhat simplistic—framing of collaboration. In truth, collaboration occupies a broader and more diverse spectrum of forms. We were forced to conclude that there is no single one-size-fits-all organisational model for effective collaboration.

However, the investigations did conclude that there are two broad sets of characteristics that are common to, and necessary for, effective collaborations. These are:

1. Collaborative *practice*—the behaviours, attitudes and values that support and sustain collaborative endeavour, which are part of CQ.
2. An authorising environment that creates the organisational spaces within which collaboration can occur.

The existence of CQ and organisational intelligence—or an *amiable* authorising environment—together is a necessary precondition for successful collaboration.

Organisational intelligence

Organisational intelligence refers to the collective understanding of an organisation and the structured permissions from leaders of organisations that enable collaboration. Organisations with organisational intelligence support collaboration by creating systems that help collaboration thrive and provide clear, unambiguous authority to the collaboration team— often outside normal operating processes. These organisations will also have an understanding of the challenges to collaboration, the relational nature of collaboration and, therefore, some patience for collaboration. We can see how important this organisational intelligence and permission is by discussing the operating spaces in and around which collaboration works.

Primary and secondary operating spaces

For the most part, collaboration occurs in a secondary (informal) operating space in which many of the conventions of the primary (formal) operating space do not apply in quite the same way. This 'dual operating system', which Kotter (2012) identified, comprises a 'management-driven hierarchy' and a second operating system, which is 'devoted to the design and implementation of strategy, that uses an agile, network-like structure and a very different set of processes' (Kotter 2012: 46–47). This second operating space is more nimble than the primary space, which allows it to 'address the challenges produced by mounting complexity and rapid change' (Kotter 2012: 46).

Furthermore, the operational and behavioural norms that will apply in this secondary operating space are to a large extent undefined— at least at the outset—and need to be co-designed and coproduced by participants. For most participants, this means *unlearning* old norms and attitudes while creating and signing up to new ones. This can liberate individuals and information from 'silos and hierarchical layers' and enable the second operating space to flow with far greater freedom and speed (Kotter 2012: 50).

These new norms might apply only within the collaboration space and thus require participants to become, effectively, bicultural as they transition back and forth across a shifting boundary between secondary operating spaces and the primary operating spaces where the dominant, normative operating culture of partner organisations resides and within which formal authorisation for collaboration occurs.

This second space is important as it 'permits a level of individualism, creativity, and innovation that the bureaucratic hierarchy cannot provide', and it is essential that the secondary space does not come to be viewed as a 'rogue operation' by the primary operators but is 'treated as a legitimate part of the organisation, or the hierarchy will crush it' (Kotter 2012: 51).

Indeed, one interviewee told us:

> A typical bureaucratic behaviour is that once something starts to happen that you don't like, you divest yourself from the process and you start to brief upwards about the negative effects of it. If they get wind that somebody's going to come into their patch and start to change the way they do things and break down their happy little fiefdoms—that's just my language—you end up with an internal political problem. (Throughcare)

Internal 'political problems' can inhibit the development of collaborative work, especially when collaboration is seen to impinge on established lines of managerial demarcation. Secondary operating spaces also establish bounded areas in which experimentation can occur: operating spaces in which occasional failures are acceptable and the risks of failure are minimised. The flexibility or nimbleness of such a space allows for collaboration between groups to grow.

Authorising environment

The kind of authorising environment in which any collaboration is set is also a determinant of success or failure. Having the right authorising environment is important: a supportive authorising environment is one that exhibits the qualities of 'interagency collaborative capacity' (Bardach 1998)—one that is capable of devolving authority to the leadership of a collaboration and that allows time to build relationships of trust between collaboration partners and empowers stakeholders to establish a governance framework adapted to the specific needs of the collaboration.

It might be expected—in fact, it is highly likely—in collaboration settings that participants will bring to the table different expectations, framings, norms, skills and priorities. These can act as barriers to working collaboratively in some settings as priorities and areas of focus become sources of tension. On the other hand, agreeing not to be fettered by particular organisational, cultural and/or disciplinary legacies can liberate imaginations and stoke enthusiasm and commitment.

The siloed behaviour of public sector organisations represents a significant barrier to effective collaboration insofar as it impedes the kind of authorising environment necessary to create a 'licence' for collaboration. The notion of a licence to collaborate applies as much to the negotiation of collaborative relationships between partner organisations as it does to the relationship between the collaboration and the affected constituencies of interest.

Similarly, bureaucratic rigidity and prescription can act as an impediment to collaboration. This is often evident where collaboration partners wish to pursue localised responses that depart from standardised approaches. Here bureaucratic actors can behave like 'gatekeepers'. As one interviewee observed, bureaucracies often forget that they are a 'resource'; they are not the 'main game'.

A critical aspect of authorising environments in which collaborative approaches can take hold is the extent to which collaboration partners enjoy executive backing. Executive backing confers political and operational licence to collaborate and offers protection for collaborative spaces. However, as Merchant (2011) observes, the fluidity and absence of hierarchy in collaborative settings can be uncomfortable terrain for executives, which shows the importance of developing organisational intelligence through an understanding of collaboration and what it needs to thrive.

Thus, we can say that partner organisations need to offer clear, unambiguous authority to collaborate. It is essential that they acknowledge and accept that there might be an accentuated level of risk associated with the collaboration by virtue of the complexity of the operating environment. Moreover, it is important to acknowledge that the integrity of the collaborative process is a function of reciprocal flows of authority from the executive to collaboration leads and assurance from collaboration leads and partners to the executive; collaborators need permission and support while bureaucratic heads need assurance of appropriateness, likelihood of success and alignment of goals.

Successful collaborations are formed in a supportive authorising environment in which it is possible for the collaboration to forge strong relationships with key constituencies through a mix of formal and informal networks (Jupp 2000: 8; Bryson et al. 2009). Authorisers can enable collaboration to succeed by providing a licence to collaborate and support for building the relationships crucial to collaboration.

Although many people working in the public and community sectors exhibit a capacity for high CQ, differences in organisational culture can either encourage or inhibit its expression. In the community sector, whose authorising environment is shaped by fidelity to mission and values, CQ can flourish. In much of the public sector, however, with an authorising environment often shaped by fidelity to protocol and process, CQ can struggle to find expression. The success of collaboration can be reliant on organisational intelligence, which buffers the processes of collaboration and allows it to flourish.

If the environment for collaboration is lacking, no amount of CQ will be able to overcome an obstinate authorising environment. Part of a good collaborating environment is the attention given to the importance of long-term relationships between partners in collaboration. A supportive authorising environment is one that aids in the maintenance of these relationships over time and ensures that those individuals with higher CQ are involved in collaboration. Without a supportive authorising environment (see Chapter 3) and CQ, collaboration is unlikely to succeed as the relationships necessary for collaboration will not be built.

The quality of collaboration also depends to a significant degree on the program/partnership logics brought to the collaboration by partners—for example, organisations steeped in 'transactional' logics might struggle with many aspects of collaboration, whereas organisations that are more 'relational' in outlook might fare better.

Final observations

Interviewees across all cases spoke about the importance of relationships— and relationship-building—as the bedrock of effective collaboration. Constructive relationships—interpersonal and interorganisational—are the precursors of trust, credibility and legitimacy. Collaboration is all about relationships and, to win the confidence of stakeholders, participants need to have insight into the ways in which attitudes and conduct are shaped by organisational history, pre-existing networks, traditions, habits and learned behaviours. Partners in collaboration need the skill set of CQ to engage with others, instil trust, respond constructively to resistance or suspicion and diffuse tensions; to generate buy-in, reassure, persuade, upwardly manage, negotiate compromises and adapt to changing circumstances.

Effective collaborations can encourage multiple opinions and provide safe spaces in which to air differences. However, it is important not to underestimate the emotional labour that goes into building collaborative relationships and that fuels the willingness of people to be involved. A capacity for adaptation and a tolerance for changeability are important. Also important is the capacity to exploit cultural tensions within and between organisations towards collaborative aims. Workers at the coalface need to be skilled and empowered to incentivise and upwardly manage middle managers, who can be key blockers of collaborative effort.

It might be said that the personality traits and skills that make up CQ differ from the primary skill sets traditionally valued in many organisations. Most often, CQ is learnt 'on the job' as practitioners respond adaptively to the challenges of collaboration.

That said, CQ alone is not enough for a successful collaboration: a nimble and supportive authorising environment is vital for collaborative efforts to flourish.

CQ is an important ingredient in the collaborative process because it embodies the skills required to build trust and relationships between individuals and their organisations. After all, people, not organisations, build relationships and a supportive authorising environment is necessary to help maintain those relationships for successful collaboration over time.

Practice considerations

1. Does your organisation have honest and full discussions regarding the nature of and challenges associated with successful collaboration, including in relation to whether or not it would genuinely support a collaborative process?

2. Does it recognise and discuss the idea of CQ, including to identify where the traditional governance structures may restrict the opportunity for effective collaboration?

3. Does your organisation have a written resource describing collaborative processes, the challenges faced and potential mitigations needed to communicate effectively?

4. Does your organisation value, encourage and reward attitudes, behaviours and practices that are consistent with CQ, including in relation to its performance management processes and activities?

5. Can you identify those aspects of your organisation's culture or business practices that either: a) inhibit the expression of CQ, or b) recognise and foster CQ?

6. Does your organisation value and offer incentives for measured risk-taking and forging relationships with internal and external stakeholders?

7. Are there potential CQ exemplars in your organisation who might be enlisted to act as CQ 'champions'?

8. Do the recruitment practices and reward frameworks of your organisation support and reinforce personal qualities and attributes that are consistent with CQ?

9. What steps would you need to take to devise a 'CQ strategy' for your collaboration, and how might you capture the impact CQ has on collaboration success?

References

Bardach, Eugene. 1998. *Getting Agencies to Work Together: The practice and theory of managerial craftsmanship*. Washington, DC: Brookings Institution Press.

Bryson, John M., Barbara C. Crosby, Melissa M. Stone, and Emily O. Saunoi-Sandgren. 2009. *Designing and managing cross-sector collaboration: A case study in reducing traffic congestion*. Collaboration: Networks and Partnerships Series Report. Washington, DC: IBM Center for The Business of Government.

Daymond, Jarryd. 2015. Practitioners' perspectives on cross-sector collaborations. PhD thesis, Macquarie University, Sydney.

Jupp, Ben. 2000. *Working Together: Creating a better environment for cross-sector partnerships*. London: Demos.

Kotter, John. 2012. 'Accelerate!' *Harvard Business Review* 90(11): 44–58.

Merchant, Nilofer. 2011. 'Eight dangers of collaboration.' *Harvard Business Review*, 1 December.

5

DESIGNING THE COLLABORATION AND ITS OPERATIONAL FRAMEWORK

Introduction

It is important to ensure that the collaboration model is fit for purpose. That said, collaboration is not always the 'answer' and can sometimes look very much like a solution in search of a problem. In this chapter, we look to the collaboration literature and to the experiences of people in our case studies for guidance about designing successful multiparty collaborations.

Collaboration needs more than good intentions; it also needs to be designed, built and implemented. Collaborations have many moving parts; ensuring that the operational framework for the collaboration is fit for purpose is a core design challenge. Attention to the character—and history—of stakeholder relationships is critical, as is attention to the degree of fit (or lack of fit) between legacy systems, operating norms and formal rules. For not only do each of the collaboration partners and stakeholders bring their own, often distinct, institutional and administrative histories to the table, they also have diverse perspectives and interests that affect how collaboration works. Purposive design of the collaboration framework can address such differences head-on and provide the basis for a new synthesis: a renewed understanding of the problem and what needs to be done.

Collaborations work best when there is clarity about aims, strategy, process, communication and conduct. However, respectful, cordial communication can sometimes be difficult, especially when strong personalities are involved and/or parties bring divergent views to the table (Kahane 2017). It is essential, therefore, that collaboration partners forge a shared understanding of the collaboration's purpose, objectives, rationale, strategic direction and proposed actions, based on a common language. It is important to identify the things on which collaboration partners agree and those on which they disagree. Where there is disagreement, it might be possible to establish protocols to guide discussion and so avoid conflict and fallout. Independent collaboration brokers can play a positive role by helping to bridge gaps and resolve conflicts in nomenclature and understanding.

It is important to acknowledge that all collaborations are highly context dependent and, in some ways, unique. Collaborative strategies need to be built on a comprehensive understanding of the presenting problem(s) and the social, political and policy ecologies in which they arise. Typically, the kinds of problems that collaboration seeks to address tend to be multifactorial in nature and do not fall wholly within the responsibility— or capability—of any single entity or jurisdiction. Nor are they amenable to resolution by multiple entities or jurisdictions acting separately because the interstices of bureaucratic and programmatic boundaries are where people and communities can fall through the cracks.

Collaboration is about hope

Despair is a natural and understandable reaction to complex—or 'wicked'—problems. It is easy to become resigned to a status quo that is demonstrably not achieving the desired results. It is altogether too easy to arrive at an acceptance that systemic, institutional and cultural barriers to change are insurmountable. In part, this is a product of *path dependence*—a process in which decisions made in the present context are shaped by the legacy of past decisions, even when past circumstances are no longer relevant. Path dependence can explain why it is sometimes difficult for policymakers and practitioners to think outside the square and visualise alternative ways of working. Equally, complexity—and its bedfellows, fragmentation, incoherence and uncertainty—also creates opportunities for *path creation*, which is a process in which actors look to the past, not necessarily to repeat or avoid what happened previously, but, instead, to generate new options (Garud et al. 2010).

In New Zealand, the local Children's Team in Gisborne coined the term 'too many cars in the driveway' to give expression to the frustrations of families and communities in crisis who had long struggled to make sense of, and get help from, the multiple agencies and officials involved in their lives. We strongly suspect that, for many frontline workers, 'too many cars in the driveway' is a potent metaphor for ineffective systems and lost opportunities. In Gisborne, it provided a rallying cry to create greater coherence, provide clear entry points and pathways, reduce administrative duplication and gaps/inconsistencies in service delivery and generally provide a platform for bespoke responses to complex problems.

To be sure, 'complexity' entails challenges on multiple fronts: political, operational, informational and institutional (among others). Challenges can also present opportunities; there is fluidity in complexity that creates spaces for innovative, disruptive solutions to complex problems. A large part of the collaboration challenge is often about how best to leverage 'complexity' and 'interests' to mobilise support for a collaborative approach. There can also be an element of serendipity about collaboration: collaborative responses sometimes arise from a fortuitous collision of interests.

Be clear about the problem and demonstrate the case for collaboration

Collaboration is only one of many strategies that might be utilised to leverage responses to complex social problems—responses that are fit for purpose. Deciding whether collaboration is the most appropriate strategy requires a clear understanding of the social, geographic and/or historical characteristics of the problem(s) to be addressed (see Chapter 9). Evidence about the nature and scale of the problem is critical, as is a plan for gathering evidence about the practical impact of any collaboration (see Chapter 3). Crucially, authorisers and prospective partners need to be provided with evidence that collaboration offers a necessary and viable catalyst for change. This might include evidence that existing attempts to address the problem have not been effective and are unlikely to be effective into the future.

Bear in mind that collaboration is not always the appropriate solution to a problem. Some problems are amenable to relatively simple linear solutions and, sometimes, mandating collaboration can make problems more difficult than they need to be or even deflect effort away from the problem. Pell (2016), for example, argues *against* the pursuit of collaboration as a policy goal of government. She contends that focusing on collaboration 'joins up documents, not services' and does not of itself solve the problem of fragmentation; rather, it 'wastes money, fosters compliance and creates a new layer of bureaucracy' while the 'true cause of fragmented services goes unaddressed' (Pell 2016: 4).

Although Pell concedes that criticising collaboration is 'a little heretical', she suggests that when 'the interface between the citizen and the organisations they interact with' is examined empirically, one finds that 'specialisation, targets, thresholds and eligibility criteria cause fragmented services' (Pell 2016: 5). According to Pell (2016: 5), 'services are fragmented because we design them to be' and the priority for policymakers should be to reverse the functional design of public services to ensure they 'work for citizens and communities from their point of view'.

Establish a lingua franca for collaboration

It is essential to bear in mind that different stakeholders might bring to the table different understandings or framings of the problem, as well as different language, differing capacity and capability and different motivations or values. There is a broad consensus in the collaboration literature that it is important to establish a commonly understood language among the collaboration partners. This is especially relevant in collaborations that bring together practitioners from different disciplines. For example:

- Some stakeholders might attribute the causes of violence against women to poverty, dispossession, a lack of education or substance abuse, whereas others might look to broader historical or cultural reasons for the perpetuation of gendered violence.
- In the childhood obesity space, clinical practitioners—dieticians, general practitioners and community nurses—might tend to 'medicalise' the problem, whereas others might take a wider 'systems perspective' that accommodates a wider array of reinforcing factors including food industry practices, marketing, the cost and availability of healthy food options and public awareness.

- In the disaster recovery space, many first responders will view the problem through the lens of a command structure concerned primarily with the deployment of physical assets, whereas others might see resilience as primarily a function of social cohesion and the mobilisation of 'soft' assets (social capital).

As well as having a common language to describe the problem, it is also essential to have a common language to describe the operational framework for collaboration. According to one of Australia's foremost collaboration experts, Robyn Keast (2016: 39–40), clarity of language is important because different understandings and expectations can lead to confusion and frustration, and potentially to dysfunctional or suboptimal outcomes.

Devise an appropriate operational framework

Keast (2016: 34) distinguishes between the various ways in which interorganisational relationships might be expressed in operational terms, and the subtle (and not-so-subtle) taxonomic differences between interorganisational *entities* such as amalgamations/mergers, alliances, networks, joint ventures, consortiums, coalitions and partnerships. These are summarised in Table 5.1.

Table 5.1 Summary of interorganisational entity features

Term	Purpose/focus	Defining features
Amalgamation/ merger	Formed to achieve efficiency	Vertical coordination via hierarchical/ formalised authority
Alliance	Joining of resources/forces to meet a common purpose (protection, trade)	Limited number of partners (exclusive) Close relations by affinity, similar or shared interests (strong lock-in) Pooling of resources Incomplete contracts, detailed negotiations and communication
Joint venture	Legal association for the purpose of mutual profit	Entity owned by two or more independent entities Variance in terms of legal basis Can be a product of alliance
Network	Aggregate grouping of (three or more) entities around a common function or task	Based on flow of resources, and affect, and cohesion of effort Open system of interpersonal relationship Self-organising (loose lock-in) Inclusive membership

Term	Purpose/focus	Defining features
Consortium	Loose association for the purpose of engaging in a joint venture, working together to achieve chosen objective	Interagency agreements, such as MOUs Incomplete contractual agreements Members responsible to others in terms of agreed actions Pooling of resources
Coalition	Temporary alliance formed for the purpose of defence against attack, advocacy, to gain access/support	Interagency agreements such as MOUs Clear rules and operating principles Temporary or time-limited arrangement
Partnership	a. Formal, legal association for the purpose of shared profit/loss b. Informal connecting relationship	Unincorporated Smaller number of partners Linked by written (formal) or verbal (informal) agreements Incomplete contracts Time limited by agreement

Source: Keast (2016: 39).

Although there is often a strongly intuitive aspect to collaboration, as a purposive activity, it is essential for collaboration to be informed by logical, strategic thinking. Collaboration needs to be led—even if it utilises some form of distributed or shared leadership. The ways in which leadership is exercised need to be established and agreed among the partners. Protocols for communication and external representation need to be set out and adhered to. Behavioural expectations and processes for resolving disagreements need to be established. Systems for reporting achievements and measuring impact need to be devised. Agreements need to be reached about who does what. Collaborations also need an agreed framework for accountability and the management of risk (financial, legal, reputational and political). Above all, these functions need to 'work' for each of the partners. It might not always be possible to achieve a neat fit with the internal policies and business systems used by partner organisations, and some forbearance and flexibility will sometimes be required.

Adaptivity and risk

Two preconditions are implicit in any decision to engage in collaboration:

1. The recognition of a need to devise and navigate new ways of working (see Chapter 2).
2. Collaboration represents an attempt to work flexibly and adaptively in complex, uncertain and dynamic environments.

Unfortunately, adaptive, flexible, person-centred processes are too often lacking in the typical operating environments of public sector organisations, where cultures of risk-aversion have long favoured standardised, rules-based operating systems.

Organisations operating in the public sector often adopt a failsafe attitude to risk, which can significantly fetter collaboration partners and impair the achievement of collaboration aims. What collaboration in fact requires is a risk environment in which it is 'safe to fail' (Butcher and Gilchrist 2016: 372–73). The contrasting notions of 'failsafe' and 'safe to fail' were set out 45 years ago by Jones et al. (1975: 2):

> Two poles on the spectrum of strategies are fail-safe and safe-fail. The goal of a fail-safe policy strives to assure that nothing will go wrong. Systems are designed to be foolproof and strong enough to withstand any eventuality. Efforts are made to radically reduce the probability of failure. Often the managers of such systems operate as if that probability were zero.

> A safe-fail policy acknowledges that failure is inevitable and seeks systems that can easily survive failure when it comes. Rather than rely on reducing the occurrence of failure, this policy aims at reducing the cost of that failure.

It is important, therefore, for people participating in collaborative initiatives to ensure that authorisers understand that collaboration entails both uncertainty and risk, and to obtain their commitment to putting in place the expertise and resources to manage proportionate risk (*not* eliminate it). It is also important to accept the possibility of failure; and to clearly distinguish between 'blameworthy failure' (that is, failure that entails corruption, incompetence or unethical behaviour) and 'praiseworthy failure' (that is, things did not quite go as planned, but we can learn from the experience and do better in the future) (Edmondson 2011).

An appropriate governance framework

Often in multiparty collaboration, especially involving the public sector, there is academic concern about the constraining effect of path dependence and, in particular, the constraining effects of legacy rules, systems and processes in public sector agencies (Heuer 2011). To overcome this, it is important to consider the design of the collaboration architecture, including:

- The instruments that will give effect to the collaboration—for example, an MOU, contract or other form of agreement.
- The process for reaching agreement about the nature of the problem to be addressed—for example, an investigation phase including consultations with stakeholders and relevant policy networks.
- The means by which the problem will be addressed—especially when a departure from past practices is contemplated.
- The respective contributions of the parties—including funding, information exchange and practical operational supports.
- The governance framework that will guide the collaboration—for example, a steering group, a governance group or some other form of oversight (Alam et al. 2014; Wilson et al. 2016).

Each of these elements can be set out in formal terms of reference (TOR). TOR provide a useful starting point for collaboration; however, if used as a compliance tool and applied in the form of 'rules', TOR can impede the realisation of collaborative purpose. It is important to allow the collaboration to make necessary adaptations as required by changing circumstances. This need not impair accountability so long as partner organisations are kept informed via the agreed governance framework about the emergence, extent and management of risk arising in the collaboration, and about required changes in operating procedures.

Trust-effective collaborations employ explicit strategies for the purpose of building trust, establishing credibility, confirming legitimacy and communicating the purposes of collaboration (Jupp 2000; Leat 2009; Bryson et al. 2009b; Corwin et al. 2012; Daymond 2015). However, trust can be hard to win because collaboration is often offered as an antidote to a history of policy failure and vexed relationships. Collaboration can struggle in the face of:

- cynicism: 'Everything else has been tried, why should this work?'
- impatience: 'We have been waiting a long time for signs of change; we want results now'
- doubt: 'Collaboration is all talk and no follow through'
- urgency: 'The situation is getting dire, do something quick'.

Each of these puts pressure on the collaboration advocates and leaders and accentuates the risk of collaboration failure. (See Chapter 10 for a more expansive exploration of trust, credibility and legitimacy.)

Collaboration is a way of thinking, not a model

Effective collaborations have an organic quality; they are shaped and sustained by the relationships between partners and stakeholders. In short, collaboration is not an organisational model; it is a 'headspace'—a way of thinking and behaving. And, for this reason, it is unwise to unilaterally mandate a prescriptive model for collaboration. Although collaboration frameworks are expected to demonstrate accepted standards for operational performance, they should not be prescriptive policy artefacts. Our investigation leads us to conclude that, although all collaborations operate with a similar rationale, are obliged to address a similar set of practical and strategic problems and employ a similar suite of operational and governance disciplines, each collaboration is also unique in its own way in that it seeks to respond to a set of circumstances occurring in a unique context. And while collaboration partners remain accountable to their employing organisation (where relevant), it is also expected that they will exhibit fidelity to the purpose, aims and codes of behaviour established and agreed to by the collaboration partners.

Of course, many organisations do not exhibit collaborative behaviour *internally*, let alone in their relationships with external partners. It is reasonable to ask, therefore: 'If people can't work collaboratively *within* their organisations, what are the chances that they will be able to work collaboratively *between* organisations?' (see Chapter 7). Ultimately, a cultural predisposition for collaboration *within* partner organisations is likely to be a stronger predictor of successful collaborative relationships with external partners than the most elegantly crafted model.

Don't forget silos

The public sector is often accused of operating in policy and programmatic silos. These silos—reinforced by legal demarcation, budgetary appropriation and organisational culture—are blamed for the kinds of fragmentation and incoherence that plague the lives of disadvantaged and vulnerable people. Conversely, it is frequently asserted that the collaborative mindset is part of the DNA of the not-for-profit sector. The truth lies somewhere between the two: it is possible to find many examples of people in the public sector working effectively across organisational and sectoral boundaries (although they do so quietly and informally with no fanfare); and it is possible to find examples of intense rivalry between not-for-profit organisations. Although not-for-profit service-providing organisations often employ the rhetoric of partnership, their participation in the competitive human services market over the past three decades has somewhat muted the kind of collegiality that had been a hallmark of the sector (Butcher and Freyens 2011).

'Zippering' as a means for bonding collaborators

A 'zippered' relationship is one in which multiple people have multiple points of interaction with other entities and organisations. This can be contrasted with a 'button' relationship that relies on a single point of contact. Zippering applies both to the broader relationship strategies of organisations and to collaboration specifically. Effective partnerships require peer-to-peer connections at all levels of the organisation: executive to executive, middle manager to middle manager and coalface worker to coalface worker. Collaboration or partnership strategies utilising a 'button' approach run the risk that their primary point of contact: 1) might not have sufficient seniority or authority to influence decision-making or to make commitments on behalf of the partner organisation, or 2) might be unable or unwilling to transmit key messages about the collaboration/partnership within the organisation. Zippering offers the best platform for assurance about organisational alignment with the purpose, aims and strategies proposed for the collaboration, and the best platform for achieving results. It also supports the vertical alignment of core understandings within the organisation as well as horizontal alignment between organisations. Bear in mind, however, that zippering might constitute a departure from 'business as usual'.

Collaborative best practice

It *is* possible to identify elements of better practice when designing a collaboration framework. These are set out in Table 5.2.

Table 5.2 Key elements of better practice when designing a collaboration framework

Key element	Guide for collaborative best practice
Purpose	Work towards a clear, inclusive and shared understanding about aims, strategy, process, communication and conduct.
Communication	Encourage clear, unambiguous, consistent, open and respectful flows of information between all stakeholders.
Expectations	Ensure that expectations and goals are agreed and understood by all stakeholders.

Key element	Guide for collaborative best practice
Evidence	Compile documented evidence of the problem(s) being addressed and previously attempted fixes (or failures).
Systems mapping	Build a comprehensive picture of the environment in which the collaboration intends to operate, including the identification of key systems, institutions, administrative bottlenecks, gaps, barriers, stakeholders, influencers and gatekeepers.
Consult stakeholders and experts	Comprehensively canvass the views of all relevant internal and external stakeholders to identify potential synergies, sources of resistance, untapped capacity and capability, conflicting perspectives, sources of legitimacy and barriers to trust.
Authorising environment	Match collaborative rhetoric with formal authorisation; assess partner/stakeholder capacity and capability; identify and commit resources (for example, funding, material support, reputation and information); and confirm political and social licences to collaborate.
Executive/ leadership backing	Ensure that the collaboration has clear and unambiguous backing by the executive/leadership in each of the partner organisations/groups, and that the executive/leadership understands the rationale, strategy, time frame, resource implications and risks of collaboration—in other words, make sure that authorisers know what they are signing up to.
Roles and contributions	Identify and agree to the respective roles played by partners/stakeholders and ensure these are understood and supported by authorisers.
'Zippered' relationships	Establish peer-to-peer relationships for the purpose of supporting actions flowing from collaboration.
Collaboration space	Establish a curated—and protected—collaboration space governed by operating procedures and decision-making frameworks agreed to by collaboration partners and supported by authorisers.
Independent facilitation	Where appropriate, utilise independent collaboration brokers to facilitate conversations about the shape of the collaboration; these might include respected thought leaders or social-purpose organisations and/or consultants with relevant expertise.
Governance	Create a governance framework for the purposes of providing assurance to authorisers and stakeholders about the decisions, actions and achievements of the collaboration.
Sustainability	Demonstrate executive sanction for collaboration leaders to participate in decision-making forums and engage with stakeholders over the long term.
Conflict resolution	Identify the things on which collaboration partners agree and the things on which they disagree; acknowledge differences in priority and perspective; and establish protocols to guide discussion and resolve conflict.
Futureproofing	Futureproof collaboration by acknowledging the collective knowledge of partners and stakeholders, leveraging corporate memory, undertaking scenario-setting and succession planning, and documenting the collaboration journey.

What the cases tell us

The collaborations we examined highlight the fact that every collaboration is different and there is, therefore, no stock standard approach. Identifying the ways in which collaborative efforts differ can inform the design of new collaborations. In principle, we would strongly advise anyone contemplating a collaborative approach to investigate a number of existing collaborations to understand their similarities and differences.

A time and energy-intensive process

In the establishment phase of collaboration, it is important to understand and manage the expectations of authorisers, partners, stakeholders and communities of interest. A consistent feature in each of the cases examined for this study was the skill with which collaboration leaders engaged in respectful conversations with a wide range of stakeholders about the purpose of the collaboration. Such conversations are not simply about informing; they are also about eliciting information and soliciting views, demonstrating a capacity to listen and to give weight to people's opinions.

Building relationships and trust and establishing shared expectations and procedural norms require significant upfront investments of time, effort and emotional energy. As one interviewee observed:

> We realised, 'Gosh, just to set this up took way longer than we ever imagined', just getting people on board with the concept of it let alone to actually come together and work together and actually achieve some results ... That was one of the key learnings: collaboration takes time and continual energy from everyone. These are not words Treasury takes kindly to, and we really struggled to get their support. We had to compromise each budget cycle and got less and less funding each time. [It's] ironic of course that there are many other initiatives that also struggle to identify outcomes, but the reality was there was more political support for them and not so much for us.

Managing communications and flows of information to and from internal and external stakeholders is a particularly important practice element (see Chapter 8). Stakeholders and authorisers need to understand that building trust takes time:

> I think one of the key messages that's been good for people is that it is a four to five-year journey. (Official, Children's Action Plan, New Zealand)

> Our core leadership group didn't really cement itself for at least 18 months, two years. By that stage, we've ended up with a really lovely breadth of people with some very diverse experience banks in there. (CBEM, Emerald, Victoria)

Sometimes, however, a level of trust needs to be established as a precursor to the sharing of information. More than one interviewee alluded to the political risk attached to information sharing:

> Keep your minister safe. You cannot be the person at the front line who shares information … There's nervousness at all levels of the system, because you don't want to be the one who ends up on the front page of the paper.

The importance of evidence

A capacity to offer evidence in support of a collaborative approach is essential to win support for collaboration from partner organisations and from external stakeholders who might be concerned about any change to existing systems and processes (even where existing systems are not working). Each of the examples in this study has supported the case for a collaborative approach with evidence about the nature and scale of the problem, and about the degree to which existing systems and programs have failed to demonstrate impact. Each has also been keen to demonstrate that collaborative approaches are impactful. While evidence about the nature and scale of the problem is crucial to winning institutional and community support for collaboration, evidence of failure of the status quo to address the problem is essential to sustain the formal authorisation and social licence that enable collaboration to occur (see Chapter 10).

Demonstrating impact

Authorisers and other stakeholders are often impatient for results and do not always appreciate that a definitive impact might not be immediately apparent (see Chapter 3). A senior official involved in the establishment of the Throughcare initiative in the Australian Capital Territory expressed some exasperation on this score:

> I get annoyed sometimes about, 'Can you evaluate it? Can you tell us what's happening?' These things take time in terms of how you manage them. And it takes away the human context.

This same official is credited with creating an authorising environment that allowed Throughcare to grow organically and with resisting pressure to set key performance indicators to avoid shifting the focus from collaboration to a fixation on deliverables.

Similarly, an official involved in the establishment of Children's Teams in New Zealand lamented that 'people expected results instantly'. She went on to point out, however, that collaborations cannot rely on anecdotal evidence for long:

> We should have made our performance metrics way tighter … we still would have struggled over time frames, but I'd now be able to give a clearer story based on the data rather than relying on anecdotal evidence for too long … We're starting to get way better at it, but we should have done better with this particular initiative by better managing our performance and the measurements associated with that.

Importance of executive backing

High-level backing is a critical ingredient for successful collaboration. The executives and leaders of partner organisations need to offer clear, unambiguous authority for collaboration:

> You have to have people at the top giving the message, whether that's about the values of your organisation or whether it's about what you're committed to. Your staff are not going to get excited, are they, if those at the top are not? You want your staff to be excited about what they're doing and feeling good about what they're doing. (Senior executive, Throughcare, Australian Capital Territory)

Executive backing confers political and operational licence to collaborate and offers protection for collaborative spaces:

> I think the buy-in from [the] upper-level executive and the capacity and the resources to be able to go out and do our job with the support makes it a lot easier, especially when we're doing something that hasn't been done before. (WHO STOPS, SEA Change, Portland, Victoria)

Ongoing executive backing depends upon regular, and robust, demonstrations of impact. Authorisers need assurance that the collaboration is worth the effort:

I think it's important that there's a continuation of providing evidence in terms of outcomes back to the executive. So, you can go back and report on the latest findings and how that's looking, [and] benchmark against world-best practice. (WHO STOPS, SEA Change, Portland, Victoria)

Brokers, champions and influencers

Sometimes, collaboration needs a bit of help. As we have already observed, collaboration is both hard to do and sometimes requires bespoke approaches that take into account the institutional histories and dynamics of particular policy fields. In response, we have seen the emergence of what Daymond (2015: 45) calls 'an industry of cross-sector collaboration practitioners' who work with stakeholders to design and facilitate the implementation of multiparty collaborations. Expert facilitation serves to defuse and reconcile differences and helps to establish credibility and legitimacy (see Chapters 8 and 10).

Independent collaboration brokers can play a positive role by helping to facilitate a shared understanding of the rationale for, and objects of, collaboration. Facilitation by a disinterested third party can help to break down barriers, establish commonalities, address differences and create trust in shared endeavours (Bowden and Ciesielska 2016: 24; Corwin et al. 2012; Bryson et al. 2009a; Daymond 2015; Jupp 2000; Leat 2009).

Prospective collaborations might consider the value of engaging a collaborative intermediary organisation, which Hamann and April (2013: 12) define as 'intermediary organisations that create platforms for deliberation and collaboration between diverse stakeholders'. The necessary capabilities of collaborative intermediary organisations— and indeed of any party acting in a facilitation role—are:

- the ability to translate diverging value frames and perspectives
- an explicit comfort in spaces of high complexity and ambiguity
- the ability to frame conflict and tensions as an opportunity for creativity and innovation (Hamann and April 2013: 20).

Among the collaborations investigated for our study, Change the Story and WHO STOPS took advantage of expert third-party facilitation in their early stages to help collaboration partners and other stakeholders to arrive at a shared understanding of the problem and a shared vision of the way forward.

Other collaborations have, to some degree, looked to individual champions or influencers to help bring diverse stakeholders to the table. Champions might be people with both influence and formal authority who are able to advocate within organisations on behalf of the collaboration. Influencers, on the other hand, might be people who, while not having formal authority, are well regarded and whose support for collaboration is reassuring to diverse stakeholders:

> We've looked at people in positions of authority, so … councillors, leaders of organisations. Then we've looked at a few of those people that are just change-makers in the community, those people who just make things happen and are known through the community or people that are just well connected so that if it goes up on her Facebook, for example, everyone reads her posts or whatever. (Great South Coast Change)

Importantly, champions are people who embrace opportunities for innovation. Said one interviewee of their primary agency contact:

> [He is] working almost against the bureaucratic intent in some ways and bringing a personal approach to the bureaucratic intent. And that's what you need. But bureaucracies don't even realise they need that. So, they employ people who can carry out their bureaucratic intent, and it's just good luck if they get someone who knows how to translate that into a community development function. (CBEM, Emerald, Victoria)

It is also advisable to cultivate multiple collaboration champions because, in a real sense, every person engaged in collaboration has the potential to act as a champion.

Co-design grounded in lived experience

Ideally, collaborative aims and actions should be shaped via processes of co-design, including, wherever possible, tapping into the lived experiences of the people and communities that are the focus of the collaboration. One interviewee emphasised the importance of 'allowing multiple opportunities for people to feed back in and reflect':

> I think there are certain things you can build in. It is a bit about the design of a process and some of that is about not just saying to people, 'Well, look, you can go away, but we need your feedback by next Friday', for example. It is being able to have a range of different ways in which that feedback is given, checking back in with key stakeholders, having that awareness where there are people who are saying, 'This is not working for me', having an awareness that you might have to do some extra work. I think … a big part of it is a willingness to participate in a process that is a partnership approach rather than a power dynamic … If the process had been given in a really rigid way that was lacking in reflection and self-reflection, the whole thing would have crumbled. (Change the Story)

It is worth noting, however, that the concept and practice of co-design are not universally understood. As one interviewee involved in the implementation of the Children's Action Plan put it:

> I think co-design would have been a really brand-new buzzword at that time. So, nobody quite knew what that was. When we were all pulled together after the five-minute cup of tea to sort of co-design something, we all turned up not quite knowing what that meant, what it was going to do. Quite a few people after a few weeks sitting left still not quite knowing what it was and what it was going to do … So, people all came to the table with different ideas of what co-design was and then got frustrated when it wasn't what they thought it was.

Another interviewee offered a slightly more nuanced reflection:

> I think co-design is overused and misunderstood, quite frankly … We should have gone to technical experts in the field to help us be more disciplined around what and how we were trying to do … When you try and retrofit co-design on something that's already started to evolve, I think you're in trouble. In theory, it's pretty good and I think you should be able to do it, but you've got to start at the grassroots. As soon as you get the idea, start properly, right from the beginning. (Senior official, Children's Action Plan Directorate)

Corporate memory

Corporate memory and knowledge are tremendous assets in the collaboration space. Owing to the dynamic, volatile nature of collaborations, collective memory is often not recorded or accorded its true value. Changes in personnel and administrative structures can result in a loss of corporate memory and the substitution of operational orthodoxy in place of the collaborative ethos. There can also be an inherent fragility to executive-level support for collaboration owing to mobility and changing personnel, or changes in the political or operating environment. According to one interviewee, this is especially true for not-for-profit organisations:

> Because we're so limited, I don't have someone who comes to these meetings with me because we couldn't afford to have two people sitting around in those meetings. But in government they'll have three or four people at different places in the hierarchy attending the meeting, and that's a good thing. (Throughcare, Australian Capital Territory)

Final observations

It is worth restating that there is no one-size-fits-all template for collaboration. That said, while all collaborations are unique in that they represent singular responses to a particular set of environmental, historical and institutional circumstances, they also have many features in common. Although there is truth in the proposition that collaboration is a mindset, not a method, effective and sustainable collaboration is underpinned by a suite of practical and strategic activities and practice elements. Our research has revealed a set of broad principles that might be used to guide better practice:

1. Collaboration is about mobilising people and organisations in support of an alternative approach to solving complex problems.

2. It is essential to clearly articulate the problem and demonstrate the case for collaboration.

3. Participants in collaboration need a common understanding of the problem and a common language to frame solutions.

4. Authorisers need to: a) understand the nature, and likelihood, of any risks associated with collaboration, and b) empower people at the collaboration front line to manage those risks without undue interference.

5. An appropriate governance framework is required to provide assurance to authorisers and others who have a stake in the outcomes of the collaboration.

6. Trust, credibility and legitimacy are the foundations of collaboration, and require open, authentic processes.

7. Authorisers need to understand that collaboration is a time and energy-intensive process and that it will take time for results to become apparent.

8. The case for collaboration needs to be supported by evidence and the path to impact needs to be fully mapped out.

9. Collaboration cannot succeed without strong executive backing in partner organisations.

10. Collaboration brokers, champions and influencers can help to win support for collaboration and sustain ongoing commitment to the purposes and approaches of the collaboration strategy.

11. Collaboration needs to be grounded in lived experience.

12. It is important to value and preserve collaborative 'memory' through attention to succession planning and by documenting the collaboration journey.

Practice considerations

1. Set out the case for *and* against collaboration, taking into account the fact that collaboration is not the answer to *every* problem. Would another form of working together be more appropriate to the task at hand? Is there a shared vision about the task to be undertaken or about the problem that needs to be addressed?

2. Reflect on how historical factors, the intersection of policy spaces, organisational culture and stakeholder relationships contribute to the problem/task; identify what needs to change and assess the potential barriers to change.

3. Identify all relevant stakeholders and potential collaboration partners: who is onside and who needs to be persuaded? Appraise the trustworthiness and credibility of key agencies, institutions and actors from the perspective of major stakeholders. Consider how any trust/credibility deficits might be addressed as well as how established trust/credibility might be leveraged in support of collaboration aims.

4. Carry out a SWOT (strengths, weaknesses, opportunities and threats) analysis of the key systems, behaviours, processes, institutions and actors that need to change to address the problem or carry out the task.

5. Assess the amount of executive-level backing for a collaborative approach. Assess the potential for a 'zippered' approach that entails peer-to-peer interactions with partner organisations (taking care to spell out the risks of a 'button' approach). Identify potential champions and influencers inside and outside all partner organisations and devise a strategy to mobilise their support for collaboration.

6. Assess whether partner organisations are 'collaboration ready'. What aspects of their organisational culture present barriers to collaboration? What aspects of their culture enhance the prospects of collaboration? Is there an organisational commitment to 'moving the dial' where impediments exist? Do partner organisations have a track record of innovation?

7. Assess authorisers' appetite for risk: Do partner organisations understand the risks associated with collaboration? Do they embrace uncertainty? And are they prepared to accept and learn from failure?

8. Assess the level of decision-making authority brought to the table by collaboration partners. Do participants have the knowledge, skill and authority to participate in decision-making? What resources are available to build the collaborative capacity of collaboration leaders and other participants? Consider engaging expert brokerage/facilitation in the formative stages.

9. Construct a governance framework that will provide: a) clarity about the respective roles and responsibilities of collaboration partners, and b) the assurance necessary for authorisers in partner organisations to embrace the kind of risk associated with collaboration.

10. Think about how impact might be demonstrated over the course of the collaboration, including indirect indicators (for example, evidence of more effective multiparty working) and direct indicators (evidence of improved outcomes). Enlist the assistance of people and institutions with relevant expertise in the formulation of appropriate indicators.

11. Formulate realistic timelines/targets for each stage of the collaboration—wherever possible, taking account of learnings from other collaborations—and, using the governance framework, ensure that authorisers and stakeholders know what to expect over the short, medium and longer terms.

12. Develop a communication/consultation strategy and associated protocols to guide engagement with internal stakeholders (that is, within partner organisations) and external stakeholders (that is, individuals, groups and communities likely to be affected by the collaboration) around the rationale, purpose and proposed strategies for collaboration. Ensure consistent, transparent messaging. Actively manage stakeholder expectations.

References

Alam, Quamrul, Md Humayun Kabir, and Vivek Chaudhri. 2014. 'Managing infrastructure projects in Australia: A shift from a contractual to a collaborative public management strategy.' *Administration & Society* 46(4): 422–49. doi.org/10.1177/0095399712459728.

Bowden, Alistair, and Malgorzata Ciesielska. 2016. 'Ecomuseums as cross-sector partnerships: Governance, strategy and leadership.' *Public Money & Management* 36(1): 23–30. doi.org/10.1080/09540962.2016.1103414.

Bryson, John M., Barbara C. Crosby, Melissa M. Stone, and Emily O. Saunoi-Sandgren. 2009a. *Designing and managing cross-sector collaboration: A case study in reducing traffic congestion*. Collaboration: Networks and Partnerships Series Report. Washington, DC: IBM Center for The Business of Government.

Bryson, John M., Barbara C. Crosby, Melissa M. Stone, and Emily O. Saunoi-Sandgren. 2009b. 'Designing and managing cross-sector collaboration: A case study in reducing traffic congestion.' *The Business of Government* (Fall/Winter): 78–81.

Butcher, John R., and Benoît Freyens. 2011. 'Competition and collaboration in the contracting of family relationship centres.' *Australian Journal of Public Administration* 70(1): 15–33. doi.org/10.1111/j.1467-8500.2010.00708.x.

Butcher, John R., and David J. Gilchrist. 2016. *The Three Sector Solution: Delivering public policy in collaboration with not-for-profits and business*. Canberra: ANU Press. doi.org/10.22459/TSS.07.2016.

Corbin, H., L. Corwin and M.B. Mittelmark. 2012. 'Producing synergy in collaborations: A successful hospital innovation.' *The Innovation Journal: The Public Sector Innovation Journal* 17(1): Article 5.

Daymond, Jarryd. 2015. Practitioners' perspectives on cross-sector collaborations. Masters thesis, Macquarie University, Sydney.

Edmondson, Amy C. 2011. 'Strategies of learning from failure.' *Harvard Business Review* 89(4): 48–55, 137.

Garud, Raghu, Arun Kumaraswamy, and Peter Karnøe. 2010. 'Path dependence or path creation?' *Journal of Management Studies* 47(4): 760–73. doi.org/10.1111/j.1467-6486.2009.00914.x.

Hamann, Ralph, and Kurt April. 2013. 'On the role and capabilities of collaborative intermediary organisations in urban sustainability transitions.' *Journal of Cleaner Production* 50: 12–21. doi.org/10.1016/j.jclepro.2012.11.017.

Heuer, Mark. 2011. 'Ecosystem cross-sector collaboration: Conceptualizing an adaptive approach to sustainability governance.' *Business Strategy and the Environment* 20(4): 211–21. doi.org/10.1002/bse.673.

Jones, Dixon D., C.S. Holling, and R. Peterman. 1975. *Fail-safe vs. safe-fail catastrophes*. IIASA Working Paper, WP-75-93, August. Vienna: International Institute for Applied Systems Analysis.

Jupp, Ben. 2000. *Working Together: Creating a better environment for cross-sector partnerships*. London: Demos.

Kahane, Adam. 2017. *Collaborating with the Enemy: How to work with people you don't agree with or like or trust*. Oakland, CA: Berrett-Koehler Publishers.

Keast, Robyn. 2016. 'Integration terms: Same or different?' In *Grassroots to Government: Creating joined-up working in Australia*, ed. Gemma Carey, pp. 25–46. Melbourne: Melbourne University Press.

Leat, D. 2009. *More than Money: The potential of cross-sector relationships*. Leicester, UK: Taylor Bloxham.

Merchant, Nilofer. 2011. 'Eight dangers of collaboration.' *Harvard Business Review*, 1 December.

Pell, Charlotte. 2016. 'Debate: Against collaboration.' *Public Money & Management* 36(1): 4–5. doi.org/10.1080/09540962.2016.1103410.

Wilson, Rob, Paul Jackson, and Martin Ferguson. 2016. 'Editorial: Science or alchemy in collaborative public service? Challenges and future directions for the management and organization of joined-up government.' *Public Money & Management* 36(1): 1–4. doi.org/10.1080/09540962.2016.1103408.

6

AUTHORISATION, GOVERNANCE AND ASSURANCE

Introduction

Australian governments at all levels now embrace collaboration as a core organising principle guiding the implementation of policy, the design of program architecture and the delivery of services. Even so, collaboration continues to represent a challenge for many public sector organisations. As the APSC observed in a 2012 report:

> It is clear that existing public sector institutions and structures were, by and large, not designed with a primary goal of supporting collaborative inter-organisational work. It can be challenging enough to implement governance arrangements and foster cultures that facilitate collaboration across internal organisational boundaries within hierarchical, vertically structured organisations. (APSC 2012: 17)

Authorisation, governance and assurance are important aspects of building and sustaining collaborations. However, the governance frameworks traditionally used by public sector organisations might not necessarily meet the needs of collaboration. Insofar as it tends to emphasise assurance through demonstrated compliance with rules-based systems, traditional hierarchical governance might not offer the kind of latitude that multiparty collaboration demands. Whereas traditional governance tends to emphasise upwards accountability framed around fidelity to process, collaboration governance emphasises reciprocal flows of accountability framed around fidelity to collaborative purpose. To put it plainly, the former is rules-based and the latter is mission-based.

To be clear, fidelity to mission does not preclude accountability for good process; it is not a case of 'any means to an end' nor a case for cutting corners. Rather, good collaboration governance is framed around the principle of pushing leadership and authority down to the collaboration front line within an overarching framework of collective accountability. This entails an acceptance—indeed, the embrace—of three pillars of collaboration: distributed leadership, decentred authority and collective accountability.

The meaning of 'trust' in a governance context

Trust is one of the most important elements of any successful collaboration (see Chapter 10), where 'success' is, in part, a function of: 1) partners' shared understanding of, and commitment to, the collaboration's rationale, purpose, aims and means; and 2) the obligations and possible benefits that flow from/to each partner (Jupp 2000; Corwin et al. 2012). Trust is also an important factor in collaboration governance and, in this context, it has many dimensions:

1. Intra-organisational trust: Trust between authorisers, frontline collaboration workers and key personnel/business units providing operational support to the collaboration (for example, information technology, financial management, human resources, communications).

2. Interorganisational trust: 'Zippered' peer-to-peer relationships between partner organisations (see Chapter 5).

3. Trust between individual partners and key external constituencies including clients/customers, policy communities, representative organisations and/or professional bodies/trade unions; this involves questions of reputation, capability, reliability and legitimacy.

4. Trust between the collaboration itself, as a forum for goal-setting and decision-making, and authorisers as well as external stakeholders.

In general terms, trust involves notions of honesty, reliability, truthfulness and safety. The same qualities of trust also hold true in the context of corporate governance and can be re-expressed in terms of the core attributes of *good* governance. To better appreciate this point, it is useful to refresh our understanding of the meaning and function of 'governance'. The Governance Institute of Australia defines governance as:

> the system by which an organisation is controlled and operates, and the mechanisms by which it, and its people, are held to account. Ethics, risk management, compliance and administration are all elements of governance. (Governance Institute of Australia n.d.)

Using the above definition as a starting point, we can readily see that, from a governance perspective, trust is fundamentally concerned with accountability and assurance. For example:

1. *Ethics*: Authorisers 'trust' that their people, and those employed by/representing their partner organisations, will conduct themselves according to the highest probity standards.

2. *Risk management*: Authorisers 'trust' that their people, and those employed by/representing their partner organisations, have: identified all material risks (financial, operational, representational and political); put into place appropriate strategies for risk mitigation and risk response; and have systems in place to keep authorisers apprised of any changes in the risk environment.

3. *Compliance*: Authorisers 'trust' that their people, and those employed by/representing their partner organisations, comply with all relevant guidelines, policies and legal requirements and, where necessary and appropriate, seek a formal documented variation of those requirements to meet the particular circumstances of the collaboration.

4. *Administration*: Authorisers 'trust' that their people, and those employed by/representing their partner organisations, apply best-practice standards when administering the collaboration to provide a high level of assurance in relation to the documentation of decision-making, financial controls, payments, agreement-making and contracts, human resource management, communications, data storage and sharing, and communications.

Collaborative/network governance

Over the past dozen or so years, policy thinkers have argued for the advantages of collaborative or networked governance as a means for realising greater nimbleness and adaptability in the delivery of public programs and services (Goldsmith and Eggers 2005; Eggers 2008; Smyth 2008). A countervailing view is that governing through networks can make already difficult policy problems even harder to address (McGuire and O'Neill 2008: 239–40; Wanna 2008: 9–10). Public policy aims can be difficult to achieve even *within* organisational and domain boundaries, *despite* governance structures that exhibit strong vertical integration and mature systems for internal control. Consider, then, the inherent difficulty of managing multiple relationships in networked systems characterised by asymmetries of knowledge, power and authority, as well as variegated cultures, values, business systems and capabilities (Huxham and Vangen 2008).

Provan and Kenis (2008: 234–36) identify three basic forms of network governance:

1. **Participant governance**, which is described as 'the simplest and most common form' and is governed by network members. Participant governance entails no separate or unique governance entity and can be accomplished either formally (for example, through regular meetings of designated representatives) or informally (for example, through the ongoing but uncoordinated efforts of those who have a stake in the network's success). Participant-governed networks can be highly decentralised or they may be highly centralised, governed by and through a lead organisation that is also a network member (although, in theory, no single entity represents the network as a whole).

2. **Lead organisation governance**, in which all major network-level activities and key decisions are coordinated through and by a lead organisation. This form is 'highly centralised and brokered, with asymmetrical power'. The lead organisation 'provides administration for the network and/or facilitates the activities of member organisations'. Network goals 'may be closely aligned with the goals of the lead organisation', which may underwrite the cost of network administration on its own, receive resource contributions from network members or facilitate access to external funding through grants or government funding.

3. **Network administrative organisation** (NAO), in which a separate and centralised administrative entity is set up specifically to govern the network and its activities. The NAO coordinates and sustains the network but, unlike the lead organisation model, the NAO is not another member organisation. Instead, the NAO is established for the exclusive purpose of network governance. The NAO may be a government entity, an existing not-for-profit organisation or a unique not-for-profit organisation or for-profit corporation established for the express purpose of governing the network. An NAO may be modest in scale (for example, consisting of a single individual acting as network facilitator or broker) or it may be a formal organisation, consisting of an executive director, staff and board operating out of a physically distinct office.

Provan and Kenis (2008: 238) suggest that shared governance is most likely to be effective when 'trust is pervasive throughout the network':

> Trust need not be deep, but it cannot simply be a collection of dyad-based relationships. Rather, trust ties must be dense, so that perceptions of trust are shared among and between network members. As with the density of connections, trust density means that many people in the network trust one another, thereby providing a dense web of trust-based ties. In the absence of this, shared governance will not be effective since there will be little basis for collaboration among network members.

Finally, as discussed in Chapter 4, working collaboratively in multiparty settings requires a skill set different to that traditionally found in the Australian public sector (Bourgon 2008; Edwards 2001; Considine and Lewis 1999; Stewart 2007; Gazely and Brudney 2007). Former Australian prime minister Julia Gillard (2013) summed up the situation neatly:

> [W]e are so far beyond the command and control models of the past: now it is about collaboration, about delegation, about seeking and getting people's consent about mobilising teams. I think it is those skills that will be the really precious ones in the future.

There is clearly a need to further develop the skills necessary to support and sustain collaborative governance (Edwards 2001; Shergold 2008a, 2008b). However, barriers to effective multiparty work sometimes arise as a result of conflicting values (Stewart 2007), failure to recognise shared values (Moore 2000) and tensions between 'top-down' (directive) and 'bottom-up' (participatory) approaches to policy formulation and implementation (Dollery and Wallis 2003: 169–72).

Governance in secondary operating spaces

Collaboration frequently occurs in secondary operating spaces (Kotter 2012). These are semiformal or informal operating environments that are less tightly bound by the normal requirements of the dominant primary operating spaces. Secondary operating spaces allow partners to establish operational norms and ways of working that meet the needs of collaboration and provide assurance to authorisers. Secondary spaces coexist in dynamic tension with—and at the discretion of—dominant traditional organisational cultures (see Chapter 4). The pre-existing operating culture could be thought of as a primary operating space in which long-established systems, norms and rules govern what can and cannot be done.

(Kotter 2012: 48) observes:

> Hierarchies and standard managerial processes, even when minimally bureaucratic, are inherently risk-averse and resistant to change. Part of the problem is political: Managers are loath to take chances without permission from superiors. Part of the problem is cultural: People cling to their habits and fear loss of power and stature—two essential elements of hierarchies. And part of the problem is that all hierarchies, with their specialized units, rules, and optimized processes, crave stability and default to doing what they already know how to do.

Secondary operating spaces are presented as a solution to this problem as they can be built on a set of different processes that are more agile and based on relationships rather than transactions. They can be discrete and isolated from the primary operating spaces—those that are more archetypal of modern corporate management structures—thus allowing for increased experimentation without authorisers becoming concerned that the atypical processes and behaviours of value in collaborative environments will be seen to threaten the traditional structures valued by most managers.

Although Kotter is in this instance referring to private sector enterprises, his observations also hold for the public sector, whose traditional modus operandi continues to be challenged by changing environmental conditions and political/societal expectations—in particular, the expectation that organisations will work collaboratively for the public benefit. In many ways, traditional bureaucratic systems are inimical to working across programmatic, organisational or sectoral boundaries—particularly where there are misalignments of priorities, outlook and norms.

What the cases tell us

Each of the collaborations investigated for this study exhibited a set of arrangements that enables collective deliberation about:

- the rationale for and purpose of the collaboration
- the risk environment in which collaboration will occur
- how the collaboration will operate
- what the collaboration seeks to deliver
- the contributions of partner organisations
- how best to engage internal and external stakeholders
- the provision of assurance and the demonstration of impact.

Some form of written instrument, such as an MOU or a contract, might prescribe the governance framework. Or the framework might be far less formal and operate through implicit reciprocal arrangements. The framework might take the form of a dedicated governance group, a steering committee or a partnership group.

Whatever form it takes, governance, like collaboration itself, is about managing. Our observation is that collaboration appears to occur within something much like Kotter's secondary operating space. Importantly, this secondary operating space connects to the hierarchy through people who populate both spaces and, ideally, works to liberate information from 'silos and hierarchical layers' and enable it to flow with far greater freedom and speed (Kotter 2012). This secondary operating space creates spaces in which to be transgressive (see Chapter 2). Often, participants (and collaboration leaders in particular) find themselves in the position of forcing operational or cultural change in the face of institutional or organisational resistance. Individual participants in collaborative forums typically transit back and forth between primary and secondary spaces— an experience that can be disorienting and conflicted.

Formal governance provides a mechanism for authorisation to collaborate and assurance that collaboration is occurring. Although formal governance is indispensable, informal governance also serves important purposes. Whereas formal governance is usually exercised via agreed protocols or rules of engagement, and might be guided by terms of reference agreed among the parties, informal governance is more 'relational' than 'procedural'. Informal governance is concerned more with maintaining communications, listening to concerns, modelling behaviours and creating legitimacy. Formal and informal governance were strongly in evidence in each of our five cases.

In each of the cases, collaboration is subject to formal governance through a backbone group and/or a governance group consisting of partner organisations and, in some cases, organisations representing principal stakeholder interests. A governance group comprising all collaboration partners is an indispensable forum for sharing information, managing expectations, anticipating and mitigating risk, providing assurance to stakeholders and taking stock of the environment in which collaboration is occurring. As one interviewee observed:

> One of the reasons why the steering group is so important [is] because at that level the steering group talks about such things as different triggers within a community, different personalities within a community, people who are ready to take on a new idea as against those that aren't. So, having a bit of an idea of how people work is a really important tool. (WHO STOPS, SEA Change)

Governance as a conduit for authority

The governance framework allows for the authority to collaborate to flow from partner organisations to those charged with making collaboration happen. The governance framework might comprise delegates from partner organisations and might even include other stakeholders, such as representatives from particular communities of interest. Although it is not unusual for the delegates to have differing levels of seniority, it is important that members have a commensurate level of authority, legitimacy and experience that enables them to engage confidently and contribute to decision-making. As one interviewee observed of their governance group:

> It was mostly very senior people, but there were some more junior bureaucrats there, and that's okay because they can build some corporate knowledge. Often with those things it's very senior people that participate in them, and it's good to have some depth. (Throughcare)

Another interviewee described a difficulty associated with delegates whose authority to collaborate is conditional or unclear, or who have insufficient seniority or confidence to act with authority:

> They feel inhibited, plus they often don't have the incentives. Most public servants still have their line responsibilities through their agencies, which goes to a budget requirement in an outcome statement for their portfolio. (Throughcare)

In addition to participating in deliberation and decision-making, delegates to any governance framework also play a role as collaboration *champions* or *ambassadors* within their organisations and constituencies—defined succinctly by one interviewee as 'people that hold key influence, just influence and pull within the community'.

Collaboration partners need not only be able to maintain the confidence and goodwill of people around the table, but also to provide appropriate assurance to their executive and board (and support the executive and board, who might themselves be called on to provide assurances to ministers or other constituencies). Partners also need to be outward-looking and able to offer assurance to a range of external stakeholders—some of whom might have perspectives that are not fully aligned with the organising themes of the collaboration. Formal pathways for authority and assurance can be enhanced by the appointment of senior collaboration champions.

Locus of decision-making

The capacity of governance frameworks to facilitate decision-making might vary according to circumstances. Some governing frameworks primarily support advisory functions, although, depending on the seniority and formal authority of the delegates, it might be argued that the provision of advice amounts to de facto decision-making, as illustrated in the following quote:

> Well, in terms of what the authority was, the terms of reference of the … governance group … [stated] very clearly that we were advisory. We didn't have decision-making authority. It was about recommendations and suggestions.

> That said, I think we were in the best of both worlds in that, because of the very good relations around the table, we were, in a sense, doing a bit of policy co-design tweaking as we went so that [the lead agency CEO], who was virtually at every meeting, would take quite seriously what was being discussed and proposed. She'd actually push back when she needed to and say, 'Well, that's not going to fly with the minister', or whatever. She would be quite frank. (Throughcare)

Other governance frameworks—particularly those that are part of a more distributed collaboration process (see Chapter 5)—take a more directive role:

> That was the thing in those meetings that I thought was refreshing: we'd go to the meeting, we'd make a decision and it would happen. It wasn't that we'd go to the meeting, there'd be a discussion and then a decision would happen somewhere else later on, which may or may not be what the community people were looking for. (Throughcare)

Bottom-up or top-down?

Good governance provides collaborators with an idea of how the collaboration will operate, what the collaboration seeks to deliver and what the contributions of partner organisations will be. When governance is not clear, however, it leads to questions about whether the collaboration will use a centralised or localised approach—otherwise expressed as a bottom-up or top-down approach. Although both approaches are valid, it is important that collaborators make it clear what kind of approach they will take.

In cases such as WHO STOPS or CBEM, there is an evident emphasis on locally empowered and locally led initiatives. Each is steered from below—either from the community or from a community of interest—while using top-down processes to moderate community views and shape a practicable path forward. One of the architects of the Australian Capital Territory's Throughcare initiative offered the view that frontline staff sometimes know best:

> When you engage with the people who are at the service delivery end, in my view, they're more practice-exposed so they have a sense for innovation, learning lessons from what they do on a day-to-day basis—things like that.

By contrast, in the case of the Children's Action Plan (CAP), there was an evident tension between the local Children's Teams and governance groups and the CAP directorate/ministry in Wellington. As one Children's Team member expressed it:

> I think the Children's Team approach seemed to go through a bit of a phase of being very, very prescriptive on everything, and that hasn't sat particularly well with a desire to do things that are more aligned with an indigenous approach. So, I think that is also something where we've got a rub ... it's a challenge for collaboration in any space with prescriptive elements—the need for flexibility and agility.

A similar view was offered by a member of a Children's Team governance group:

> I think we had a number of kicks back around: 'No, don't accept that. That's not how we roll here. This is what we want to do.' I think [the Children's Team director] was continuously going back and saying, 'Yeah, no'—'Yeah, I hear what you're saying, but no, that's not going to work.'

A member of another governance group described a situation in which the local Children's Team successfully pushed back against the prescriptive elements of the model:

> We actually went back and instead of reporting negatively to Wellington, we said: 'We're not going to do this. We're not going to achieve those. We're not going to stick to those KPIs [key performance indicators] for these reasons. But look at the fantastic work we've done. We've engaged with all these families, all these kids, all these success stories.' It was at that point that we were given a bit of a free rein to go for it and operate independently of what all the other Children's Teams were doing, who were still working to their prescriptive, centre-led regime.

However, one former official offered a candid appraisal of the tensions involved:

> I think there were shifts at a policy level around the degree of prescription versus the degree of flexibility. And I think that caused mixed messages for teams on the ground. So, that kind of desire to be prescriptive as a means of driving the momentum, I don't think it had that effect. I think it served to confuse and cause people to resist a little bit where it didn't work at a local level. That has been a bit of a journey, really, of trying to capture almost a cookie-cutter prescription that would allow rapid rollout and then a realisation that that wasn't actually achieving its purpose and that we needed a great deal more flexibility in what suited each location.

Some officials working in the CAP directorate in Wellington took the view—for essentially sound reasons—that there needed to be some consistency between the practice and operational elements of the Children's Teams to support the collection of data and to compare social impacts. Within this consistency, they felt, there was ample room to tailor local responses and build on local strengths. This tension was neatly encapsulated by one former CAP official:

> There was too much say from the centre about how things had to be done, but there were reasons for that that the communities couldn't see. So, we came with templates and we were telling them that they must do this, they must do that, they must do the next thing. At a local level, they really resented that. But what they couldn't see at that local level was the pressure that the centre was under to make sure that whatever you did there, you were recording it in a nationally consistent way. So, there was always this tension between the two.

The importance of unambiguous executive management support

It is essential to establish strong management pathways to enable formal authority to cascade down to the collaboration and assurance to flow up to executive management. Where there are many groups working in collaboration, these groups often have different expectations or goals. These can act as barriers to working collaboratively in some settings. It is important to be able to communicate with collaborative partners to create common goals and expectations. To create common goals, some compromise may be required. This can only be enabled by inclusive leadership and with a supportive authorising environment.

The functions that support collaboration need to be formally recognised and appropriately resourced. Sadly, declarations of collaborative intent are not necessarily accompanied by the reallocation of existing resources. To the extent that resource allocation is often a function of programmatic rules formulated in primary operating spaces, authorisers might be constrained in their ability—or willingness—to exercise discretion about how resources are deployed. It is one thing for governments and senior executives to give rhetorical support for collaborative working, but if that support is not matched with appropriate authorisation and resources, it becomes meaningless and, worse, dispiriting.

Corporate memory and knowledge are tremendous assets in the collaboration space. Owing to the dynamic, volatile nature of collaborations, collective memory is often not recorded or accorded its true value. Changes in personnel and administrative structures can result in a loss of corporate memory and the substitution of operational orthodoxy in place of the collaborative ethos. Appropriate systems need to be established for the purpose of capturing, documenting and sharing knowledge that might otherwise be lost through bureaucratic 'churn'.

Final observations

Collaborative action cannot be effective or sustained in the absence of an appropriate and robust governance framework. As the conduit for formal authority, legitimacy and assurance, governance is an essential element in the provision of surety for collaboration. Whereas authorisation establishes a licence to collaborate and confers authority, the governance framework establishes the mechanisms for accountability, a forum for the assessment of risk and the ratification of decisions, and pathways for the provision of assurance to authorisers and stakeholders.

Ideally, governance frameworks should be benchmarked against other frameworks established for similar purposes. Although there is no single template for sound governance, governance nevertheless entails core functions such as strategic direction, relationship management, risk management, financial control, operational oversight, etc. Above all, any governance framework established to guide collaborative endeavour must be 'fit for purpose' and must engender the confidence of authorisers, participants and stakeholders.

Practice considerations

1. Distributed leadership, decentred authority and collective accountability are the three pillars of effective collaboration. Assess the degree to which these principles are consistent with the mission, values and operating culture of each partner organisation. Identify potential impediments (for example, inconsistent understandings about what these principles mean in practice) or constraints (for example, the statutory framework within which partner organisations are obliged to operate) and possible solutions.

2. Undertake a comprehensive risk assessment that addresses:
   - the risks (reputational, industrial, operational, legal or political) that might arise as a consequence of entering into a collaborative arrangement
   - the risks that might arise as a result of not collaborating (for example, continuation or worsening of existing problems)
   - the levels of trust prevailing between partner organisations and within organisations (for example, between business units or program areas affected by the proposed collaboration)
   - the legacy of past relationships between partners, especially where there is a history of mistrust or conflict
   - any policy gaps or misalignment of priorities and approaches that have contributed to the problems the collaboration is intended to address
   - the respective risk appetite of partner organisations and any differences in their respective risk management frameworks that might affect collaborative action.

   It is essential that all collaboration partners contribute to the exercise in an open and forthright manner, even if the conclusions drawn from the assessment make for uncomfortable reading.

3. Prepare an analysis of the advantages and disadvantages of competing governance models, including (but not limited to) participant governance, lead organisation governance or the establishment of a networked administration organisation (or some combination of the three).

4. To the extent that the proposed collaboration will exist in a secondary operating space, consider the implications for each of the partners with a special emphasis on the delegation of authority for decision-making and the provision of assurance.

5. Identify any skills, knowledge or information gaps that might in some way affect the capacity of partner organisations to engage in the collaborative endeavour and propose strategies to address these. Specify how preferred strategies will be resourced and implemented. Identify any existing internal capability within partner organisations that can be deployed to address the problem, and/or indicate whether external expertise will be required and how it might be sourced.

6. Specify how and where decision-making will occur with respect to the collaboration and the level of authority and delegation capable of being exercised by the representatives of partner organisations. Set out clear protocols stipulating the manner in which the governance/backbone group advises authorisers about decisions taken and/or requests approval from authorisers for recommended actions. These protocols need to be able to identify points of disagreement between partner organisations, timely communication of approval and/or pathways for the timely resolution of disagreements.

7. Set out the expectations that will apply to each partner organisation and to delegates participating in any governance/backbone group. These might include expectations about financial contributions, the provision of operational support (for example, operating premises, payroll, financial management, human resource management, information technology, and so on) and 'behavioural' expectations (for example, ethical conduct, conflict resolution, internal and external communications and sharing of information and knowledge).

8. Consider the need to codify the governance framework for the proposed collaboration in the form of a written instrument, such as a contract, head agreement or MOU. Also consider whether to set out the same expectations and processes in a 'mission statement' for the purposes of providing assurance to a wider range of stakeholders.

References

Australian Public Service Commission (APSC). 2012. *Tackling Wicked Problems: A public policy perspective*. Canberra: APSC.

Bourgon, Jocelyne. 2008. 'The future of public service: A search for a new balance.' *Australian Journal of Public Administration* 67(4): 390–404. doi.org/10.1111/j.1467-8500.2008.00597.x.

Considine, Mark, and Jenny M. Lewis. 1999. 'Governance at ground level: The frontline bureaucrat in the age of markets and networks.' *Public Administration Review* 59(6): 467–80. doi.org/10.2307/3110295.

Corbin, H., L. Corwin and M.B. Mittelmark. 2012. 'Producing synergy in collaborations: A successful hospital innovation.' *The Innovation Journal: The Public Sector Innovation Journal* 17(1): Article 5.

Dollery, B.E., and J.L. Wallis. 2003. *The Political Economy of the Voluntary Sector: A reappraisal of the comparative institutional advantage of voluntary organisations*. Cheltenham, UK: Edward Elgar.

Edwards, Meredith. 2001. 'Participatory governance into the future: Roles of the government and community sectors.' *Australian Journal of Public Administration* 60(3): 78–88. doi.org/10.1111/1467-8500.00226.

Eggers, William D. 2008. 'The changing nature of government: Network governance.' In *Collaborative Governance: A new era of public policy in Australia?* Eds Janine O'Flynn and John Wanna, pp. 23–28. Canberra: ANU Press. doi.org/10.22459/CG.12.2008.03.

Gazely, Beth, and Jeffrey L. Brudney. 2007. 'The purpose (and perils) of government–nonprofit partnership.' *Nonprofit and Voluntary Sector Quarterly* 36: 389–415. doi.org/10.1177/0899764006295997.

Gillard, Julia. 2013. Video of conversation with Julia Gillard. Broadcast 30 September. [Online]. Available from: annesummers.com.au/2013/10/video-of-sydney-conversation-with-julia-gillard/.

Goldsmith, Stephen, and William D. Eggers. 2005. *Governing by Network: The new shape of the public sector*. Washington, DC: Brookings Institution Press.

Governance Institute of Australia. n.d. *What is Governance?* [Online]. Sydney: Governance Institute of Australia. Available from: www.governanceinstitute.com.au/resources/what-is-governance/.

Huxham, Chris, and Siv Vangen. 2008. 'Doing things collaboratively: Realising the advantage or succumbing to inertia?' In *Collaborative Governance: A new era of public policy in Australia?* eds Janine O'Flynn and John Wanna, pp. 29–44. Canberra: ANU E Press. doi.org/10.22459/CG.12.2008.04.

Jupp, Ben. 2000. *Working Together: Creating a better environment for cross-sector partnerships*. London: Demos.

Kotter, John. 2012. 'Accelerate!' *Harvard Business Review* 90(11): 44–58.

McGuire, L., and D. O'Neill. 2008. 'The report on government services: A new piece in the accountability matrix?' In *Strategic Issues of the Not-For-Profit Sector*, ed. J. Barraket, pp. 236–62. Sydney: UNSW Press.

Merchant, Nilofer. 2011. 'Eight dangers of collaboration.' *Harvard Business Review*, 1 December.

Moore, Mark H. 2000. 'Managing for value: Organisational strategy in for-profit, non-profit, and governmental organisations.' *Nonprofit and Voluntary Sector Quarterly* 29(1): 183–204. doi.org/10.1177/0899764000773746391.

Provan, Keith G., and Patrick Kenis. 2008. 'Modes of network governance: Structure, management, and effectiveness.' *Journal of Public Administration Research and Theory* 18(2): 229–52. doi.org/10.1093/jopart/mum015.

Shergold, Peter. 2008a. 'Governing through collaboration.' In *Collaborative Governance: A new era of public policy in Australia?* eds Janine O'Flynn and John Wanna, pp. 13–22. Canberra: ANU E Press. doi.org/10.22459/CG.12.2008.02.

Shergold, Peter. 2008b. Contracting out government: Collaboration or control? Neil Walker Memorial Lecture, Centre for Social Impact, University of New South Wales, Sydney.

Smyth, Paul. 2008. 'Collaborative governance: The community sector and collaborative network governance.' In *Collaborative Governance: A new era of public policy in Australia?* eds Janine O'Flynn and John Wanna, pp. 51–57. Canberra: ANU E Press. doi.org/10.22459/CG.12.2008.06.

Stewart, J. 2007. 'Managing across boundaries: The problem of conflicting values.' *Third Sector Review* 13(2): 71–85.

Wanna, John. 2008. 'Collaborative government: Meanings, dimensions, drivers and outcomes.' In *Collaborative Governance: A new era of public policy in Australia?* eds Janine O'Flynn and John Wanna, pp. 3–12. Canberra: ANU E Press. doi.org/10.22459/CG.12.2008.01.

7

LEADING COLLABORATION

Introduction

Those involved in collaborations often report difficulties in reaching agreement about the purpose of the collaboration and in maintaining the necessary levels of personal and organisational commitment over the longer term. These difficulties can be accentuated when collaborators encounter doubt, distrust or institutional and/or stakeholder resistance. Multiparty collaboration is complex. It often requires partners to navigate uncharted organisational and operational terrain, and to understand and reconcile diverse perspectives, priorities and needs. Collaboration is often undertaken in circumstances of uncertainty and the precise trajectory of collaborative endeavour can take unanticipated turns.

For all these reasons, collaboration needs to be led with sensitivity and insight. Leading collaboration is not project management nor is it a linear sequence of tasks with predefined, predictable results. Instead, it is an organic process. Understandably, the 'organic' aspects of collaboration sometimes conflict with the formal rules, protocols or habitual behaviours of organisations and institutions. Working across organisational, domain and sectoral boundaries to solve complex public problems places a greatly enhanced emphasis on skills relating to conflict resolution, engaging the public and balancing ethical priorities (Getha-Taylor and Morse 2013: 75).

The practice and attributes of effective leadership in the context of collaboration can be quite different to the leadership attributes often sought after in a traditional management role, and there is abundant emerging evidence that collaborative governance requires a set of leadership competencies quite distinct from those traditionally rooted in hierarchy and formal authority (Getha-Taylor and Morse 2013: 95). In this chapter, we discuss leadership as a critical factor in effective collaboration. We also consider two dimensions of collaborative leadership: first, the personal/individual qualities, attributes and competencies required by collaboration leaders; and second, collaborative leadership as a process.

Leadership in the public, private and not-for-profit sectors

The subject of leadership is under greater scrutiny than ever before (Terry et al. 2019). It is all very well to stress the importance of leadership in collaboration, but what kind of leadership does collaboration require? And, in multiparty collaborations involving participants from different sectors, what account needs to be taken of any differences between leadership traditions or paradigms that prevail in the public, private and not-for-profit sectors, and to what extent might these differences—presuming they exist—affect collaboration?

Relationships between public sector entities and their not-for-profit partners can be distorted by power differentials and by the market logics underpinning contractual relationships (Furneaux and Ryan 2014: 1131). Babiak and Thibault (2009: 138) suggest that partnerships formed across multiple sectoral boundaries involve the union of different—and potentially incompatible—missions, goals and values. They also contend that 'feelings of ambiguity, resentment, uncertainty, and suspicion' can result from 'perceived power imbalances' arising from resource inequities and political backing (Babiak and Thibault 2009: 137).

Orazi et al. (2013: 486) suggest that administrative leaders in the public sector behave differently from their counterparts in the business world, and point to the need for leadership development programs that 'focus on these differences instead of merely mimicking programs designed for leaders in the private sector'. Their research suggests the emergence of a distinctive style of public sector leadership that is more dispersed, and shared, and on the whole more conducive to networks of peer organisations and collaborative governance (Orazi et al. 2013: 497). The authors suggest that, compared with their private sector counterparts, public sector leaders 'have to ensure higher accountability to different stakeholders and face higher levels of formalisation and red tape' (Orazi et al. 2013: 492). In addition, while public sector leaders exhibit 'lower levels of satisfaction due to excessive constraints', they have, on the whole, a stronger sense of 'public service motivation' (Orazi et al. 2013: 492).

Whereas the contemporary public sector leans more towards 'participative' leadership styles that rely on dialogue and coaching, cooperation and delegation, the private sector, by contrast, is more inclined towards 'directive' leadership styles based on the application of rules and instructions aimed at implementing readymade, established strategies (Vogel and Masal 2012; Hansen and Villadsen 2010). Such a finding might, at first blush, seem surprising and even counterintuitive. Vogel and Massal (2012: 12) explain that managers working in complex environments—such as those characteristic of large parts of the public sector—tend to favour the participative leadership style:

> Complex issues are presumably solved more effectively by involving the employees than by means of rules and control mechanisms … In contrast, however, if the working environment is not seen as being very complex, it would seem that autonomy is limited and the role definition is less clear. In this case, the directive leadership style is preferred, which by means of rules and control mechanisms can deal more effectively with the circumstance of limited autonomy and lack of clear role definition,

Andersen (2010: 140) notes that both public and private sector leaders 'face the same challenges of achieving organisational goals with or through other people'. Even so, leaders in both sectors display marked differences in behaviour: whereas both public and private sector leaders employ intuitive decision-making styles, the former tend to be 'change-oriented' (insofar as they are open to new and different ways of doing things) while the latter tend to be more 'relationship-oriented' (in that they are sensitive to the nature and quality of their relationships with colleagues) (Andersen 2010: 133, 135). Also, public sector leaders tend to be motivated by 'achievement' (a desire to excel, to do something unique or surpass some standard of excellence) whereas private sector leaders tend to be motivated by 'power' (to make powerful actions, make an impression or secure reputation and position) (Andersen 2010: 133–37).

According to Terry et al. (2019), there is neither a clear evidence base nor a consensus about what constitutes 'good' leadership in the not-for-profit sector. They note that structural challenges confronting the sector have contributed to the emergence of a 'deficit' view of not-for-profit leadership—a view that reflects a 'widespread belief that voluntary organisations lack leadership skills—and that if these could be identified and distilled, they could then be imparted and embedded via leadership development programmes' (Terry et al. 2019: 2). However, they point to a lack of convincing evidence for such a proposition, instead suggesting the way forward is to 'reject theories and models that traditionally place the focus on individuals and on hierarchical models of leadership', focusing instead on 'conceptualisations of leadership that emphasise its collective nature' (Terry et al. 2019: 2).

Terry et al. (2019: 10) conclude that there has been excessive focus on the characteristics and skills of individuals in formal leadership positions, and only limited exploration of leadership *processes*:

> [M]edia narratives all too often associate the achievements of voluntary sector organisations with the heroic endeavours of extraordinary individuals (a yearning to identify and celebrate such individuals is also apparent in the wider culture), and failure with the character failings of occupants of senior positions.

This emphasis on the 'person', they suggest, encourages an 'elusive search for heroic leaders' and is potentially elitist in its consequences (Terry et al. 2019: 10). Terry et al. (2019: 10) challenge the heroic leader narrative and argue instead for 'collective' approaches in which leadership responsibilities are dispersed and shared and that have the capacity to encourage more diverse sources of leadership and 'offer more bottom-up relational organisations ways of understanding and exploring leadership that resonate with their values'. Collective approaches to leadership, they say, offer a *process perspective* in which individuals and stakeholders influence one another relationally, share responsibilities and hold one another accountable (Terry et al. 2019: 10). Viewed from a process perspective, leadership is about *how* leaders get things done (Terry et al. 2019: 3).

Leadership in collaboration

The initiation of a collaboration or partnership requires catalytic leadership in the form of a powerful convenor or brokering organisation able to leverage influence and social capital to overcome institutional or cultural resistance. Once this has been established, leaders need to be able to balance diversity and resolve tensions between stakeholders (Bowden and Ciesielska 2016: 24).

Ansell and Gash (2012: 18) argue that the distinctive quality of collaborative leadership is that it is *facilitative* rather than *directive*, in that facilitative leadership creates 'the conditions that support the contributions of stakeholders to the collaborative process and effective transactions among them'. In this respect, Ansell and Gash appear to view facilitative leadership very much through the kind of *process* lens advocated by Terry et al. (2019).

Ansell and Gash (2012: 18) identify three types of facilitative leaders:

1. *Stewards*, who facilitate the collaborative process 'by protecting the integrity of the collaborative process itself'.
2. *Mediators*, who facilitate 'by helping to arbitrate and nurture relationships between stakeholders'.
3. *Catalysts*, who help stakeholders 'to identify and realize value-creating opportunities'.

They also propose that facilitative leadership typically requires leaders to 'play all three of these roles', although their relative prominence will be influenced by 'antecedent conditions, systems context, and collaborative goals' (Ansell and Gash 2012: 18). This they refer to as a 'contingency approach' to collaborative governance in which it is assumed that leadership styles will be shaped by the distinctive demands of particular tasks, goals and contexts (Ansell and Gash 2012: 3).

Ansell and Gash (2012: 18) extend their analysis to identify two different styles of facilitative leadership:

1. The *professional facilitator*, who 'adopts a neutral stance towards outcomes, comes from outside the community, and is independent of any of the stakeholders'.
2. The *organic leader*, who 'comes from the stakeholder community, and can generally draw on extensive social capital, but may not be neutral with respect to outcomes'.

Table 7.1 The collaborative leadership role

Collaborative leadership roles	General definition	Skills and strategies	Distinctive role of professional facilitator	Distinctive role of organic leader
Steward	Establishes and protects the integrity of the collaborative process	Lends reputation and social capital to convene the process Establishes the inclusiveness, transparency, neutrality and civic character of the process Manages the image and identity of the collaborative process	Professional facilitator may be more important in establishing process ground rules than in initially convening the process	Organic leader may be critical in convening a collaborative process, because an organic leader has reputation and social capital to invest
Mediator	Arbitrates and nurtures relationships between stakeholders	Serves as 'honest broker' in mediating disputes Facilitates the construction of shared meaning Restores process to positive interaction Builds trust among stakeholders (specific strategies depend on goals and baseline trust)	Professional facilitator role may have an easier time establishing credentials as 'honest broker'; professionals often have sophisticated communication and negotiation skills	Organic leaders may be more effective in intervening to move difficult processes forward; may have context-specific knowledge valuable for adjudication
Catalyst	Identifies value-creating opportunities and mobilises stakeholders to pursue them	Engages in 'systems thinking' Frames or reframes problems Creates mutually reinforcing links between collaboration and innovation	Professional facilitators are probably less likely to engage in catalytic leadership	Organic leaders are likely to draw on contextual knowledge and unique relationships to act catalytically

Source: Ansell and Gash (2012: 8).

Although both types of leader can serve as 'honest brokers', Ansell and Gash argue that the professional facilitator 'will have an easier time establishing their neutrality, but a harder time motivating and persuading stakeholders to make effective contributions', whereas organic leaders can 'cajole and mobilise, but may have trouble convincing stakeholders of their neutrality':

> Thus, the professional facilitator will probably not have much luck in convening stakeholders, but may do a good job of maintaining the integrity of the process. Organic leaders may do a good job convening collaborative forums, but may also become the target of distrust as collaboration unfolds. With respect to mediation, professional facilitators will easily stand 'above the fray' and will have the professional skills to effectively mediate. Organic leaders, however, may have advantages in arbitrage that requires translation between different specialised idioms. Finally, with respect to catalytic leadership, our expectation is that organic leaders will have the advantage, since recognition of value-creating opportunities often requires a deep familiarity with the substantive issues at stake. Our expectation is that collaborative governance that aims for creative problem-solving will require strong catalytic leadership from organic leaders. (Ansell and Gash 2012: 18)

Collaboration leadership

The role of a leader in a collaborative endeavour is different to the role of the traditional manager, who, more often than not, is obliged to function in a hierarchical, as well as a vertically and horizontally segmented, operating environment. Instead, successful collaboration leaders predominantly work in a non-hierarchical manner where they will likely need to manage the expectations of internal and external stakeholders and engage with collaboration partners to come to mutual understandings about the articulation of goals, methods, timelines and reporting processes (Luke 1997: 24).

Unlike traditional governing roles based on rules, protocols and chains of command, leading collaboration is about curating and cultivating relationships, resolving differences and sharing control (Archer and Cameron 2012). Collaboration leaders are generally more 'facilitative' than 'directive'; indeed, 'captain's calls' or executive decisions by leaders can undermine trust in, and commitment to, collaboration.

Trust is a kind of currency or lubricant that allows people to engage in reciprocal risk-taking and work towards shared goals and objectives (Williams 2002: 114), and building trust is one of the most important activities of collaborative leaders (Atchison and Bujak 2001; Crosby and Bryson 2010; Ansell and Gash 2012; Williams 2002). Collaboration leaders use the trust they have built up to mediate or broker discussion between stakeholders, thereby helping to reduce the potential for conflict (Ansell and Gash 2012; Gray 2008). (For an expanded discussion, see Chapter 10.)

In the complex environments characteristic of collaboration, contradictions and tensions sometimes arise between the collaboration leadership and the prevailing values and norms in partner organisations. It is essential, therefore, that trust also exists between authorisers and collaboration leaders (see Chapter 6).

Effective collaboration leaders also invest time in building diverse networks to allow different points of view to be voiced in discussions and reflected in decisions made (Archer and Cameron 2012). This requires collaboration leaders to use both formal and informal processes to engage their fellow collaborators, share responsibility and ensure that all partners feel they are an important part of the process. This includes being especially attentive to any power imbalances between partners and stakeholders (Fletcher and Käufer 2003).

Collaboration leaders also need to be able to protect collaborative processes politically and adapt to what is likely to be an ever-changing environment while keeping the collaboration objectives in sight.

The importance of 'boundary-spanners'

Multiparty collaboration is at its most effective when it is led by people who are adept at building and sustaining relationships, managing within non-hierarchical environments, managing complexity and understanding the motives, roles and responsibilities of collaboration partners (Williams 2002: 103). These are the 'boundary-spanners'—people with exceptional networking skills who are able to cultivate interpersonal relationships, who have 'an appreciation of the interdependencies around the structure of problems and their potential solutions', who are able to facilitate communication over 'social ground' rather than between 'institutional grounds', who are entrepreneurial and 'creative lateral thinking rule breakers', and who are able to bring unlikely partners together, break through red tape and frame problems in a different way (Williams 2002: 109–10).

Williams (2002: 109–10) points out that boundary-spanners play an important role in instilling and reinforcing trust within collaborative networks. A note of caution is warranted, however. Although the kind of social bonding that takes place through interpersonal networking can be extremely positive, there are potential downsides associated with informality and an overreliance on personal relationships, which could be inherently fragile (Williams 2002: 110).

Williams notes that boundary-spanners generally consider that their employing organisation has 'the first call on their responsibility', but they also recognise that there are multiple sources of authority and legitimacy in multipartner settings:

> A poor partner is perceived as one who slavishly or dogmatically ploughs a representative furrow in partnership arenas and, irritatingly, has to 'report back' everything to the home organization. Conversely, the more effective partners are those who are empowered, within certain negotiated parameters, to engage constructively with other partners. They have a feel for what may or may not be acceptable to their home organizations and are ready to play the partnership game. (Williams 2002: 120)

Williams (2002) has distilled the 'art of boundary-spanning', which is summarised in Table 7.2.

Table 7.2 The art of boundary-spanning

Key elements of boundary-spanning	Key competencies of boundary-spanning
Building sustainable relationships by understanding people and the organisations they represent, and managing difference in the pursuit of mutually beneficial agendas	**Communicating and listening:** Searching for shared meanings through a two-way process in which receiving information (listening) is as important as giving information **Understanding, empathising and resolving conflict:** Building robust relationships that can manage conflict and criticism while retaining a willingness to move on without harming the relationship **Personality:** People with the defining traits of respect, honesty, openness, tolerance, approachability, reliability, sensitivity and an ability to divest themselves of organisational and professional baggage **Trust:** A key variable influencing the effectiveness of collaborative relationships and essentially a condition constituted in the relationships between individuals, although by implication organisations can acquire a reputation for being more or less trustworthy, thus underscoring the inherent difficulty of disentangling personal from institutionalised forms of trust
Managing through influencing and negotiation in environments characterised by power relationships that are more contested and dispersed than is often the case in traditional bureaucracies	**Influencing:** Being persuasive and diplomatic, being constructive and nonjudgemental, leading on some occasions but facilitating in others and being acutely aware of political and personal sensibilities **Negotiation** over aims, funding proposals, operational programs, priorities, resource allocation and so on **Brokering:** Devising solutions informed by an acute understanding of interdependencies between problems, solutions and organisations **Networking:** Involving exchanges of information, having access to new ideas, seeking support from and influencing others, learning about resource opportunities (often, and most effectively, via conversations that occur outside formal decision-making structures)
Managing complexity and interdependencies through the application of interorganisational experience, transdisciplinary knowledge and cognitive capability	**Making sense:** An appreciation of connections and interrelationships manifested in different ways at different stages in the partnership process; dealing with often-disparate bodies of technical knowledge and professional expertise; partner search, problem diagnosis, defining roles and responsibilities, negotiating goals and developing crosscutting agendas **Innovation:** The ability to collaboratively fashion new solutions to previously intractable problems through the skilful negotiation of sustainable partnership agreements and the successful mobilisation or levering-in of resources

Key elements of boundary-spanning	Key competencies of boundary-spanning
Managing roles, accountabilities and motivations through an acute awareness of the configuration of roles and responsibilities between agencies within an existing or emerging interorganisational domain, and the political and professional sensibilities that encompass them	**Awareness** of the potential conflict between one's role as organisational representative and that of a partner in a multi-organisational endeavour; of conflicting accountabilities and multiple sources of accountability **Understanding** the parameters and constraints of each partner

Source: Williams (2002: 114–21).

Collaboration as a process

Just over 25 years ago, Hood et al. (1993: 14) made the following observations:

> Cross-sectoral collaborations are unusual groups in many ways. They bring together individuals, primarily leaders, from divergent sectors in the community to work together on a problem or concern they share …

> The goals, values, and ideologies of the individual participants may differ greatly, and they are expected to solve a problem of large magnitude and over a long-term duration. Each collaborative group develops a sense of the group-as-a-whole, where norms and cultures emerge that are singular to that group. The subgroups that form may be based upon ideology, or they may form according to social status, gender, ethnic origin, or basic personality factors. Interpersonal factors, including communication processes, trust, and conflict, will either contribute to or detract from the success of the collaboration.

These observations remain as true today as when they were first published.

Working with external stakeholders entails a different set of activities and requisite competencies than goal-oriented organisational leadership (Getha-Taylor and Morse 2013: 78). Getha-Taylor and Morse (2013)— drawing on Morse and Stephens (2012), among others—have attempted to distil the broad phases of collaboration and core collaborative competencies (see Table 7.3) at the heart of which is a set of behaviours (and related attributes and skills) that revolves around: understanding and identifying stakeholders, convening them, designing appropriate processes for them, facilitating agreements among them, designing appropriate governance arrangements for agreements reached and keeping them together to implement what is decided.

Table 7.3 Phases of collaboration and collaborative competencies

Phases of collaboration			
Assessment	**Initiation**	**Deliberation**	**Implementation**
Issue analysis	Stakeholder engagement	Group facilitation	Developing action plans
Environmental assessment	Political/community organisation	Team-building and group dynamics	Designing governance structures
Stakeholder identification	Building social capital	Listening	Public engagement
Strategic thinking	Process design	Consensus-building	Network management
		Interest-based negotiation	Conflict resolution
			Performance evaluation
Collaborative competencies			
Collaborative mindset Passion for creating public value Systems thinking		Openness and risk-taking Sense of mutuality and connectedness Humility or measured ego	

Source: Getha-Taylor and Morse (2013: 78).

Consistent with many other researchers and commentators, Perrault et al. (2011: 296) emphasise the process-intensive nature of collaboration: 'Implementing collaborations is not easy. The cost of participation is high, requiring a commitment of time and resources that must be outweighed by the benefits of collaboration.'

Pointing to the challenges of collaboration, 'not the least of which is the cost, time, and patience required to collaborate', Perrault et al. (2011: 283) identify three important success factors for collaboration:

1. Established informal relationships and communication links (personal connections).
2. The attention paid to the development of mutual respect, understanding and trust.
3. A norm of shared leadership incorporating a 'learning purpose' at both the individual and the organisational levels (p. 296).

Shared leadership

Bowden and Ciesielska (2016: 29) consider that public sector managers 'do not need to hold the naturally powerful, collaborative leadership roles—convenor, conduit and funder—that they used to'. Instead, they suggest, public sector managers need to adapt to the new role of 'leveraging the legitimacy gained through their technical assistance provider role to influence the direction and content of cross-sector partnerships' (Bowden and Ciesielska 2016: 29).

Shared leadership can be very positive for collaborations. Crosby and Bryson (2005: 184) observe:

> A central challenge for leaders is to bring diverse stakeholders together in shared-power arrangements in which they can pool information, other resources and activities around a common purpose. The focus should be on key stakeholders—those most affected by a social need or public problem or who have important resources for meeting the need.

In collaboration, unlike traditional hierarchical leadership, there are no direct lines of authority over partners. Collaboration works on the basis of consensus, equality and win–win solutions, requiring the application of skills such as negotiation, mediation, bargaining and brokering (Williams 2002). By sharing, leadership partners will feel empowered to engage constructively with one another. As Crosby and Bryson (2010: 222) observe, cross-sector collaborations are more likely to succeed if leaders use resources and tactics to help equalise power, to avoid imposed solutions and to effectively manage conflict.

Crucially, this requires those leading the collaboration to both understand the needs of partners and stakeholders and work towards a shared understanding of each participant's respective needs and priorities. It is not necessary for the needs and priorities of each partner or stakeholder to be identical; it *does* require a willingness to understand and respect the differing motivations of partners and key stakeholders and bring goodwill to the task of agreeing to feasible and constructive actions and strategies.

Succession, structure and governance

It is sometimes said of collaborations that they are 'hero led'—meaning they are often led by charismatic 'policy entrepreneurs', who, through the force of their energy, imagination and connections, are able to spearhead new initiatives or win support for new ideas, even in the face of organisational or institutional resistance. There is, however, an inherent fragility to hero-led initiatives. Former head of the Australian Department of the Prime Minister and Cabinet Peter Shergold offered the following observation in a 2018 interview with public health think tank the Sax Institute:

> Too often I have seen excellent collaborative partnerships falter when leadership 'heroes' move on to different organisations. Somehow the culture of collaboration must be embedded into governance structures to ensure its longevity. (Shergold 2018: 2)

Collaboration should not have to depend on charismatic heroes. Rather, all organisations operating in environments characterised by complexity and interdependency—regardless of which sector they inhabit—need to inculcate the range of competencies required for successful boundary-spanning. Collaborative behaviours should be habitual, not exceptional. For this to happen, all members of the leadership teams of partner organisations need to 'walk the talk'. In this way, collaboration leads can have some confidence that authorisers 'have their back'.

Authorisers and collaboration partners need to be mindful of the risks flowing from the person-centred nature of collaboration leadership: burnout and the turnover of key personnel can lead to a loss of corporate memory, and the departure of leaders—heroic leaders, in particular—can undermine collaborative purpose and strategic intent (Butcher et al. 2019; Ansell and Gash 2012). These are foreseeable and manageable risks that can be mitigated by the adoption of a governance framework that builds capacity for the future needs of the collaboration and includes provisions for business continuity and succession planning.

What the cases tell us

Collaboration leadership

In some respects, collaboration is about reconciling—or at least accommodating—diverse and nuanced perspectives on problems and contributing to solving those problems. Each of the policy spaces in which our cases operate involves stakeholders who work from quite different vantage points. A capacity to acknowledge, balance and valorise differences of perspective—whether cultural, institutional or disciplinary—is an essential component of collaboration leadership.

However, as discussed above, leadership sometimes has an ephemeral quality that tends to reside in individuals and is not necessarily endemic in organisational culture. As one Throughcare interviewee observed:

> If I think about the collaborations that happen between organisations outside of government, the longevity of those depends on the longevity of key leaders staying the same. In government, it's very rare for key leaders to be in their roles for really long periods of time. So, the collaborations are time-limited because they're limited by the people … When you get the right people with the right skill set and the right leadership capability, they find the opportunities to make things happen.

Another interviewee observed that collaboration leadership 'is a cultural issue', noting that authorisation to engage collaboratively:

> has to cascade downward from [executive] leadership …

> People acting entrepreneurially off their own bat can achieve a lot, but if they're hobbling around with a ball and chain then they can only go so far. (CAP)

It is also possible that, over time, as a collaborative initiative evolves, the style and skill mix required to carry the initiative forward might change:

> I remember a boss saying to me once when I went into a role that he was looking for someone very different to fill the same role when I came on board than the person that preceded me because they'd done a certain lot of things and taken things to a level and achieved what they needed, but now as a result of that they actually needed something quite different. So that does lead

> me to wonder about not just that conundrum of everything being
> dependent on the individual but also about our overall leadership
> that sees us needing to have one person there for the longevity of
> an initiative and whether that's viable. (CAP)

Leadership can, as one interviewee observed, come from a number of
different quarters: it might come from someone assigned a formal
management role, from a respected member of the community or from
someone in another organisation who 'steps up'. It might be all three.
However, leadership does sometimes need to be 'nudged':

> What do we do to get the right leadership … I think if we'd had
> a leadership change implementation program going alongside the
> implementation of the initiative, we would have been much more
> successful. (CAP)

Two themes that emerged from the interviews—often in conjunction—
were the 'conundrum' of person-centred leadership and the predominance
of an operational/transactional leadership paradigm that fails to
incorporate the attributes or skills essential for collaboration:

> Reflecting back on your question around the leadership ending
> up being very dependent on the personality in a role, it does
> prompt me to think and ask, if we acknowledge that it is about
> some unique individuals, then how do we cultivate a pool of
> that kind of individual? Normally we cultivate—certainly in the
> government sector—subject matter experts; we don't cultivate
> leaders that have these intrinsic things that certainly help the
> collaborative approach. (CAP)

A competency framework for collaboration

Leading collaboration requires good, innate facilitation skills. Collaborative
leaders have a sound understanding of the constraints under which
partners and stakeholders are obliged to operate. They know when to step
in, and when to step back. As one interviewee suggested:

> I think a good leader probably knows when it's time for them
> to step out of their own spotlight and do what they are there
> for but also is able to surround themselves with smart expertise
> within their team and put those people forward when it is more
> appropriate. (Change the Story)

Collaboration leaders need to be able to inspire people to action, demonstrate empathy and manage egos. They require the capacity to obtain a nuanced understanding of the community, institutional and policy spaces in which they work or which are impacted by the collaborative project, and they understand what shapes people's perceptions and what fuels their fears and their hopes. Collaborative leadership is about enabling key players to contribute to shared leadership:

> I see leadership as about setting directions, but it's also about giving others the wherewithal to assist in getting there. And it's also about succession planning. It is not just about individuals; it is about having a group of people that can share that leadership. (Throughcare)

Of course, leadership also has practical, instrumental applications, as expressed by another interviewee:

> A function of leadership is direction, protection and order. So, having the ability to let them know that risk-taking is acceptable; giving them the protection that you're going to back them up, which is not a common public service mantra; and creating an … ordered environment. (Throughcare)

Importantly, leading collaboration does not rely solely on formal instrumental leadership. Success resides in the judicious empowerment of frontline workers and communities:

> I think that one of the learnings has been that we need to engage, that you really need to have both mandated leadership—the support of mandated leadership of CEOs and those sorts of people to give their workers a mandate to work in a particular way—as well as leadership in the broader sense of good community leadership. Both of them are important … the people who are employed by the health services have got a very limited mandate, really. Unless their leaders, their managers, have a broad view about the work being done in the community rather than in delivering services then they really are very limited. (WHO STOPS, GSC Change)

A recurring theme in the interviews is that personal qualities are as important to the success of collaboration as technical or business skills:

> The personal qualities of people to implement things have the greatest influence on the success of an initiative, more than the clinical ones and more than the technical ones. You need those, but they are not as important. I think that's what's coming

to be known: people's personal strengths about staying calm, being in control, resilience, maintaining the bigger, longer-term picture, supporting people who are less confident about those things, more anxious about why isn't it working now—they are the leadership skills that are required longer term to be successful. (CAP)

Creative rule-breakers

Collaboration leaders are also operating in spaces where normative organisational rules are blurred. They need to have a clear understanding of normative boundaries while also being prepared to step over those boundaries. The following quote captures a common sentiment:

> There are some fantastic people out there who just do the right thing regardless of all of those kinds of rules or regulations. But they are very rare in my experience. (CAP)

Effective collaboration leaders are creative, often charismatic, rule-breakers; however, they are most effective when they have express authorisation to exercise initiative and when they have confidence that authorisers will back them up. Conversely, authorisers need to have confidence in the judgement of collaboration leaders and assurance that they will be kept informed about any real or potential risks:

> At a leadership level, it's giving your staff permission to share information and managing and then having trust and confidence that you will manage that risk. (CAP)

Collaboration leaders are trusted sources of information; they are also 'myth busters', being less concerned with enacting 'bureaucratic intent' and more focused on community activation and fostering constructive relationships based on trust and reciprocity. And because the levels of collaboration skills represented around the table are often uneven, it is a prime objective of collaboration leaders to raise the collective collaborative intelligence of others and bring diverse, complementary skills and knowledge to the collaboration:

> It's about being able to inspire people to want to go over and above what it is that their formal job description might be.
>
> … Being able to be discerning, being quite strategic, being able to manage egos and being able to inspire people. I don't think that it's smart for any of us to think that as one individual we will have all of those skill sets and that alone we are going to be the reason why this program stands up or falls down. We won't. (CBEM)

Finally, collaboration leaders often succeed in spite of the bureaucracies in which they are employed—bureaucracies that do not necessarily realise that these are the very people they need:

> It's the entrepreneurialship [sic], I think, that we don't look for enough. People who are going to push boundaries and challenge. We can all be great public servants and stick to all the rules and stuff. We've got to find some rule-breakers and get them into leadership roles. Then we'll really start to see some change, I believe. (CAP)

Leave your ego at the door

One interviewee from Victoria suggested that ego can be toxic in collaboration settings and added that 'reluctant leaders are best'. A good leader is one who can 'abandon their ego to the talent of others' (De Pree 1987). While acknowledging the importance of formal authority (often associated with seniority) to drive a collaboration agenda, interviewees often cited the attributes of humility and a willingness to listen as indispensable features of effective collaboration leadership:

> We had enough people with sufficient seniority who wanted to see the program get up, but they were also willing to work with people with sufficient knowledge and expertise to design a good program. So, we got that sweet spot of people with sufficient authority to drive a change agenda but with sufficient humility to be guided. That's a hard thing to land in that sweet spot. Usually the style of leadership is, 'I have authority and I'll make decisions', whereas these people said: 'I have authority, and I will listen and I'm prepared to change my mind.' (Throughcare)

Of course, one of the challenges facing any collaboration leader is managing the egos of other stakeholders. One interviewee encapsulated the problem as follows:

> It is about dealing with other people's egos, and that is not exclusive to the agencies or the departments. We're dealing with the egos of other community representatives at any given time and in any community. So, if their ego is bigger than what they've actually got to offer in the short, medium and long term to an initiative then for me that's a game changer. Because now my passenger is obstructive for starters because that ego is getting in the way, and we are now needing to carry that inefficiency and do it in such a way that that ego continues to be massaged, and that is exhausting and unhelpful and unproductive. (CBEM)

Relaxing institutional rules

The nurturing of collaborative approaches depends heavily on executive sponsorship and the selective relaxation of the usual institutional rules. The quid pro quo in these understandings is that the collaboration leader will act judiciously and provide timely information and assurance to the executive. This is a 'no surprises' relationship but not a 'no risk' relationship. However, there can also be an inherent fragility in executive-level support for collaboration owing to mobility and changing personnel or changes in the political or operating environment.

A sentiment commonly expressed in the interviews is that leaders with the skills necessary to both maintain respectful relationships at the coalface *and* deftly manage the executive are uncommon and hard to recruit because, as one interviewee astutely observed:

> You needed someone that could do both, and that was very hard to find someone that could do both that also had the trust of both sides. It was very hard to do that. And more often than not it didn't work. There were trade-offs along the way, and it just didn't work. You either got one or you got the other. (CAP)

Other interviewees speculated about the reasons for this difficulty:

> That's not often how you advertise a job. You advertise with particular academic qualifications or experience. To have to steel the person to be able to weed through some of these tensions, and also to be able to do this sort of work in the prevention space, where ultimately you're sitting across all of these jurisdictions, literal differences, both at a macro and [a] micro level, being able to do that stuff sensitively and with a sense of humour. I think the sense of humour bit is the only bit that probably gets you through when you get into some of the really dark, sticky bits. But being able to reach out across communities and acknowledge your privilege in the space but also that sensitivity to different things. (Change the Story)

Yet another said:

> I mean [I] know you've got to work within the political context and stuff like that, but there's always little things you can do within the system, if you like, that kind of challenges that stuff … And there'll be pockets of brilliance and it's kind of like how do you recognise that talent and not knock the stuffing out of them through rules of bureaucracy, because that's often what happens to those people, isn't it? (CAP)

Continuous communication

Collaboration leaders and partners invest an extraordinary amount of time in communication—with each other, with the executive, middle management and frontline workers of their own organisations, agencies or community groups, and with the range of external stakeholders who are in some way affected by the collaboration:

> There has to be a [recognition] amongst the stakeholders that there's a problem. The collaboration, to me, is getting the stakeholders together around a common problem and then using the collaborational [sic] approach to try and agree on what is the path forward to resolve that problem. (Change the Story)

As such, and confirming this analysis, three consistent messages from each of the cases investigated for this study are: communication is the bedrock of collaboration, communication is both labour-intensive and time-intensive and effective communication requires empathy, active listening and patience:

> It's the style of leadership; it's the style of collaboration. At the end of the day, if you spent an hour with people, they could feel very involved, very listened to, [that they] very much own the process when they leave. You could spend two hours with people and they could feel like they were never consulted. So, it's not so much the time and the money; it's the quality of the time that's spent with them. (Change the Story)

Final observations

The personal qualities and skills collaboration leaders bring to the table can make or break any collaboration. Importantly, effective collaboration leaders must enjoy the trust, confidence and backing of authorisers in their respective employing organisations. In the early stages of collaboration, partner organisations need to decide what kind of leadership model might offer the best chance of getting buy-in from stakeholders, especially those who might believe themselves to be disadvantaged in terms of power or influence. It is also essential to ensure the best fit between the aptitudes and skills around the collaboration table and the core attributes and competencies that effective collaboration demands. Authorisers and partner organisations need to commit to building the capacity of collaboration leaders through the provision of training, mentoring or specialist facilitation. While leadership is an important factor in the effectiveness of any collaboration, the leadership role need not be vested in any one organisation or individual. For most multiparty collaborations, shared leadership might offer the best prospects for reaching agreement about ends and means, reinforcing a sense of shared purpose, managing power imbalances and instilling trust and commitment. Moreover, all partner organisations need to be supportive of the leadership model selected for the collaboration and back the modus operandi of collaboration leaders.

Practice considerations

1. Consider who might be best to exercise leadership roles within the collaboration. Ensure that you are selecting potential collaboration leaders based on collaboration competencies rather than on rank, position or formal responsibilities.

2. Give careful consideration to the leadership model you think is most appropriate to this collaboration. Give careful consideration to potential power imbalances between collaboration partners and key stakeholders. Carefully assess any sensitivities that might arise and how these might be ameliorated by sharing or distributing leadership roles within the collaboration partnership.

3. Benchmark your proposed collaboration leadership against other, comparable initiatives. Speak to the leaders of other collaborations to find out what works and what does not. Use available, relevant self-assessment tools such as the Collaboration Health Assessment Tool developed by the Centre for Social Impact.[1]

4. Take stock of the skills mix within the collaboration, including any gaps in key collaboration leadership competencies. Identify strategies to address those gaps and to leverage the strengths of partners. Identify sources of support or training within partner organisations or externally, including specialist consultants or facilitators. Identify potential mentors within partner and stakeholder organisations who might work individually or collectively with the collaboration team.

5. Formulate a leadership plan that takes into account any developmental needs of key partners such as the:

    a. competencies required to support boundary-spanning activities

    b. competencies required for each phase of collaboration.

6. Formulate a strategy for the purpose of socialising the collaboration among authorisers, partners and stakeholders, and for addressing and resolving any differences that might arise.

7. Ensure that authorisers understand the dynamics of collaboration leadership and the nature and desirability of shared accountability within a leadership group. Keep authorisers apprised of any issues that arise and the manner in which any disagreement about the aims, goals, strategies or means will be resolved.

8. Develop a business continuity and succession plan in anticipation of possible changes in key personnel to ensure that the collaboration stays on track.

---

1   To access the Collaboration Health Assessment Tool, go to: www.csi.edu.au/chat/about/.

References

Andersen, Jon Aarum. 2010. 'Public versus private managers: How public and private managers differ in leadership behavior.' *Public Administration Review* 70(1): 131–41. doi.org/10.1111/j.1540-6210.2009.02117.x.

Ansell, Chris, and Alison Gash. 2012. 'Stewards, mediators, and catalysts: Toward a model of collaborative leadership.' *The Innovation Journal* 17(1): 2–21.

Archer, David, and Alex Cameron. 2012. 'Collaborative leadership.' *Training Journal*: 35–38.

Atchison, Thomas A., and Joseph S. Bujak. 2001. *Leading Transformational Change: The physician–executive partnership*. Chicago: Health Administration Press.

Babiak, Kathy, and Lucie Thibault. 2009. 'Challenges in multiple cross-sector partnerships.' *Nonprofit and Voluntary Sector Quarterly* 38(1): 117–43. doi.org/10.1177/0899764008316054.

Bowden, Alistair, and Malgorzata Ciesielska. 2016. 'Ecomuseums as cross-sector partnerships: Governance, strategy and leadership.' *Public Money & Management* 36(1): 23–30. doi.org/10.1080/09540962.2016.1103414.

Butcher, John R., David J. Gilchrist, John Phillimore, and John Wanna. 2019. 'Attributes of effective collaboration: Insights from five case studies in Australia and New Zealand.' *Policy Design and Practice* 2(1): 75–89. doi.org/10.1080/25741292.2018.1561815.

Crosby, Barbara C., and John M. Bryson. 2005. 'A leadership framework for cross-sector collaboration.' *Public Management Review* 7(2): 177–201. doi.org/10.1080/14719030500090519.

Crosby, Barbara C., and John M. Bryson. 2010. 'Integrative leadership and the creation and maintenance of cross-sector collaborations.' *The Leadership Quarterly* 21(2): 211–30. doi.org/10.1016/j.leaqua.2010.01.003.

De Pree, Max. 1987. *Leadership is an Art*. East Lansing, MI: Michigan State University Press.

Fletcher, Joyce K., and Katrin Käufer. 2003. 'Shared leadership: Paradox and possibility.' In *Shared Leadership: Reframing the hows and whys of leadership*, eds Craig L. Pearce and Jay A. Conger, pp. 21–47. Thousand Oaks, CA: Sage. doi.org/10.4135/9781452229539.n2.

Furneaux, Craig, and Neal Ryan. 2014. 'Modelling NPO–government relations: Australian case studies.' *Public Management Review* 16(8): 1113–140. doi.org/10.1080/14719037.2014.895030.

Getha-Taylor, Heather, and Ricardo S. Morse. 2013. 'Collaborative leadership development for local government officials: Exploring competencies and program impact.' *Public Administration Quarterly* 37(1): 71–102.

Gray, Barbara. 2008. *Intervening to Improve Inter-Organizational Partnerships.* Oxford: Oxford University Press. doi.org/10.1093/oxfordhb/9780199282944. 003.0025.

Hansen, Jesper Rosenberg, and Anders R. Villadsen. 2010. 'Comparing public and private managers' leadership styles: Understanding the role of job context.' *International Public Management Journal* 13(3): 247–74. doi.org/10.1080/ 10967494.2010.503793.

Hood, Jacqueline N., Jeanne M. Logsdon, and Judith Kenner Thompson. 1993. 'Collaboration for social problem solving: A process model.' *Business & Society* 32(1): 1–17. doi.org/10.1177/000765039303200103.

Luke, Jeffrey Scott. 1997. *Catalytic Leadership: Strategies for an interconnected world.* San Francisco: Jossey-Bass.

Morse, Ricardo S., and John B. Stephens. 2012. 'Teaching collaborative governance: Phases, competencies, and case-based learning.' *Journal of Public Affairs Education* 18(3): 565–83. doi.org/10.1080/15236803.2012.12001700.

Orazi, Davide Christian, Alex Turrini, and Giovanni Valotti. 2013. 'Public sector leadership: New perspectives for research and practice.' *International Review of Administrative Sciences* 79(3): 486–504. doi.org/10.1177/0020852313489945.

Perrault, Ellen, Robert McClelland, Carol Austin, and Jackie Sieppert. 2011. 'Working together in collaborations: Successful process factors for community collaboration.' *Administration in Social Work* 35(3): 282–98. doi.org/10.1080/ 03643107.2011.575343.

Shergold, Peter. 2018. 'Helping refugees build new lives: From consultation to collaboration.' *Public Health Research & Practice* 28(1). doi.org/10.17061/ phrp2811801.

Terry, Vita, James Rees, and Carol Jacklin-Jarvis. 2019. 'The difference leadership makes? Debating and conceptualising leadership in the UK voluntary sector.' *Voluntary Sector Review* 10(3): 1–13. doi.org/10.1332/204080519x1563433 1938320.

Vogel, Rick, and Doris Masal. 2012. 'Publicness, motivation, and leadership: The dark side of private management concepts in the public sector.' *Revista Administratie si Management Public* 2012(19): 6–16.

Williams, Paul. 2002. 'The competent boundary spanner.' *Public Administration* 80(1): 103–24. doi.org/10.1111/1467-9299.00296.

8

ENGAGEMENT

Introduction

Complex problems in social policy are, almost by definition, multifactorial. That is, many social problems arise as the result of the interplay of multiple discrete and sometimes reinforcing factors. For instance, the collaborations investigated for this book came into being because key policy actors recognised that the problems they sought to address could not be ameliorated by one organisation or discipline acting on its own.

For example:

- Offenders re-entering the community on completion of a custodial sentence require articulated supports from a range of sources to obtain accommodation, find employment, access mental health services, get help with addiction or gambling and re-establish connections with their families and communities, among other possible needs.

- Community preparedness for bushfires, floods, extreme weather events and other hazards hinges on having clear, well-understood protocols for the coordination and deployment of community assets, including volunteer firefighters, emergency management authorities, police, state emergency services, energy providers, financial institutions, landowners, local businesses, local councils, schools, hospitals and many others.

- Reducing the incidence of childhood obesity requires local governments, businesses, schools, community health workers, primary healthcare workers, local sporting associations and citizens (among others) to work together towards a set of common goals utilising a coherent framework for action and impact.

- Violence against women and children cannot be tackled at a societal level unless governments, key social institutions, civil society organisations, researchers and community leaders can reach a broad consensus about the major contributors to gendered violence, the required actions and coherent multidisciplinary practice frameworks.
- At-risk children and families depend on teachers, school principals, primary healthcare providers, community mental health professionals, social workers, police, the courts, community leaders and others working together within a broadly agreed understanding of the nature and scope of the problem, and with a shared commitment to coordinated action.

For each of our cases, successful collaboration depends on the willingness of partners—including individuals, community groups and organisations—to:

1. commit resources (for example, people, time, expertise, facilities and money)
2. ensure that their respective authorising and management systems support (or at least do not impede) collaborative endeavour.

With respect to the latter, it is important to bear in mind that each organisation has:

1. its own operating logic, founding story and mission
2. a distinct administrative history and an organisational culture shaped by that history
3. operating systems designed to serve its core business and governance requirements
4. unique stakeholder relationships framed around its core purposes.

With respect to the last point, it is important to understand that successful collaboration depends on earning the trust, confidence and support of multiple internal and external stakeholders who bring diverse interests, perspectives, perceptions, sensitivities and power relations to the table.

Engagement strategies

The collaborations studied used a variety of formal and informal processes to engage with stakeholders.

Table 8.1 Engagement strategies

Collaboration	Principal engagement strategies
Change the Story	The national framework for the primary prevention of violence against women and their children was informed by extensive consultations undertaken around the country with researchers, practitioners and policymakers—from community and non-governmental organisations, services and networks to government agencies at all levels.
Community-Based Emergency Management	The reform of Victoria's emergency management arrangements was built on a public conversation about three seminal documents: the 2011 *Green Paper: Towards a More Disaster Resilient and Safer Victoria*, the 2012 *White Paper: Victorian Emergency Management Reform* and a 2017 discussion paper, *Resilient Recovery*, which proposed a Resilient Recovery Model intended to empower communities, government, agencies and businesses to plan for and achieve recovery outcomes.
WHO STOPS	WHO STOPS involves a facilitated community engagement process in which local leaders bring people together to: create an agreed systems map of childhood obesity causes for a community; identify intervention opportunities through leveraging the dynamic aspects of the system; and convert these understandings into community-built, systems-oriented action plans. Local backbone groups based in Portland and Hamilton, Victoria, engage with a wide range of external stakeholders, including health practitioners, primary healthcare providers, local government, schools, clubs and local associations and businesses, to raise awareness of the causes of and contributors to childhood obesity, and to stimulate community responses to the problem and encourage population-level behaviour change.
Throughcare	The Extended Throughcare Governance Group, co-chaired by the CEO of ACT Corrective Services and a representative of the Australian Capital Territory's community sector, was established to oversee the implementation of the initiative. The co-chairing model was intended to encourage the community sector to take a primary role as a partner and has had the effect of encouraging strong community buy-in as well as helping to make the program more responsive to the diverse needs of its client base. The governance group was the primary forum in which community-sector views were brought to the table for discussion and action. The model relied more on informal caucusing among stakeholders than on any formal engagement strategy. One government group member conceded that engagement occurred primarily at an organisational level, and not directly with prisoners themselves.

Collaboration	Principal engagement strategies
Children's Teams	The Children's Action Plan flows from: a 2011 green paper probing community views about the adequacy of responses to the needs of vulnerable children and families; a 2012 white paper that set out the New Zealand Government's commitment to establish local Children's Teams that would bring together professionals to assess the needs of vulnerable children using a common assessment approach and, where required, form a joined-up intervention plan; and a 2015 expert panel that identified a number of structural and systemic deficiencies with the delivery of services for vulnerable children and their families. Public consultations in the formative stages of the action plan were undertaken in various parts of the country, and the feedback from these conferred legitimacy on the government's actions. Since their establishment, Children's Teams Local Governance Groups — consisting of senior managers from core service delivery agencies and, where appropriate, other key partners such as non-governmental organisations, *iwi* (tribes) and local government representatives — have provided the primary interface for community engagement.

Collaboration practice

Head (2008: 739) notes that much of the literature on collaborative networks focuses on good processes using the lens of 'practice' knowledge. Head identifies eight process and relationship issues that are likely to be critical for the success of networked governance arrangements:

1. Aligning the perspectives of different kinds of stakeholder groups and, in so doing, managing diversity and making good use of diverse skills.

2. Eliciting a strong political mandate to find acceptable solutions to the problem and to fund the strategies arising from joint efforts.

3. Focusing on local capacity-building, especially in relation to local and regional initiatives.

4. Building trust through a confidence-building process (noting that trust is rarely a starting point but is 'earned').

5. Cultivating a learning orientation that enables the collaborative entity to develop and review common goals, adjust strategies in the light of experience, build long-term relationships, avoid a culture of blame, provide sufficient time for processes to work and learn to deal with the dual identity of participants (as members of the collaborative entity and as representatives of their employing organisations).

6. Adopting clear rules for decision-making, governance and accountabilities for key tasks.

7. Encouraging and nurturing skills in bridging and linking among the sectoral stakeholder groups.

8. Leadership capabilities including 'bridging' skills (linking to external resources), 'mobilising' skills (making best use of existing assets and strengths), 'persuasive' skills (selling and marketing the benefits and strategic opportunities) and 'adaptive' skills (the capacity to deal with changing contexts and challenges, such as changing expectations and aspirations, turnover of membership, and reform fatigue) (Head 2008: 739–41).

Collaboration process

Emerson et al. (2012) suggest that collaborative practice comprises three process components:

1. Principled engagement, which encompasses the four process elements of discovery, definition, deliberation and determination.

2. Shared motivation, which consists of trust, mutual understanding, internal legitimacy and shared commitment.

3. Capacity for joint action, consisting of procedural and institutional arrangements, leadership, knowledge and resources (Emerson et al. 2012: 20).

Principled engagement

The process of 'principled engagement' is one in which 'people with differing content, relational, and identity goals work across their respective institutional, sectoral, or jurisdictional boundaries to solve problems, resolve conflicts, or create value' (Emerson et al. 2012: 10). Principled engagement enables partners to 'develop a shared sense of purpose and a shared theory of action for achieving that purpose' through the application of four basic process elements:

1. Discovery, which refers to 'the revealing of individual and shared interests, concerns, and values, as well as to the identification and analysis of relevant and significant information and its implications'.

2. Definition, which refers to 'continuous efforts to build shared meaning by articulating common purpose and objectives; agreeing on the concepts and terminology participants will use to describe and discuss problems and opportunities; clarifying and adjusting tasks and expectations of one another; and setting forth shared criteria with which to assess information and alternatives'.

3. Deliberation, in which a safe space is provided for '[h]ard conversations, constructive self-assertion, asking and answering challenging questions, and expressing honest disagreements'.

4. Determination, in the form of procedural decisions about operational matters or implementation, and substantive determinations concerning the outputs or end products of collaboration (Emerson et al. 2012: 10–11).

Shared motivation

'Shared motivation' is defined as 'a self-reinforcing cycle consisting of four elements: mutual trust, understanding, internal legitimacy, and commitment' (Emerson et al. 2012: 13). Trust 'happens over time as parties work together, get to know each other, and prove to each other that they are reasonable, predictable, and dependable' and has been found to be 'instrumental in reducing transaction costs, improving investments and stability in relations, and stimulating learning, knowledge exchange, and innovation' (Emerson et al. 2012: 13). Trust 'generates mutual understanding, which in turn generates legitimacy and finally commitment' (Emerson et al. 2012: 13).

According to Emerson et al. (2012: 14), 'mutual understanding' refers to the ability to understand and respect the positions and interests of others in ways that confirm that participants in a collective endeavour are 'trustworthy and credible with compatible and interdependent interests'. Mutual understanding 'legitimises and motivates ongoing collaboration' and leads to 'shared commitment' (Emerson et al. 2012: 14).

Capacity for joint action

Collaborative governance requires the generation of 'new capacity for joint action that did not exist before and sustain or grow that capacity for the duration of the shared purpose' (Emerson et al. 2012: 14). Emerson et al. (2012: 14) conceptualise the capacity for joint action as the combination of procedural and institutional arrangements, leadership, knowledge and resources.

Ten propositions for principled engagement

Emerson et al. (2012) summarise their findings in the form of 10 propositions.

- **Proposition One:** One or more of the drivers of leadership, consequential incentives, interdependence or uncertainty are necessary for a collaborative governance regime (CGR) to begin. The more drivers that are present and recognised by participants, the more likely it is a CGR will be initiated (Emerson et al. 2012: 10).

- **Proposition Two:** Principled engagement is generated and sustained by the interactive processes of discovery, definition, deliberation and determination. The effectiveness of principled engagement is determined, in part, by the quality of these interactive processes (Emerson et al. 2012: 13).

- **Proposition Three:** Repeated quality interactions through principled engagement will help foster trust, mutual understanding, internal legitimacy and shared commitment, thereby generating and sustaining shared motivation (Emerson et al. 2012: 14).

- **Proposition Four:** Once generated, shared motivation will enhance and help sustain principled engagement and vice versa in a 'virtuous cycle' (Emerson et al. 2012: 14).

- **Proposition Five:** Principled engagement and shared motivation will stimulate the development of institutional arrangements, leadership, knowledge and resources, thereby generating and sustaining capacity for joint action (Emerson et al. 2012: 15).

- **Proposition Six:** The necessary levels for the four elements of capacity for joint action are determined by the CGR's purpose, shared theory of action and targeted outcomes (Emerson et al. 2012: 15).

- **Proposition Seven:** The quality and extent of collaborative dynamics depend on the productive and self-reinforcing interactions among principled engagement, shared motivation and the capacity for joint action (Emerson et al. 2012: 17).

- **Proposition Eight:** Collaborative actions are more likely to be implemented if: 1) a shared theory of action is identified explicitly among the collaboration partners, and 2) the collaborative dynamics function to generate the needed capacity for joint action (Emerson et al. 2012: 18).

- **Proposition Nine:** The impacts resulting from collaborative action are likely to be closer to the targeted outcomes with fewer unintended negative consequences when they are specified and derived from a shared theory of action during collaborative dynamics (Emerson et al. 2012: 18).
- **Proposition Ten:** CGRs will be more sustainable over time when they adapt to the nature and level of impacts resulting from their joint actions (Emerson et al. 2012: 19).

What the cases tell us

As might be expected, each of our cases exhibited contextually unique features. Importantly, all of the cases evidenced important commonalities from which we might draw a number of generalisable 'lessons'.

It is all about relationships

Interviewees across all cases spoke about the importance of relationships—and relationship-building—as the bedrock of effective collaboration. Constructive relationships—interpersonal and interorganisational—are the precursors of trust, credibility and legitimacy. For many working on the front line, the interpersonal takes precedence over the interorganisational:

> It comes down to individual personalities and people type. I know because I worked on the front line for a very long time. But, if I needed something done, I knew who to pick up the phone and talk to and who would move the mountains for me and who wouldn't. (Senior official, Children's Action Plan Directorate)

And, when it comes to earning the trust of external stakeholders, connectedness to local communities is a distinct advantage:

> Part of the primary operating mechanism or principle is, if you don't have a relationship then you can't earn the trust. So, you've got to work through it. You've got to grow the relationship to then earn the trust to then get the social licence. I think that's why 99 times out of 100 having someone that's local but with credibility is quite important. (Whangarei Children's Team)

Respectful conversations

A consistent element in each of the cases examined for this study is the capacity for leaders to engage in respectful conversations with a wide range of stakeholders about the purpose of the collaboration. Such conversations are not simply about informing, but also about eliciting information and soliciting views and about demonstrating a capacity to listen and give weight to people's opinions (see also Chapter 7). These conversations can be a catalyst for the reframing of issues and the articulation of new solutions and approaches. One interviewee from New Zealand emphasised that it is imperative to 'listen louder':

> Listen louder, because you can't go into a collaboration with preconceived ideas about how other people might work, how other organisations might work. You have to learn that and understand that through experience. So, if there's only one thing I say, it's 'listen louder'. You need to understand it before you can start passing judgement and before you can start influencing.

Internal and external stakeholders

The 'relational' element of collaboration cannot be understated: like any relationship or set of relationships, things generally go better when participants have some understanding and tolerance of the motivations, world views and needs of all who have an interest or 'stakeholding' in the core purposes and operations of the collaboration.

Internal stakeholders might include the following:

1. People who are accountable for partner organisations' performance, such as the executive or board, who need to be kept aware of relational, financial, legal, reputational or political risks that might arise from collaborative action.

2. People responsible for administering a partner organisation's programs and services (that is, output activities), especially where they are responsible for the delivery of services (including contracted service provision) to people, groups or communities directly affected by collaborative action.

3. People within partner organisations who are accountable for specific corporate support functions (for example, input activities such as human resource management, branding and communications, information

management, financial reporting, occupational health and safety, professional standards and statutory obligations) that might come into conflict with some of the operational aspects of collaborative action.

External stakeholders might include the following:

1. Professional associations, unions or accreditation bodies that might have an interest in the potential implications for their members of collaborative action.
2. Communities in which collaborative action occurs, and which might be affected in some way (including local government, residents' groups, community associations or other localised interest groups).
3. Peak organisations, industry associations, advocacy groups or other representative bodies that claim to represent the interests of the groups or communities that are the focus of collaborative action.
4. Policy communities (in government, civil society or academia) that are curators/holders/mediators of knowledge about the particular problems or issues that are the focus of collaborative action.

Constructive engagement with both internal and external stakeholders around the rationale for collaboration is an essential element in any collaboration strategy. It helps to:

- reduce institutional and stakeholder resistance
- ensure adequate resourcing
- maintain the support of authorisers.

Middle-management resistance

Organisational collaboration partners often focus their engagement efforts outwardly in an attempt to persuade and reassure external stakeholders, leading them to overlook various internal stakeholders on whose goodwill and cooperation collaboration sometimes depends. A major barrier to effective collaboration is the prevailing incentives that discourage the kinds of trust and relationship-building on which collaboration rests. Those tasked with making collaboration happen should not blithely assume that executive-level authorisation necessarily means that all personnel within the organisation—particularly those exercising key 'gatekeeper' functions—are on board.

In those cases where collaboration has its origins in policy decisions promulgated by agency leadership in partner organisations, and implementation rests largely with frontline officers/workers, it has been observed that mid-tier managers can be a source of resistance because the incentive structures under which they operate tend to reward fidelity to operational protocols rather than risk-taking. Typically, such resistance was described in terms of territoriality—mid-tier managers protecting their 'turf'. What is particularly interesting is that collaboration partners report encountering resistance from mid-tier bureaucrats within their own organisations in spite of unambiguous executive-level support for collaboration.

It is at this level, perhaps, where the dominant incentive structures reward territoriality, conservatism, risk aversion and excessive focus on outputs— all qualities that militate against genuine collaboration. It cannot be assumed that understanding or support for collaborative approaches exists at all levels within partner organisations; whereas communication strategies around collaboration tend to focus on external audiences, it is possible that internal messaging tends to be neglected:

> We've had management buy-in, once we get the leadership buy-in. Then to implement it at an organisational level, what we are seeing is there needs to be that next level middle-management buy-in. Otherwise you're going to hit roadblocks and it stalls. And they're some of the challenges that we're coming across at the moment. (WHO STOPS, GenR8 Change)

Champions and influencers

Collaboration champions (within partner organisations) and influencers (within affected communities) can play an important role by championing the purpose, aims and methods of the collaboration and, in so doing, leveraging internal and external support. In the main, these are people who are capable of exercising influence within their organisations and constituencies and who are also supportive of the collaboration. The 'soft diplomacy' exercised by champions—in part, by sharing good news stories and celebrating achievements—should not be underestimated (see Chapter 3).

Expert facilitation

Some of the cases—Change the Story, WHO STOPS and CBEM—have taken advantage of expert third-party facilitation in the early stages of their establishment to help the parties to arrive at a shared understanding of the problem and a shared vision of the way forward. Facilitation helps to break down barriers, establish commonalities, address differences and create trust in shared endeavour:

> There's a mammoth range of views in the community about it and lots of people arguing—fighting—about things. We said: 'Hold on.' We convened a town hall meeting. We had maybe 130 people—no agencies, just people. We had it facilitated so that everybody got a chance to say what they thought about it and everybody else got a chance to hear that. And I think in lots of ways that was a good proof point to the groups in the community that, 'Hey, these guys mean what they're saying. They're just facilitating rather than trying to take decisions or lead.' (CBEM, Anglesea, Victoria)

To some degree, other cases have also relied on individuals exercising a brokerage role to bring parties to the table and to assist the collaboration team in its communications with external stakeholders (thereby building legitimacy).

Establishing trust and legitimacy

Authenticity is critical in winning the trust and cooperation of stakeholders and in demonstrating legitimacy and earning a licence to collaborate. Being local is not sufficient on its own. A number of interviewees emphasised the importance of authenticity—illustrated by the following account of the consultation process underpinning Change the Story:

> I think authenticity had to sit at the core of it, because otherwise the whole thing would crumble. You can't speak to this audience and that audience using language that is common to both and [that] brings in difficult theories and framings for some people without there being authenticity at the core of the process, the consultation, the partnership. That's tough stuff; it's not something you can necessarily articulate and say, 'This is how you do it' … I think process wise, you can say this is what makes co-design different from just going out and doing it prior to your consultation, but I also think a big part of it is a willingness to participate in a process that is a partnership approach rather than a power dynamic.

In another setting, a former Children's Action Plan (CAP) official remarked on the esteem in which local Children's Team leaders are held and the trust accorded to them in their local communities as important factors in the success of teams in Rotorua and Gisborne:

> That's what it was all predicated on: genuine, authentic, open-minded. But also the passion and the commitment—absolutely wanting to make the difference for the community. Community-minded people that wanted the best for their community and the children and families in it. Those aspects you'd rate 10 out of 10 in those two communities. They are just very evident, and that's what's important that they can teach the others. What did they do to get that? It wasn't just saying it will happen; they showed it. They demonstrated it. Their actions every day showed that. They went the extra mile all the time.

Another interviewee—again with regard to the implementation of regional Children's Teams—observed the importance of 'soft conversations' with stakeholders, and emphasised the importance of starting the conversation early while accepting that people might join the conversation at different stages:

> A lot of that sitting around and talking and building [the team] and spending a lot of time before that Children's Team came together was a good way to actually get everybody to get along. You'd see it, people that had come from the start that were going along, that had turned up to every meeting, that were really buying into it by the end against some people that came in, say, three-quarters of the way through and had missed all of that soft conversation that you have that gets everybody on the same page. They had missed all of that, and then they're suddenly like, 'Why are we doing it this way?' That was very frustrating. There was quite a bit of that. If you didn't make sure that you had everybody on board right at the beginning, you lost something later on, especially if they were someone important or noisy or something.

Trust-building forms an integral part of building collaborative ways of working. In general, trust-building needs to be led and, in general, it might be expected that in any collaboration there will be a lead entity. The lead entity need not always be the organisation with the largest financial exposure; it is perfectly possible for collaborations to be led by entities that have a perceived legitimacy or moral authority that exceeds their financial investment. And, in fact, it is possible that such a delegation might enhance, overall, the perceived legitimacy of the collaboration among affected communities of interest.

Three of the cases in particular—Change the Story, Children's Teams and WHO STOPS—emphasised the importance of utilising analytics to aid 'sense-making'. This was particularly important in making the case for a collaborative approach, authorising the deployment of assets and resources, building trust and support among varied stakeholders and gaining legitimacy. In the case of WHO STOPS, the involvement of researchers from Deakin University added considerable weight by conferring authority and legitimacy on key messages about obesity.

Final observations

Top-down 'command' systems no longer hold sway in modern public sector management. Indeed, they have not held sway for some time, although it must be said that practice has been slow to follow theory. Sicilia et al. (2016) observe that public managers are obliged to listen to service users and affected community groups, to mobilise collective resources and knowledge in the public interest and to nurture coproductive behaviours. This is good advice in general, especially in the context of collaborative approaches to complex social problems.

Our aim in this text is to offer practitioners a pathway from 'platitudes' to impact. What does it mean, in practice, to listen to service users and communities of interest? How, in practice, do we mobilise resources and knowledge in the public interest? And how do we nurture coproductive behaviours?

The cases from this study offer useful lessons:

1. **Change the Story** involved three organisations working together in the family and domestic violence space to develop a coherent, evidence-based national practice framework. Our Watch, VicHealth and Australia's National Research Organisation for Women's Safety (ANROWS) first reached a consensus on an agenda for action that included the comprehensive mapping of the peer-reviewed literature, the identification of and engagement with expert communities and open and robust consultations with government agencies, community

sector organisations, practitioner communities and advocacy groups around the country. This initiative demonstrated strong 'listening' with both service users and communities of interest. Change the Story explicitly sought to mobilise resources and knowledge in the public interest. The proposed framework had a strong evidential base; it was subjected to thorough expert review, and the final proposals were effectively communicated to diverse audiences. In so doing, Change the Story not only earned broad trust and buy-in, it also served to enlist the support of diverse communities of interest for the adoption of the framework by state and territory governments—thus amounting to a form of coproduction.

2. Victoria's **CBEM** initiative is one product of a long period of soul-searching, public dialogue and institutional reform following natural disasters in that state that caused significant loss of life, extensive damage to private property and public infrastructure and enormous personal and collective trauma for survivors and communities. A new government entity, Emergency Management Victoria (EMV), was established to work with communities, government, agencies and business to 'strengthen their capacity to withstand, plan for, respond to and recover from emergencies'.[1] CBEM operates by working with local organisations and community leaders to facilitate the crafting of locally led strategies to instil community resilience and build effective and sustainable relationships involving a range of community actors.

3. **WHO STOPS** is a collaboration between the Victorian Department of Health and Human Services and Deakin University. At the time of interviews, WHO STOPS provided oversight of two local collaborations, SEA Change (based in the coastal town of Portland) and GenR8 Change (based in the inland town of Hamilton). The two local initiatives are linked via the involvement of the Southern Grampians and Glenelg Primary Care Partnership. WHO STOPS aims to strengthen existing community capacity and confer community ownership on efforts to prevent childhood obesity (Allender et al. 2016). This occurred through a facilitated community engagement process led by researchers from Deakin University involving the provision of intensive training and support oriented around strengthening community leadership, workforce development, resources, partners, networks and intelligence.

---

1   See Emergency Management Victoria's website: www.emv.vic.gov.au/about-us/what-we-do/our-role.

4. In New Zealand, the establishment of **Children's Teams** followed a similar trajectory. The Children's Action Plan (CAP) differed in the degree to which the process was government-led and formalised by the establishment of a government directorate comprising staff seconded from relevant ministries and agencies. The process entailed the production of a green paper and a white paper, which provided a platform for community consultations (or *hui*) throughout the country. As with Change the Story, the CAP was evidenced-based and the case for the creation of Children's Teams was made to agencies, unions, local government, professional groups, practitioners, civil society organisations and, in communities where Māori form a significant proportion of affected families, Māori community leaders. In communities such as Rotorua, Whangarei and Gisborne, local governance—or backbone—groups formed to brainstorm and implement the Children's Team model. Although the ideal of coproduction was somewhat challenged by occasional tensions with the directorate based in Wellington around what the local backbone group perceived to be an undue level of 'prescription', in the main, the Children's Teams in these locales can be said to be genuinely 'locally led'.

Our findings suggest that stakeholder engagement around collaboration differs from conventional approaches to engagement around policy or programmatic choices facing government. Whereas much government-led consultation centres on communicating and gaining public support for the substance of policy proposals or government initiatives, engagement around collaboration is much more about finding common ground in relation to the framing of problems, the identification of practicable solutions and obtaining a shared commitment to action. It is far less about 'box ticking' and is more about nurturing and sustaining an ongoing conversation that leads to impactful action.

Practice considerations

1. Identify all organisational, community and individual relationships that are to some degree important to the collaboration. Try to characterise the nature of those relationships—for example, are they constructive or adversarial? Comprehensively map the 'ecosystem' in which the collaboration needs to operate.

2. Who are the internal and external stakeholders who need to be 'brought into the tent'? Remember, stakeholders can be organisations, individuals or communities of interest. Within organisations, what functional or business lines need to be on side?

3. Think hard about the core messages at the heart of the collaboration; test assumptions and consider all sources of evidence that support or challenge the collaboration's central value proposition.

4. Work hard to have respectful conversations. Think carefully about what respectful conversations look like. Identify sources of available knowledge and/ or expertise that might be used to inform or guide an effective and consistent communication strategy.

5. Identify potential sources of middle-management resistance. Which core business functions within partner organisations are key to the operational success of the collaboration? For example, key players in communications, marketing, branding, legal, finance or human relations might need to be brought on board with the aims of the consultation. What strategies are available to gain the cooperation and/or support of these key gatekeepers?

6. Who are the potential collaboration champions in partner organisations? What avenues are available to enlist their support? Are they sufficiently well placed and well regarded, both in their organisations and externally? What opportunities exist to bring them into conversations with internal and external stakeholders?

7. Are there external influencers who might be enlisted to help promote the aims of the collaboration and build support among a wide range of stakeholders? These might include community leaders, leaders in civil society or business and others with a positive public profile and the capacity to reach multiple stakeholder audiences.

8. Consider the potential benefits of using an expert third-party facilitator to assist with the tasks of communication and building trust. This might be a private consultant or someone from an academic institution who has a professional interest in the objects of the collaboration, or it might be someone drawn from a community sector/civil society organisation who has standing within the relevant communities of interest.

9. It is important that any person acting in a facilitation role is seen to be impartial. Moreover, the facilitator must be capable of earning the respect of participants and stakeholders as well as being able to respond constructively to any disagreements or conflicts that might arise.

10. If engaging a consultant to perform this role, it will be necessary to confirm the availability of funds for the purpose (and, in this regard, it might be necessary to equitably share the costs between collaboration partners to ensure equal ownership of the process). It would also be advisable for collaboration partners to come to a consensus view about the brief provided to the facilitator and to ensure the brief is authorised by the executive of each partner organisation.

References

Allender, Steven, Lynne Millar, Peter Hovmand, Colin Bell, Marj Moodie, Rob Carter, Boyd Swinburn, Claudia Strugnell, Janette Lowe, Kayla de la Haye, Liliana Orellana, and Sue Morgan. 2016. 'Whole of Systems Trial of Prevention Strategies for Childhood Obesity: WHO STOPS Childhood Obesity.' *International Journal of Environmental Research and Public Health* 13(11): 1–12. doi.org/10.3390/ijerph13111143.

Emerson, Kirk, Tina Nabatchi, and Stephen Balogh. 2012. 'An integrative framework for collaborative governance.' *Journal of Public Administration Research and Theory* 22(1): 1–29. doi.org/10.1093/jopart/mur011.

Head, Brian W. 2008. 'Assessing network-based collaborations.' *Public Management Review* 10(6): 733–49. doi.org/10.1080/14719030802423087.

Sicilia, Mariafrancesca, Enrico Guarini, Alessandro Sancino, Martino Andreani, and Renato Ruffini. 2016. 'Public services management and co-production in multi-level governance settings.' *International Review of Administrative Sciences* 82(1): 8–27. doi.org/10.1177/0020852314566008.

9

ENABLING PLACE-BASED SOLUTIONS

Introduction

Collaboration is all about 'doing with', not 'doing for' or 'doing to', and one of its strengths is the potential to develop bespoke solutions that reflect local circumstances and preferences. Whereas bureaucracies traditionally favour standardised systems for service delivery in which treatments of social problems are constrained by organisational, portfolio and/or programmatic silos, collaboration can create opportunities to involve a set of diverse actors in processes of defining problems and agreeing on strategies.

One needs to bear in mind that collaboration is sometimes offered either as a remedy for resource scarcity or when traditional approaches have demonstrably failed. Understandably, past failures might predispose some stakeholders to scepticism. In addition, collaborative approaches can reveal tensions within and between partner organisations and within communities.

In this chapter, we consider the Community-Based Emergency Management (CBEM) initiative in Victoria, which has embraced a community-led approach to disaster readiness and community resilience. We also look at the Whole of Systems Trial of Prevention Strategies for Childhood Obesity (WHO STOPS Childhood Obesity, or WHO STOPS), operating in two communities in the Southern Grampians and Glenelg shires, in Western Victoria.

We reflect on the inherent difficulties of mandating a standardised format for collaboration. In this regard, we consider the experience of New Zealand's Children's Action Plan, for which attempts to impose a standardised operating framework for local Children's Teams met with resistance from community stakeholders.

What do we mean by 'place-based solutions'?

Place-based approaches reflect an understanding of the particular circumstances that shape the lives of a community and its people. They offer a customised response rather than a one-size-fits-all program. Ideally, a place-based model engages with a community and utilises existing social and physical assets in ways that are beneficial to the community generally, and to the intended beneficiaries of the approach in particular (House of Representatives Select Committee on Intergenerational Welfare Dependence 2019: 35–36). Place-based approaches are grounded in the lived experiences of people and communities.

The Australian Institute of Family Studies (AIFS) defines place-based initiatives as

> programs designed and delivered with the intention of targeting a specific geographical location(s) and particular population group(s) in order to respond to complex social problems. [Place-based initiatives] typically focus on areas and communities with entrenched disadvantage or deprivation. (Wilks et al. 2015: viii)

Place-based approaches might be employed in circumstances in which:

- problems are complex and multifactorial
- the service system is fragmented
- policy silos are unconnected and poorly coordinated
- there are multiple sources of advocacy
- programs, eligibility and intake rules are highly segmented
- knowledge and trust deficits create barriers to access.

The Queensland Government's framework for place-based approaches employs the following definition:

Place-based approaches join up the efforts of all community stakeholders (citizens, industry, diverse non-government organisations and all levels of government) to improve the social, economic and physical wellbeing of a defined geographical location. These approaches are highly collaborative, take time and are ideally characterised by partnering and shared design, shared stewardship, and shared accountability for outcomes and impacts. Place-based approaches are often used to respond to complex, interrelated or challenging issues such as social and economic disadvantage, natural disasters or environmental problems. (Department of Communities, Disability Services and Seniors 2019)

Griggs et al. (2008) observe that, 'for the most part, person- and place-based policies have been developed separately and sometimes in isolation from each other'. This, they say,

reflects the responsibilities of government departments influenced by their different approaches and traditions. The reality, of course, is that all people live in places, contribute to places and are affected by places. Poverty and disadvantage are mediated by place, and places are affected by the poverty or otherwise of their inhabitants. Hence, it is reasonable to suspect that policies that dissociate people from places and vice versa may perform poorly. (Griggs et al. 2008: 1)

Griggs et al. (2008) note that different place-based policy responses embody different priorities and assumptions concerning the interactions between people and places. They categorise policy responses into five broad policy types, which are set out in Table 9.1.

Table 9.1 Person and place: Policy types

Policy type	Major focus	Functional description
Type 1	Major focus on place to impact place	Initiatives that seek principally to enhance local infrastructure or improve degraded land as a precursor to redevelopment while paying comparatively little attention to effects on resident populations who might be affected, either positively or negatively
Type 2	Major focus on place to impact people	Initiatives that aim to improve local infrastructure but do so in ways that explicitly enhance the lives of existing and future residents
Type 3	Major focus on person to impact place	Initiatives that specifically target residents to improve an area—for example, actions that seek to prevent or reduce antisocial behaviours or otherwise enforce changes in individual behaviour for the benefit of the neighbourhood

Policy type	Major focus	Functional description
Type 4	Major focus on person to impact person	Initiatives that address individual welfare without explicit regard to local circumstances or consequences—for example, the payment of benefits that directly affect the material circumstances of individuals and families, while having incidental positive effects on place
Type 5	Simultaneous major focus on place and person to impact both	Initiatives that seek simultaneously to assist disadvantaged people and improve the built and social environments of places

Sources: Griggs et al. (2008: 2–3); Wilks et al. (2015).

What kinds of problems suit place-based approaches?

The concept of a place-based approach to problems in public policy has been around for a long time. It is possible to find in the research literature examples of the application of place-based approaches in a variety of policy settings. Examples include:

- injury prevention (Roen et al. 2006)
- energy use (Parkhill et al. 2015)
- employment, education and income disadvantage (Griggs et al. 2008)
- regional development (Barca et al. 2012)
- indigenous programs (Marsh et al. 2017)
- environmental education (Gruenewald 2005)
- child health and community health (Moore et al. 2014)
- community resilience to natural disasters (Cutter et al. 2008)
- child and family health (Moore and Fry 2011).

Other policy areas typically targeted by place-based initiatives include health, education, child development, family wellbeing, community strengthening, housing, urban regeneration, liveability, crime, employment and participation, economic development, immigrant communities, social inclusion and social exclusion (Wilks et al. 2015: viii).

It should also be noted that place-based approaches are often associated with the collective impact framework developed by Kania and Kramer (2011; AIFS 2017). Collective impact adheres to the following broad principles of practice:

- Design and implement the initiative with a priority placed on equity.
- Include community members in the collaboration.
- Recruit and co-create with cross-sector partners.
- Use data to continuously learn, adapt and improve.
- Cultivate leaders with unique systems leadership skills.
- Focus on program and system strategies.
- Build a culture that fosters relationships, trust and respect across participants.
- Customise for local context (Collective Impact Forum 2014).

Where can policy and practice guidance be found?

In their review of the conceptual and empirical literature on place-based approaches, Moore and Fry (2011: 77–78) identified the following policy considerations:

- Implementing a comprehensive place-based approach is a formidable undertaking that requires sustained commitment by many stakeholders.
- Effective, integrated place-based planning and service delivery are difficult to sustain without fit-for-purpose governance structures that are sufficiently comprehensive and binding to ensure sustained collaboration by various stakeholders and service providers.
- The incidence of disadvantage is complex and by no means homogeneous; social problems are spread across all socioeconomic strata and some geographic areas might be more likely than others to benefit from place-based approaches.
- While the literature provides some guidance about how a comprehensive community-based approach might work, there are no fully developed Australian models from which to learn, meaning it is critical to document the learnings from place-based initiatives.
- Ways of gathering and accessing small-scale data at the level of a neighbourhood or sociogeographic locality need to be developed to assess the impact of community-based approaches.
- The implementation of place-based approaches should not lead to the neglect of person-based interventions; the two complement and reinforce each other.

There are numerous sources of policy and practice guidance in an Australian and international context. A small sample of these is set out in Table 9.2.

Table 9.2 Policy and practice guidance on place-based approaches (Australian and international experience)

Title	Description	URL/hyperlink
Queensland Council of Social Service (QCOSS): Place-based approaches	QCOSS focuses on place-based work because it offers an effective platform for building strong, cohesive communities. As the state's peak body for the community sector, QCOSS seeks to support and enable place-based approaches across Queensland.	www.qcoss.org.au/ our-work/place-based-approaches/
Commonwealth Place-Based Service Delivery Initiatives: Key Learnings project	Sets out the findings of the Commonwealth Place-Based Service Delivery Initiatives: Key Learnings project commissioned by the Department of the Prime Minister and Cabinet and undertaken by the AIFS. The project aimed to identify key factors associated with successful outcomes of place-based initiatives to inform the future design, implementation and delivery of such programs.	aifs.gov.au/publications/ commonwealth-place-based-service-delivery-initiatives/
Place-based Initiatives Transforming Communities: Proceedings from the Place-based Approaches Roundtable	Place-based reform poses many challenges for governments and communities. This invitation-only roundtable brought together people from different levels of government, academics and community leaders to share knowledge and insights and forge a common framework.	www.rch.org.au/ uploadedFiles/Main/ Content/ccch/CCCH_ Place-based_initiatives_ report.pdf
Place-Based Approaches to Child and Family Services: A Literature Review	This publication synthesises the conceptual and empirical literature on place-based approaches to meeting the needs of young children and their families, with a focus on the potential contribution of place-based approaches to service reconfiguration and coordination.	www.rch.org.au/ uploadedFiles/Main/ Content/ccch/Place_ based_services_literature_ review.pdf

Title	Description	URL/hyperlink
Big Thinking on Place: Getting Place-Based Approaches Moving	This publication has been developed by the Centre for Community Child Health at The Royal Children's Hospital Melbourne and the Murdoch Children's Research Institute. It summarises expert views on the issues and opportunities using place-based approaches to promote children's wellbeing.	www.rch.org.au/ uploadedFiles/Main/ Content/ccch/CCCH_ Collaborate_for_Children_ Report_Big_Thinking_ Nov2014.pdf
Place-Based Working	This resource explores the potential for a place-based approach to enable effective work with people and communities to improve their health and wellbeing through asset-based, locally embedded, cross-sector working.	www.iriss.org.uk/ resources/irisson/place-based-working
Person- or Place-Based Policies to Tackle Disadvantage? Not knowing what works	This study reviews evaluations of person-based policies (targeted directly at individuals) and place-based policies (designed to tackle neighbourhood deprivation) to draw out key messages about what works, comparing and contrasting the effectiveness of person-based and place-based interventions. The review concentrated on policies to improve employment and educational outcomes and to increase incomes.	www.jrf.org.uk/report/ person-or-place-based-policies-tackle-disadvantage-not-knowing-what-works

What the cases tell us

Four of the five cases investigated for this study focus on problems that are clearly influenced by the characteristics of the places in which they are situated. For instance, CBEM (with its focus on community resilience), WHO STOPS (childhood obesity) and New Zealand's Children's Teams (offering multidisciplinary early intervention for children and families 'at risk') each exhibit a strong appreciation of the ways in which the characteristics of place contribute to and reinforce social problems.

One of the cases, Throughcare (which offers postcustodial support for offenders), occurred in a small jurisdiction (the Australian Capital Territory), where geographic and socioeconomic differentiation are less pronounced (hence, 'place' was effectively defined by the territorial boundary). The fifth case, Change the Story, was, in effect, a meta-collaboration insofar as it brought together diverse interests to reach consensus about a national practice framework rather than to implement solutions on the ground (although place-based approaches inform the practice model).

Of the four cases that exhibited a clear appreciation of the factors associated with place and the ways in which they contribute to the social problems being addressed, and offer potential pathways to address them, only one, WHO STOPS, explicitly modelled its approach on the collective impact model. And, in some respects, this is unsurprising, because the collective impact framework is an eminently rational approach. One might, therefore, expect rational actors pursuing collaborative approaches for social impact to adopt similar strategies.

Our study did not expressly test whether or not the cases adopted a place-based approach. For most, a focus on the characteristics of place was the default position. We *were* interested to understand how each of the collaborations framed the problems they were seeking to address as well as the dynamic relationship between that framing and the authorising environment in which the collaborations occurred. And in that regard, we look to the cases to gain insight into four key processes:

1. *Top-down versus bottom-up*: Is the model of collaboration a product of executive edict or has it been allowed to develop organically within a more 'permissive' authorising environment?

2. *Central control versus local control*: Are local collaboration partners authorised to make decisions and pursue strategies they deem to be appropriate to local circumstances and the preferences of local stakeholders?

3. *Encourage, enable and reward local innovation*: Is the capacity for local innovation encouraged or inhibited by the authorising environment in which the collaboration is obliged to operate?

4. *Scalability*: Can a fixed template for collaboration be imposed on communities without regard for local circumstances, or can collaborative actions taken in one locale be transplanted to other locales?

Bottom-up versus top-down

The collaborations represented in the cases each exhibit elements of both bottom-up and top-down approaches.

CBEM

Both CBEM and WHO STOPS emphasise the importance of local empowerment and leadership. One member of a local backbone group associated with the CBEM offered a forthright view about the importance of local leadership:

> For some of the bureaucracies it is that 'we want the community to help us do what we need to do'—and there's nothing wrong with that—but, 'We don't want them to play the game any other way except the way we play it.' Effective community work means that you take a stick to bureaucracies and you get them out of the way and realise they're a resource and not the main game. They're not the end game.

This is a message that Emergency Management Victoria (EMV) has clearly taken on board. In 2017, EMV canvassed opportunities to reform Victoria's relief and recovery arrangements (EMV 2017b). It proposed a Resilient Recovery Model (EMV 2017b), intended to create a community-focused and community-driven relief and recovery system that empowers communities, government, agencies and business to provide a pathway from recovery to resilience:

> The development of a modern, resilience-based relief and recovery system for Victorian communities is needed. We require a model that moves arrangements from welfare to wellbeing, disconnected activities to connected systems and services, unclear roles and responsibilities to agreed accountabilities, inconsistent capability to collaborative partnerships, and disparate to sustainable funding arrangements. (EMV 2017b: 5)

The Community Resilience Framework for Emergency Management formulated by EMV relies on eight guiding principles:

- Each community is unique, with existing and evolving levels of safety and resilience.
- Locally tailored planning and engagement processes are to support community and organisational leadership, through the development of mutual goals and solutions.

- These processes draw on combined community and organisational strengths.
- Information may be captured in a plan, but developing a plan is not the reason to work together.
- Collaborative processes aim to support people to manage long-term challenges (chronic stresses) while better preparing to cope with and recover from emergencies (acute shocks).
- Integrated community development principles, approaches and methodologies such as asset-based community development and appreciative inquiry also underpin this approach.
- This approach can be adapted for use before, during and after emergencies.
- Not all communities are interested or have the ability to undertake collaborative community-based decision-making processes (EMV 2016: 7; 2017a: 7).

The framework encourages local communities to develop bespoke responses to the tasks of building community readiness and resilience and putting in place sustainable local arrangements for the mobilisation of community assets and infrastructure. At the time fieldwork for this study was undertaken, local initiatives were under way in five communities—supported by EMV staff working with key actors in each community to commence, and sustain, conversations about the practical meaning of readiness, resilience and recovery in a local context.

Because trauma associated with recent Victorian experiences of disaster is the starting point for the conversation in many of these communities, and because the physical terrain (both the natural and the built environments) shaped the course of those events, the emphasis on the characteristics of place is especially profound.

WHO STOPS

Whereas the CBEM resilience framework arose as a consequence of intensive reflection on a series of extreme events and on the organisational and institutional factors that contributed to the loss of life and property, WHO STOPS has sought to proactively respond to a looming community health issue, childhood obesity.

WHO STOPS is a partnership between Deakin University, Primary Care Partnerships (PCPs) and their partners, including local councils and health services. The collaboration proceeds from an understanding that any attempt to address the systemic determinants of noncommunicable disease at a population level requires the strengthening of existing community capacity and conferring community ownership on efforts to apply systems thinking to community-wide childhood obesity prevention (Allender et al. 2016).

WHO STOPS has employed a facilitated community engagement process involving the provision at a community level of intensive training and support oriented around strengthening a set of building blocks adapted from the World Health Organization's building blocks of health systems: leadership, workforce, resources, partner networks and intelligence (WHO 2010). Researchers from Deakin University co-designed the tools and training with local community leaders and stakeholders based on systems thinking and collaborative impact models.

Deakin University is leading a five-year study funded by the National Health and Medical Research Council (NHMRC) to test whether it is possible to:

1. strengthen community action for childhood obesity prevention
2. measure the impact of increased action on risk factors for childhood obesity (ANZCTR 2016).

This quasi-experimental interventional study will:

1. assess whether the adoption of systems change interventions rapidly increases community capacity to apply evidence-informed action across community systems and affect the prevalence of childhood obesity
2. test the proposal that permanent reductions in childhood obesity are possible if the complex and dynamic causes of obesity are well understood and addressed through increased community ownership and responsibility.

It is hypothesised that a systems intervention for childhood obesity will be effective in its impact, efficient in its implementation, scalable in its delivery and sustainable in its longevity:

> The goals of this grant are to: 1) strengthen community action for childhood obesity prevention, and 2) measure the impacts of increased action on risk factors for childhood obesity.

> ... [W]e have evolved a facilitated, community engagement process which: creates an agreed systems map of childhood obesity causes for a community; identifies intervention opportunities through leveraging the dynamic aspects of the system; and converts these understandings into community-built, systems-oriented action plans. Throughout this process systems data are collected for measuring systems changes over time. Our experience to date has been that this process rapidly increases [the] capacity of community leaders to use systems thinking for community-wide obesity prevention. (ANZCTR 2016)

Partners will convene new and existing coalitions of community leaders and members (parents and leaders from local government, schools, clubs, agencies and business) who have the capacity to influence the complex drivers of childhood obesity. Examples of community-led interventions include:

- removing sugar-sweetened beverages from health services, schools and local council workplaces
- introducing healthy procurement processes for local governments
- making drinking water freely accessible in public places
- setting up 'no drive' zones 800 metres from schools to encourage active transport.

At the time fieldwork was undertaken, collaborative initiatives had been established in Portland (SEA Change) and Hamilton (GenR8 Change). Although both initiatives have the same focus (prevention of childhood obesity) and utilise a systems change approach, each has a slightly different way of operating as well as different emphases and mixes of activities. Both local initiatives have a working/steering group that provides oversight and governance and is self-sustaining and self-directed. Both groups primarily comprise mid-level state and local government officers and both rely on local ambassadors (senior-level leaders) to socialise their aims and objectives in the community and in participating organisations.

Observations

Although both CBEM and WHO STOPS have cascaded to local communities as a consequence of decisions taken at higher levels, both have fostered a locally led, bottom-up approach. In both cases, being locally led has meant encouraging the establishment of local governance/

backbone groups whose task it is to engage a wide range of stakeholders in a conversation about how community groups, institutions and interests can work together to address a set of agreed problems.

The people to whom we spoke also emphasised the importance of having a flexible attitude when it comes to how we think of 'community' and to resist the temptation to impose a particular construct. For instance, a member of the GSC Change partnership—the group overseeing the implementation of the WHO STOPS framework in Portland and Hamilton—made the following observation:

> We have quite a broad definition of 'community'. Often, it's geographically defined, and our starting point is leaders within the community with no particular requirement that they be from any specific organisation. But, of course, it tends to be the health services, primary care organisations, the local governments that already have an interest in this space and that we start working with initially. But, by design, we are trying to be as broad about where that leadership comes from as we can, and that's reflected in the group model-building processes that we run and who participates in those. (WHO STOPS, GSC Change)

Another member of the same group characterised the process of local engagement thusly:

> The building process that we go through is about bringing whoever is a potential partner or anyone passionate from the community together, and the process itself is actually understanding all those interrelationships between factors that influence obesity.
>
> Then what happens is the community self-identifies, so through the process … they actually work out, 'Well, hey, I can actually make the change here, and I'm actually part of the solution'. So, then you take them through that solution process and they actually self-nominate where they have an influence or a passion to actually make change.
>
> Within a community, that can be agencies—different agencies—through to passionate parents; anyone who wants to sign up and then act in that area. They prioritise those themselves about what they want to work on, and it really just snowballs from there. (WHO STOPS, GSC Change)

In the context of CBEM, one member of a local governance group emphasised the importance of harnessing the lived experience of local people who possess both authenticity and an intimate knowledge of 'how fire behaved in the local landscape, how communities behaved, how agencies and governments behaved'. Another pointed to the inherent fragility of local networks in the face of extreme events, and emphasised the importance of building networks that will function in a disaster recovery space:

> It's very simple: recovery needs to start before the event. In other words, the more organised, the more discussion that happens, the more involved people are in thinking about recovery before an event, the better.

> We know that when a community goes through a disaster and they come out the other end the local networks almost disappear for a short period ... if there hasn't been work done beforehand, it's very easy for what they call fracture lines to occur within the community.

> Our networks as they stand at the moment have the capacity to withstand some events but not a catastrophic event. (CBEM)

Sometimes, however, the peculiar dynamics of communities present obstacles to community-led collaborative actions. As one member of a group of 'community nudgers' wryly observed of their regional community:

> This town has been through several iterations of attempting to do community committee groups, and it's never worked—we think because it's too fractured and because often if you try this you get into, 'Who appointed you to be the committee', or 'How did you get elected to take charge and make these decisions?'. (CBEM)

The take-home messages from the preceding observations and quotes are:

1. It is essential to win community support for collaborative initiatives that aim to tackle problems in place.
2. Harnessing local insight into community dynamics, history, relationships, sensitivities and perspectives is critical.
3. It might be necessary to both invest in capacity-building and offer skilled facilitation to assist local actors to develop a workable strategy for community engagement and action.

4. One-size-fits-all approaches to locally led collaboration should be avoided; bespoke approaches that speak to the concerns of local stakeholders will enjoy greater acceptance and be more durable.

Central control versus local control

The establishment of Children's Teams in 10 New Zealand communities offered signposts to the tensions that might arise in a case where decisions about a collaborative framework are taken centrally and elements of that model are mandated locally. In the case of the CAP, there was an evident tension between the CAP directorate (later re-established as the Ministry for Vulnerable Children/Oranga Tamariki and now the Ministry for Children) in Wellington and some of the local Children's Teams and their governance groups (see Chapter 6).

Clearly, these tensions came at a cost. Fundamentally, the tensions arose because of a set of expectations arising as a result of a core policy commitment to the establishment of Children's Teams that would be nationally supported and locally led. One interviewee told us:

> It's got to be locally driven and you have to have the right people and your community should know who they are, but you have to resource external influences strongly. So, it's got to be your way, otherwise we're just following another model from somewhere else that [doesn't] fit … we drafted our own terms of reference the way we wanted them to be. It just becomes an issue about fighting for your rights. (CAP)

Staff in the CAP directorate clearly had some sympathy for the frustrations experienced by frontline Children's Team workers and members of local governance groups, as evidenced by the following reflections on the challenges inherent in finding a workable balance:

> There's a kind of constant tension, which detracts in some respects from that idea of locally led—in my mind, at least. 'Locally led' would suggest that those who were closest to your customer and the environment that the customer is in should be the best place[d] to know how to deliver what you're wanting delivered to those people. My observation and experience has [sic] been that the gap between a national office local understanding and being able to really make the collaboration work is challenging. (CAP)

This echoes a 2015 review of the CAP that found that the principal of 'nationally supported, locally led' proved difficult to manage at times. While accepting the Children's Teams' need to work in ways that suited local circumstances—in part, to gain stakeholder support—the review also concluded that 'a degree of national direction is also required to make sure the Children's Team model is implemented consistently', thus limiting the 'amount of local autonomy possible' (New Zealand Government 2015: 14).

These tensions were still in evidence in each of the three Children's Teams considered for our study. It is probably no coincidence that each was based in a region a long way from the capital, Wellington, and in places where Māori form a significant share of the total population and a disproportionate share of the at-risk population. For many Māori, contact with government agencies is viewed through a postcolonial lens. More so than in Australia, indigenous New Zealanders consider themselves to have a special relationship with the Crown, and significant progress has been made in recent decades in creating avenues for Māori self-determination. The promise of Children's Teams that are locally led was understandably embraced by Māori elders and leaders as another opportunity to address problems of social exclusion and economic dislocation in culturally appropriate ways. As we were told by one interviewee:

> There was one [Children's Team] that had very, very good trust in the community and was doing a really good job of it. But the relationship with the directorate wasn't good because they were fighting all the time to keep that local autonomy and resisting that national consistency thing. So that was probably a very successful Children's Team but there was a lot of tension with the centre. But [the team's Director] had quite a bit of support from quite senior people locally to push back against the directorate. (CAP)

In each of the communities we visited, respected and skilled Māori leaders, elders and frontline workers (including uniformed police) spoke passionately about the importance of bespoke local solutions. And in each, the local director of the Children's Team was significantly bolstered by the support of their governance group, which in turn derived its legitimacy from the wider Māori community, or *iwi*. Having said that, the role of a Children's Team director is still a challenging one, as described by another interviewee:

> I think the director was very good at managing [the tension] but was certainly hamstrung in terms of being a little bit of having two masters because she had the master at the national office level, but also you had masters around the governance table. That is a very unenviable space, I think, to be in. (CAP)

Encourage, enable and reward local innovation

Following on from the foregoing discussion, it is important to reflect on the potential costs of prescribing a standardised collaboration framework. A capacity for innovation is one of the likely casualties of any requirement imposed on local backbone/governance groups to adhere to a mandated way of working. To a large degree, this is about authorisers having confidence in the skills and judgement of people on the front line of collaboration. It also requires authorisers to embrace the principle of 'safe to fail' (as opposed to failsafe). We believe a safe-to-fail approach to social-purpose collaboration is achievable—and the attendant risks are manageable—provided the governance framework is fit for purpose (see Chapter 6).

This might be considered part of the collaboration 'journey'. As frontline collaboration partners grow in confidence and capability, authorisers recalibrate the amount of operational control they choose to exert. These are difficult trajectories to anticipate or predict, and ongoing adjustments might need to be made. A former CAP official neatly encapsulated the process:

> So, the kind of cycle of the approach became self-evident after a time and you didn't need to be so prescriptive about the number of days, weeks, that you spend at each step. You could loosen up on that. So, people stayed within that framework. It allowed a lot more innovation to occur without departure from the overall model. That was what became a review of the manual to become more descriptive rather than prescriptive and allow much more piloting of approaches and the 'locally led' factor to emerge and become stronger.

> That has happened and I think for the better. I suppose when you look at it now after three and a half years, that happened quietly as well, that loosening up was allowed to happen. There are regional differences. New Zealand might be quite small, but there are regional differences as you go north to south about your clientele, about the services that are available, and the ways that people can collaborate together are quite different.

Local innovation is a precious commodity in social policy spaces dominated by actuarial thinking and 'big data'. Of course, innovation sometimes happens under the radar and without express authority, often because of people who are adept at recognising and exploiting opportunities presented by gaps in the governance framework (often, too, these are the very people who show the greatest aptitude for collaboration).

In this sense, innovation is about accurately reading the service delivery landscape and recognising potential points of leverage, as noted in connection with the CAP:

> There are pockets of innovation that occurred even though those barriers were evident. What we tried to do was link up those that felt more uncomfortable with the constraints with those that felt less uncomfortable and had found a way to overcome it locally. So, there's some pockets of innovation that are occurring that are leading the way. (CAP)

Our observation is that, where innovation is pursued as a 'guerilla tactic', the incentives are generally about achieving results that might not otherwise have been achieved. Since the rewards and incentives flow primarily from the inherent satisfaction of finding a better way of working, this implies an essentially altruistic impulse. However, innovation can also be a consequence of deliberate design.

Innovation needs to be encouraged, enabled and rewarded. To have innovation as an integral element in collaborative work, appropriate incentive structures need to be built into the governance framework.

Scalability

One question that arose in several of the interviews was whether collaboration works better at some scales than others—or whether it is indeed 'scalable'. Four of the five cases involved collaborations operating at a local community scale. Three of these involved 'sponsor organisations' (in this case, government departments) providing the policy framework and executive authority for community-level collaboration to occur in a number of sites. Each of these—WHO STOPS, CBEM and the Children's Teams—has adopted a different approach.

WHO STOPS

WHO STOPS, influenced by the collective impact framework (Kania and Kramer 2011), has sponsored two linked but separate collaborative initiatives in two regional communities in western Victoria, Portland and Hamilton. In both communities, backbone groups have been established to encourage the formation of local networks and to devise feasible initiatives to target the root causes of childhood obesity.

The backbone groups mainly comprise people drawn from local government and regional health authorities (with ad hoc involvement by community sector organisations). These local backbone groups are, in turn, overseen by a governance group constituted under the terms of an MOU between the Geelong office of the Victorian Department of Health and Human Services (DHHS), Deakin University and the Southern Grampians and Glenelg PCP.

The PCP representative from the governance group also participates in meetings of the two backbone groups and acts as the principal conduit for information between the three. In addition, researchers from Deakin University have provided expert facilitation in each community to raise awareness about the contributors to childhood obesity and facilitate conversations about possible community-led responses.

Both the Portland and the Hamilton backbone groups have established their own local 'identity' and have looked to capitalise on community strengths. Both have sought to identify local influencers, ambassadors and champions to help gain legitimacy and buy-in from the community and key stakeholders. Neither appears to be conforming to a particular model or template for collaboration, although both have embraced a systems model for community-based approaches to chronic disease prevention (Allender et al. 2016; Nicholas et al. 2017).

CBEM/Community Resilience Framework

EMV is the key sponsor of the CBEM framework. The framework seeks, ostensibly, to promote community-led initiatives aimed at building community resilience by facilitating self-organising networks of individuals, groups and organisations within communities that can be mobilised to deal with disruption and dislocation caused by adverse events such as natural disasters or the loss of major employing industries. CBEM has fostered a number of local initiatives.

Our study interviewed participants in three community initiatives: one in the inner-city suburb of North Melbourne, another in the outer metropolitan community of Emerald and the third in the south coast community of Anglesea. Each of these initiatives has taken a bespoke approach to collaboration that reflects participants' perspectives on the nature of their risk environment and the character of their communities.

The North Melbourne initiative is auspiced by Arts House (City of Melbourne) and seeks to raise community awareness of the potential impacts on the community and society of severe climatic events such as climate change. It operates by organising themed events that bring together artists, thinkers, first responders and cultural leaders to explore the lived experiences of people and communities affected by extreme events. The initiative uses art practice as a lens through which to process that lived experience in the expectation that it contributes to broadened awareness and insight and, therefore, resilience.

The initiative in Emerald, on the other hand, takes a more conventional approach. Its focus is on mobilising community assets to build 'recovery readiness', supporting vulnerable residents who are unable to adequately safeguard against the effects of extreme events and a volunteer Emergency Support Team to supplement formal emergency services. Auspiced by Echo Youth and Family Services, this collaboration reaches out to other established community groups, organisations and influencers.

In contrast, the Anglesea Community Network (ACN) portrays itself as a 'nudge group' that seeks to facilitate connectedness by encouraging the sharing of skills, experience, knowledge and resources across community groups and organisations. The ACN comprises a small number of influencers with links to and across the Anglesea community. Although the ACN has steadfastly resisted pressures to formalise its status as a committee or legal entity, it nevertheless works closely with EMV and the Country Fire Authority to identify issues and opportunities as well as capabilities and connections.

Children's Teams

The CAP is an initiative of the New Zealand Government to provide cross-disciplinary early intervention for vulnerable children and their families. The CAP called for the establishment of Children's Teams in 10 New Zealand communities. Our study interviewed participants in three regional communities in the North Island that were among the first to establish a Children's Team: Rotorua, Gisborne and Whangarei.

Each of the local Children's Teams has worked hard to develop workable operating and practice models, and to establish credibility and legitimacy with stakeholders. Interviewees spoke of the tensions between local Children's Teams, their respective governance groups (largely comprising partner agencies in health, education, justice, police and social services) and the Ministry for Vulnerable Children/Oranga Tamariki (now the Ministry for Children) in Wellington; and between the desire for local autonomy to develop bespoke approaches and what Children's Teams regard as the imposition of a rigid, prescriptive approach from Wellington. People interviewed for each of the Children's Teams expressed a determination to develop ways of working that best reflect the needs of their communities.

What this suggests

The three cases outlined above underscore the reality that there are multiple pathways to, and organisational expressions of, collaboration. In the WHO STOPS case, an overarching governance group exerting a light touch has been effective in supporting local actors and influencers to explore approaches appropriate to their communities and form partnerships with a high degree of local ownership while still being able to provide comparable forms of assurance. The CBEM case differs again in that the two-person team responsible for facilitating community-led initiatives has shown a greater appetite for experimentation and innovation. The North Melbourne Arts House initiative, with its emphasis on looking to artists to produce works that stimulate discussions about the meaning of disaster and resilience, sits at one end of a spectrum, which also includes more traditional approaches focusing on the mobilisation of essential community assets.

The Children's Team case, on the other hand, illustrates the problematic nature of expecting community-led collaboration to exhibit organisational and operational consistency. In large part, the tension between the original desire for community-led approaches and top-down pressures for consistency was driven by political impatience for results and the desire to realise impacts on a larger geographical scale. This was neatly summarised by a former CAP official:

> We became locked into more of a managerial approach because we'd got past that first excitement and passion and we were getting into the hard yards of 'So the minister wants to see this rolled out across the country. We need to get to more sites. The only way we can get to more sites in the time span that the minister

is specifying is to make things more consistent and to be more stipulative. Because if we give everyone the time to evolve their own local version of this, we won't get there in time.' So, those [were] very practical drivers. Big change always takes longer than people want it to take.

Clearly, collaboration can operate at different organisational and geographical scales. However, collaboration frameworks cannot necessarily be transplanted from one location to another nor is it feasible to replicate a standardised collaboration framework with little regard to local circumstances and local aspirations. A major strength of collaborative approaches is the capacity to allow for the crafting of bespoke local solutions addressing local priorities with local stewardship.

When thinking about scale, we need to distinguish between processes of 'scaling down' versus those of 'scaling up'. We can think of scaling down as a process through which a model for collaboration is offered for implementation in multiple locales. The experiences of New Zealand's Children's Teams offer some cautionary lessons about top-down prescription. Scaling up, on the other hand, entails difficulties associated with trying to replicate the actions taken in one locale in other locales that might have altogether different circumstances, connections and histories. In the case of CBEM, for example, participating communities have been encouraged to draw on local knowledge and experience to develop localised strategies without any expectation that they will be upscaled. And, in the case of WHO STOPS, participating communities have been encouraged to pursue bespoke approaches informed by a consistent methodology, thus exhibiting elements of both scaling down and scaling up.

As a final observation, in scaling down place-based approaches, care should be taken to avoid restrictive operational prescription. Of course, governance arrangements need to be capable of providing assurance to authorisers but, at the same time, local collaboration partners need to be given authority to put into place localised arrangements and processes that work. On the other hand, scaling up place-based collaborations requires an acceptance of diversity in arrangements at the coalface. Understandably, bureaucracies tend to favour more uniform approaches that are subject to consistent and comparable impact metrics. However, as discussed in Chapter 2, conventional measures do not necessarily offer a definitive picture of collaborative impact.

Final observations

Drawing on the foregoing discussion, we offer a number of observations that we believe will come into play with many social-purpose collaborations:

- *Top-down versus bottom-up*: In each of the cases we examined, the decision to collaborate emanated from an overarching policy setting and, in that sense, each was 'government-led', albeit with strong community and not-for-profit sector engagement. In addition, most depended on practical implementation 'in place' by people, organisations and groups situated on the front line. In some instances, tensions arose when the expectations of authorisers were out of step with circumstances on the ground. Undoubtedly, one could find examples of collaborations that originate organically in place and which are later embraced within a policy and practice framework established to foster and sustain the collaborative action. Conversely, collaborations that have their origins in executive-level bureaucratic decisions might struggle to accommodate a focus on place within a received collaboration template.

- *Central control versus local control*: Just as the design of the collaborative practice framework might exhibit tensions between the normative expectations held by those at the top and the judgement and lived experiences of those at the bottom who are charged with the task of implementation, so, too, tensions might arise in relation to control, by which we mean the ability of frontline collaborators to exercise judgement and delegated authority for decision-making. As we have observed elsewhere, collaboration often occurs in a secondary operating space in which participants are to some extent freed from the operational constraints that usually apply in the partner organisations.

- *Geography matters*: Building and sustaining collaborative approaches require significant investments of time and energy in regional areas where distance, terrain and community identities can create multiple barriers.

- *Encourage, enable and reward local innovation*: Related to the foregoing observations is the tension that sometimes arises between authorisers' desire to standardise the collaborative practice framework. Authorisers might argue that standardisation is necessary for the purposes of comparing performance and outcomes (for example, where collaboration occurs in multiple sites under an overarching policy framework). It might also be argued that standardisation provides a platform for the replication of successful collaborations. Sometimes, the motive for standardisation results from an insistence on adherence to established processes or operational rules (heedless of the value delivered by a more permissive approach).

- *Upscaling collaboration*: Traditional bureaucratic service delivery architectures have long relied on standardised systems and modes of intervention. For the most part, this has been driven by considerations of geographic equity (offering similar services in different locations) and economic efficiency (by taking advantage of scale effects). To the extent that collaboration for social purposes is most often associated with the pursuit of bespoke strategies 'in place', collaboration sometimes sits uncomfortably with authorisers and partner agencies— particularly those in government. Authorisers might look on collaborative initiatives as pilot programs that, if proven successful, might be rolled out at a larger scale. However, collaborations might have unique features owing to the characteristics of the places in which they are situated and the relationship dynamics at work. Although it is possible to replicate collaborative approaches, the realisation of consistent outcomes or scale economies might not be possible.

Practice considerations

1. Carefully consider all of the potential characteristics of place that might have some bearing on: a) the prevalence and severity of the social problems the collaboration seeks to address; and b) the engagement of diverse local stakeholders in articulating the aims and objectives of the collaboration.

2. Factors that might have some bearing include: a) geographic factors such as distance and community infrastructure; and b) socioeconomic factors such as levels of economic participation, educational attainment, social cohesion and social exclusion.

3. Identify potential sources of relevant knowledge and expertise both within and external to the community that might be brought to bear on: a) appropriately framing the problem/s to be addressed; b) facilitating the establishment of the collaboration; c) identifying and communicating the range of feasible options; and d) articulating potential indicators of impact.

4. Identify and wherever possible co-opt influencers from within the community whose involvement or endorsement has the potential to confer informal authority and legitimacy on social-purpose collaboration and facilitate access to sections of the community that might otherwise be hard to reach.

5. Develop a communication strategy that will speak to the range of audiences that have an interest in the purposes of the collaboration, taking into account issues such as access to digital media, levels of literacy and the proportion of the population from non-English-speaking backgrounds.

6. Prior to the commencement of the collaboration, seek clarity from authorisers/partners about the authority of frontline collaboration partners to exercise decision-making and shape the collaboration in such a way as to meet the needs of place and earn the trust and cooperation of community stakeholders.

References

Allender, Steven, Lynne Millar, Peter Hovmand, Colin Bell, Marj Moodie, Rob Carter, Boyd Swinburn, Claudia Strugnell, Janette Lowe, and Kayla de la Haye. 2016. 'Whole of Systems Trial of Prevention Strategies for Childhood Obesity: WHO STOPS Childhood Obesity.' *International Journal of Environmental Research and Public Health* 13(11): 1143. doi.org/10.3390/ijerph13111143.

Australian Institute for Family Studies (AIFS). 2017. *Collective impact: Evidence and implications for practice.* CFCA Paper No. 45, November. Melbourne: AIFS. Available from: aifs.gov.au/cfca/publications/collective-impact-evidence-and-implications-practice/what-collective-impact.

Australian New Zealand Clinical Trials Registry (ANZCTR). 2016. 'Whole of Systems Trial of Prevention Strategies for Childhood Obesity: WHO STOPS Childhood Obesity.' *Trial Review.* [Online]. Available from: anzctr.org.au/Trial/Registration/TrialReview.aspx?id=371109.

Barca, Fabrizio, Philip McCann, and Andrés Rodríguez-Pose. 2012. 'The case for regional development intervention: Place-based versus place-neutral approaches.' *Journal of Regional Science* 52(1): 134–52. doi.org/10.1111/j.1467-9787.2011.00756.x.

Collective Impact Forum. 2014. 'Collective impact principles of practice'. Available from: www.collectiveimpactforum.org/resources/collective-impact-principles-practice.

Cutter, Susan L., Lindsey Barnes, Melissa Berry, Christopher Burton, Elijah Evans, Eric Tate, and Jennifer Webb. 2008. 'A place-based model for understanding community resilience to natural disasters.' *Global Environmental Change* 18(4): 598–606. doi.org/10.1016/j.gloenvcha.2008.07.013.

Department of Communities, Disability Services and Seniors. 2019. *Framework for Place-Based Approaches Supporting Our Future State: Advancing Queensland's priorities*. Brisbane: Queensland Government. Available from: www.communities.qld.gov.au/industry-partners/place-based-approaches.

Emergency Management Victoria (EMV). 2016. *Community Based Emergency Management: Working together—Before, during and after*. Melbourne: EMV.

Emergency Management Victoria (EMV). 2017a. *Community Resilience Framework for Emergency Management*. Melbourne: EMV.

Emergency Management Victoria (EMV). 2017b. *Resilient Recovery: Discussion paper*. Melbourne: EMV. Available from: files-em.em.vic.gov.au/public/EMV-web/Resilient-Recovery-Discussion-Paper.pdf.

Griggs, Julia, Adam Whitworth, Robert Walker, David McLennan, and Michael Noble. 2008. *Person or Place-Based Policies to Tackle Disadvantage: Not knowing what works*. York, UK: Joseph Rowntree Foundation.

Gruenewald, David A. 2005. 'Accountability and collaboration: Institutional barriers and strategic pathways for place-based education.' *Ethics, Place and Environment* 8(3): 261–83. doi.org/10.1080/13668790500348208.

House of Representatives Select Committee on Intergenerational Welfare Dependence. 2019. *Living on the Edge: Inquiry into intergenerational welfare dependence*. Canberra: Parliament of Australia.

Kania, John, and Mark R. Kramer. 2011. 'Collective impact.' *Stanford Social Innovation Review* 69(Winter): 36–41.

Marsh, Ian, Kate Crowley, Dennis Grube, and Richard Eccleston. 2017. 'Delivering public services: Locality, learning and reciprocity in place based practice.' *Australian Journal of Public Administration* 76(4): 443–56. doi.org/10.1111/1467-8500.12230.

Moore, T.G. and R. Fry. 2011. *Place-Based Approaches to Child and Family Services: A literature review*. Melbourne: Murdoch Children's Research Institute and The Royal Children's Hospital Centre for Community Child Health.

Moore, T.G., H. McHugh-Dillon, K. Bull, R. Fry, B. Laidlaw, and S. West. 2014. *The Evidence: What we know about place-based approaches to support children's wellbeing*. Melbourne: Murdoch Children's Research Institute and The Royal Children's Hospital Centre for Community Child Health.

New Zealand Government. 2015. *Children's Action Plan/He Taonga Te Tamariki: Identifying, supporting and protecting vulnerable children—Progress report*. Wellington: New Zealand Government.

Nicholas, Crooks, Claudia Strugnell, Colin Bell, and Steve Allender. 2017. 'Establishing a sustainable childhood obesity monitoring system in regional Victoria.' *Health Promotion Journal of Australia* 28(2): 96–102. doi.org/10.1071/HE16020.

Parkhill, Karen Anne, Fiona Shirani, Catherine Butler, K.L. Henwood, Chris Groves, and Nick F. Pidgeon. 2015. '"We are a community [but] that takes a certain amount of energy": Exploring shared visions, social action, and resilience in place-based community-led energy initiatives.' *Environmental Science & Policy* 53: 60–69. doi.org/10.1016/j.envsci.2015.05.014.

Roen, Katrina, Lisa Arai, Helen Roberts, and Jennie Popay. 2006. 'Extending systematic reviews to include evidence on implementation: Methodological work on a review of community-based initiatives to prevent injuries.' *Social Science & Medicine* 63(4): 1060–71. doi.org/10.1016/j.socscimed.2006.02.013.

Wilks, Sez, Julie Lahausse, and Ben Edwards. 2015. *Commonwealth place-based service delivery initiatives: Key learnings project.* Research Report No. 32. Melbourne: Australian Institute of Family Studies.

World Health Organization (WHO). 2010. *Monitoring the Building Blocks of Health Systems: A handbook of indicators and their measurement strategies.* Geneva: WHO.

10

EARNING TRUST, CREDIBILITY AND LEGITIMACY

Introduction

In the late 1990s, one of the pioneering scholars of multiparty collaboration, Eugene Bardach, introduced the concept of interagency collaborative capacity (ICC). ICC refers to the *potential* to engage in collaborative activities and, according to Bardach (1998: 20–21), consists of: 1) *objective components*, which take the form of formal agreements, personnel, budgetary and other resources; and 2) *subjective components*, which are mainly concerned with expectations built around:

> beliefs in the legitimacy and the desirability of collaborative action directed at certain goals, the readiness to act on this belief, and trust in the other persons whose cooperation must be relied on for success.

The objective components of collaboration are addressed elsewhere in this volume (see Chapters 5–8) and it is to *subjective components* that we now turn in this discussion of trust, credibility and legitimacy.

The processes that enable and sustain collaboration sometimes challenge established patterns of authorisation, operation and governance—especially in public sector entities. Social-purpose organisations in the public and not-for-profit sectors extol collaboration without exhibiting a strong grasp of collaborative practice. Incorporating 'collaboration' as a box that must be ticked in grant applications and other processes is a well-established ploy that attracts cynicism (Pell 2016). Even authentic attempts at collaboration can be thwarted by institutional, systemic, cultural and attitudinal barriers.

Importantly, effective collaboration relies on partners and stakeholders arriving at a mutual understanding about purpose, aims and actions. Mutual understanding 'legitimises and motivates ongoing collaboration', leads to 'shared commitment' and entails the ability to understand and respect the positions and interests of others in ways that confirm that participants in a collective endeavour are 'trustworthy and credible with compatible and interdependent interests' (Emerson et al. 2012: 14).

Successful collaboration sometimes requires stakeholders to give up power and control, to take risks and to operate outside accepted frameworks. Collaboration leaders must earn and retain the trust of stakeholders— both internal and external—and maintain legitimacy and credibility. They also need to be keenly aware of the need to provide assurance that the collaborative process is being authentically pursued and appropriately governed.

In this chapter, we consider the example of Change the Story, a collaborative initiative whose aim was the development of a comprehensive national framework for the prevention of violence against women and their children. From the outset, Change the Story confronted the challenge of forging broad agreement in a diverse and sometimes fractious policy space. Observations from other cases will also be drawn on.

We also consider the utility of social licence to operate (SLO) as a means for framing demonstrations of stakeholders' trust in collaborative processes (Butcher 2018). The relevance of SLO to collaboration will be discussed in the context of the establishment of Children's Teams in New Zealand communities in which Māori form a significant share of the local population.

The meaning of trust, credibility and legitimacy

Before we proceed, let us first consider what the terms trust, credibility and legitimacy mean in the context of multiparty collaboration. As a starting proposition, our research compels us to emphasise that the qualities of trust, credibility and legitimacy have to be *earned*; they cannot be compelled and certainly cannot be taken for granted.

Organisations operating in multiparty settings might occasionally hope to capture one or more of these qualities by *association*. For example, when government agencies purchase services from not-for-profit organisations they also benefit from the legitimacy not-for-profits confer on government-initiated and funded programs (Casey 2004).

Leadership and legitimacy

Collaborative leadership has been addressed elsewhere in this book (Chapter 7). Even so, it is essential to stress the influence of leadership on trust, credibility and legitimacy. Our observations suggest that three critical factors—integrity, competence and power—need to be addressed. Further, we believe that 'integrity' corresponds to 'trust', 'competence' corresponds to 'credibility' and 'power' corresponds to 'legitimacy'.

To a large degree, the ability of collaboration leaders to engender *trust* on the part of internal and external stakeholders will be a function of the personal qualities brought to the role. In general, the qualities that combine to create *integrity*—such as honesty, consistency, intelligence, authenticity and empathy—will go a long way towards reassuring those whose cooperation and licence are essential to the achievement of collaboration aims. And, to the extent that collaboration leaders have the backing of key authorisers, stakeholders can have assurance that their word has currency (see Chapter 7).

Collaboration leaders can influence levels of *credibility* via demonstrations of organisational and operational *competence* (see Chapter 5). The 'soft' qualities of honesty, integrity and consistency will not amount to much without the application of the 'hard' skills required to demonstrate accountability for performance. In some respects, this is about intentions versus actions. Stakeholders reasonably expect collaboration leaders and partners to *do* what they *say*, and do it competently.

Lastly, the perceived *legitimacy* of a collaboration can depend on the manner in which it addresses differences in *power* among collaboration partners, where 'power' is a function of size, formal authority and control over resources.[1] As observed by Bowden and Ciesielska (2016: 29):

> [T]hose thrust into collaborative leadership roles in cross-sector partnerships from the private and third sectors, and citizens, need to learn new capabilities to maximise their contribution and enable their cross-sector partnership to be a success.

Collaboration between not-for-profits and businesses

A major strand of the collaboration literature concerns the forging of synergistic relationships between not-for-profits and businesses. Although cross-sector partnerships between businesses and not-for-profits are a relatively new development in the Australian context, in the United States, they have existed for more than two decades in the domains of education, health care, the environment, child care, community and economic development, the arts and public safety (Googins and Rochlin 2000: 127).

Galaskiewicz and Colman (2006) and Austin and Seitanidi (2012) each propose a four-part typology for collaborations between not-for-profit organisations and businesses. Although they use different labels, the two typologies are in essence identical (see Table 10.1).

Table 10.1 Collaboration between not-for-profits and businesses

McInerney (2015: 294)	Austin and Seitanidi (2012: 736–44)
Philanthropic, which generally takes the form of unilateral payments from firms to not-for-profit organisations, but can include cooperative service delivery	Philanthropic collaborations, in which the directionality of the resource flow is primarily unilateral, from the company to the non-profit organisation
Strategic, when firms offer resources to not-for-profit organisations and receive exclusive rights to benefits in exchange	Transactional collaborations, in which the directionality of the resource flow shifts from unilateral to bilateral and entails an explicit exchange of resources and reciprocal value creation

---

1   Even partnerships between not-for-profit organisations can exhibit stark differences in power and influence, with the 'stronger' partner generally seeking to exercise a leading role and less powerful partners relegated to subsidiary roles.

McInerney (2015: 294)	Austin and Seitanidi (2012: 736–44)
Commercial involves arrangements that provide direct benefits for both parties through the sale of co-branded or licensed products or services	Integrative collaborations, in which the partners' missions, values and strategies demonstrate a high degree of congruence and collaboration and are seen as integral to the strategic success of each organisation
Political, which occurs when firms and not-for-profit organisations seek changes in political arrangements that benefit them both	Transformational collaborations, in which interdependence and collective action are the operational modalities through which large-scale social benefits can accrue to a significant segment of society or to society at large

Cross-sector partnering between not-for-profit organisations and businesses can also act as a 'powerful vehicle for implementing corporate social responsibility (CSR) and for achieving social and economic missions' (Austin and Seitanidi 2012: 728). Indeed, much of the literature concerning collaborations between businesses and not-for-profits is derived from the corporate social responsibility point of view and is concerned primarily with the advantages to be gained from collaboration, such as profitability, competitive edge and enhanced reputation (Schiller and Almog-Bar 2013: 943).

Cross-sector partnerships with not-for-profits offer a number of potential benefits to businesses, including:

- opportunities to train employees through 'service learning'
- increased employee morale through volunteering or engagement in social purposes
- access to unique data that can help define market trends for certain communities
- the potential to develop new markets and processes
- conferred legitimacy and the provision of a social licence to operate
- support during times of crisis
- support for employee interests (Googins and Rochlin 2000: 136–37).

Not-for-profits enter into collaborations with businesses to 'augment their resources, increase their exposure and networks and acquire new skills and practices' (Schiller and Almog-Bar 2013: 942–43). Among the potential benefits flowing to not-for-profits from business are:

- access to financial resources/contributions
- the provision of technical expertise/innovation

- exposure to new management practices or training
- access to volunteers/workforce
- greater opportunities to leverage relationships with other stakeholders (policymakers, funders)
- more diverse and skilled board participation/development (Googins and Rochlin 2000: 133).

Partnerships between not-for-profits and businesses can also lead to unlikely alliances between organisations that are guided by fundamentally different logics. Differences in purposes, values and strategic priorities can result in relationships that transition from confrontation to collaboration—a journey that can be assisted by third parties acting in the role of strategic allies to the collaboration (Arenas et al. 2013: 724–27). These third parties might be individuals or organisations and fall into one of four ideal types: facilitating allies, participating allies, mediators and solution-seekers (see Table 10.2).

Table 10.2 Typology of third parties involved in the transition from confrontation to collaboration between businesses and civil society

	Allies of civil society	Neutral
Not involved in the solutions	*Facilitating ally* • has influence or control over resources of company • recognised as member of organisational field • able to transfer information and knowledge	*Mediator* • trusted for an unbiased, even-handed approach • credible for expertise • able to translate meanings and knowledge • helps overcome misgivings and reluctance
Involved in the solutions	*Participating ally* • same as above, but takes active part in designing and/or implementing solutions	*Solution-seeker* • same as above, but takes part in designing and/or implementing solutions

Source: Arenas et al. (2013: 734).

Here it must be said that collaboration with business did not feature significantly in the cases we investigated for the study, although a number of the initiatives we looked at would consider that certain sectors of the business community have a notional stake in the objects of the collaboration. For example, each of the backbone groups involved in the WHO STOPS Childhood Obesity initiative have sought to enlist the participation of local businesses and chambers of commerce, focusing on the promotion of healthy food options. Likewise, the various initiatives focusing on community resilience under the CBEM are acutely aware of the role played by local businesses in supporting disaster response and recovery efforts. In the justice space, Throughcare works with local employers to provide work experience, apprenticeships and employment opportunities for offenders prior to and following release from a custodial sentence. Although in these instances engagement with the business community falls short of collaboration, it is entirely conceivable that, over time, these relationships might mature into something durable.

The concept of 'social licence'

The concept of SLO originated about three decades ago in the Canadian mining industry as a mechanism for enterprises to gain the permission for mining operations from affected communities—particularly indigenous communities. SLO has now spread to other resource industry sectors, such as forestry and renewable energy, and is also being applied in the international aid and development space. A key feature of SLO is that it most often applies when enterprises are 'operating out of place', often in postcolonial settings, and is centrally concerned with obtaining the 'permission' or 'licence' from communities for activities that affect them.

Is collaboration the right strategy?

Collaboration is not always the most appropriate—or necessary—strategy (Goldsmith and Eggers 2005). Collaboration takes time and has high transaction costs, and, in some circumstances, there might be alternative strategies that are more suitable to addressing the problem at hand (Bowden and Ciesielska 2016: 24; Hartley et al. 2013: 828). However, to the extent that 'collaboration' has become a buzzword in public policy, many organisations in the public and not-for-profit sectors might feel the need to 'tick the collaboration box'.

For example, Pell (2016: 4) suggests that a requirement to collaborate can generate *compliance* rather than *innovation* insofar as 'the ingenuity of public servants is channelled into writing convincing accounts of how collaboration has been achieved'. Having collaboration as a policy goal, she argues, can result in joined-up documents, not joined-up services, resulting in 'an immaculate track record of collaborative working on paper' (Pell 2016: 4).

Goldsmith and Eggers (2005) summarise the factors favouring a networked governance model versus a hierarchical governance model (Table 10.3).

Table 10.3 Factors determining government's choice of a governance model

Factors favouring networked model	Factors favouring hierarchical model
Need for flexibility	Stability preferred
Need for differentiated response to clients or customers	Need for uniform, rule-driven response
Need for diverse skills	Only a single professional skill needed
Many potential private players available	Government the predominant provider
Desired outcome or outputs clear	Outcome ambiguous
Private sector fills skill gap	Government has necessary experience
Leveraging private assets critical	Outside capacity not important
Partners have greater reach or credibility	Government experienced with citizens in this area
Multiple services touch same customer	Service is relatively stand-alone
Third parties can deliver service or achieve goal at lower cost than government	In-house delivery more economical
Rapidly changing technology	Service not affected by changing technology
Multiple levels of government provide service	Single level of government provides service
Multiple agencies use or need similar functions	Single agency uses or needs similar functions

Source: Goldsmith and Eggers (2005: 51).

Hilvert and Swindell (2013) suggest a decision-making framework for those considering the appropriateness of pursuing a collaborative approach (Table 10.4).

Table 10.4 A decision-making framework for choosing a collaborative approach

Examine the rationale behind collaboration	There are five prominent motivations for public sector managers to pursue collaboration: 1. It is the 'right thing' to do. 2. Levering resources. 3. Better outcomes. 4. Building constructive relationships. 5. Better processes (O'Leary and Gerard 2013). Understanding the rationale behind a collaborative effort 'will help to achieve results that will better meet the needs of the participants and work to capitalise on strengths of the relationship as well as address goals of the proposed collaboration' (Hilvert and Swindell 2013: 245).
Consider the type of collaboration that should be pursued	Public managers need to be aware of the types of collaborative arrangements that best meet the needs of the particular situation, goal or problem at hand (Hilvert and Swindell 2013: 246). Options include: 1. Public–private arrangements involving a public agency and a private firm or a not-for-profit organisation. 2. Public–public arrangements involving collaborations between at least two units of government, including: • 'vertical collaborations' across different levels of government • 'horizontal collaborations' involving at least two units at the same level of government (Hilvert and Swindell 2013: 245). Collaborations might also take the form of: 1. a 'virtual agency' that exists as a web portal or social network platform 2. a more 'traditional' model as a new agency established 'to deliver the shared service/services of interest to the partners' 3. a 'nonroutine collaboration that only comes together on shared delivery situations on an as needed basis' (for example, in an emergency services or disaster relief effort) (Hilvert and Swindell 2013: 245).
Determine the correct number of partners	Public managers should understand why they wish to collaborate to best determine the correct number of partners; there may be optimal numbers of partners in a network, but too many will increase the opportunity for 'free riding' by individual partners (Hilvert and Swindell 2013: 246).
Determine the value of asset specificity in examining the potential for collaboration	Public managers need to understand the degree of 'asset specificity' associated with public goods—being the degree to which the infrastructure or technical expertise required to provide a public service is highly specific to that service and, therefore, unlikely to be readily available in the market (Hilvert and Swindell 2013: 246).
Assess the difficulty involved with contract specification and management	Public managers need to ask how difficult it would be to manage a contract for services with 'more difficult monitoring requirements or those that are more challenging to specify in contractual language' as these might be unsuitable for delivery through collaborative arrangements (Hilvert and Swindell 2013: 246–47).

Identify the barriers	The challenges commonly associated with collaborations include opposition from government line employees, restrictive labour contracts/agreements, opposition from elected officials, turf wars, political culture, reaching consensus/buy-in, lack of mutual trust, high coordination costs and free-rider problems (Hilvert and Swindell 2013: 247).
Identify the benefits	Among the most frequently cited benefits of collaboration are economic benefits, better public service, relationship-building, more and better ideas and synergy (Hilvert and Swindell 2013: 247–48). However, managers engaged in collaborative efforts generally do not rigorously or empirically monitor these arrangements once they are in place and so fail to systematically quantify or monetise the barriers and other costs associated with the collaboration (Hilvert and Swindell 2013: 248–50).

Source: Hilvert and Swindell (2013).

As a final note, Wilson et al. (2016: 4) caution that 'institutional voids' are not easily—if ever—filled by partnerships, and suggest that, on occasion, 'partnerships have arguably crowded out other relevant interest groups or introduced "solutions" that are as controversial as the problems they were intended to address'. They also observe that, when initiating a partnership, potential collaborators face a trade-off between capitalising on the opportunity to start with a 'coalition of the willing' or investing the time and effort to establish the precise motivations of potential partners, and consensus around the exact nature of the problem (Wilson et al. 2016: 4). The difficulty of getting collaborative initiatives off the ground is compounded further by 'persistent questioning' regarding the legitimacy and effectiveness of partnerships owing to the 'hype' that collaboration is a 'panacea' for solving social problems (Wilson et al. 2016: 4).

What the cases tell us

We look to the cases for insights into matters of trust, credibility, legitimacy, social licence and community empowerment; we hear, in the voices of people who have planned, designed and led collaborative initiatives, much practical wisdom.

Collaboration 'practice'

Although trust-building is an integral part of building collaborative ways of working, the traditional incentive structures of large organisations often fail to reward—and sometimes actively discourage—the skill sets required for the kinds of trust-building on which collaboration rests.

A number of people interviewed for this study emphasised that collaboration is a 'practice' and collaborative practice is not set out in a duty statement or a job description. And, as one interviewee in North Melbourne remarked: 'I don't think it's something that you can just pick up.' Another added: 'I've learned to appreciate the whole idea of building trust and extending collaboration. That's what I've learned from this.' Rather, collaborative working is about adhering to a set of values and exhibiting behaviour consistent with those values. An interviewee in Canberra reinforced the importance of practical collaboration skills: 'I've seen many examples where [collaboration] has been attempted and it's fallen over because you haven't had the skills, the commitment, the trust.'

The skill set necessary for effective collaborative practice has been thoroughly discussed in Chapter 4 and does not need to be revisited here. Let us reiterate, however, that organisations wishing to participate in collaborations need to inculcate collaboration skills *and* ensure that those skills are valued by the organisation. This latter point is particularly important because trust is not exclusively a function of stakeholders' faith in frontline collaboration practitioners; it also depends on an authorising environment that places trust and confidence in the judgement of those same practitioners.

Collaborative practice often entails exercising discretion and judgement outside the usual comfort zones associated with formal bureaucratic systems in which fidelity to rules-based operating systems sometimes seems to take precedence over building and sustaining stakeholder relationships. Building trust with external stakeholders means allowing people working at the collaboration front line to exercise judgement, take proportionate risks and give undertakings without necessarily having to refer every matter back 'up the line'. These observations are echoed in many of the interviews conducted for this study:

> If you're thinking about public service then the key is to be outward-facing and to be engaged beyond your expertise area. (CBEM)

> I think that the relationship that [the collaboration leader] has at the CEO level is very important—that they trust. It wasn't always so, but they've developed trust in [her] expertise and leadership … There's both a personal thing about [the collaboration leader] but it [is] also about the quality of the staff that she has as well, and that you have to work with that strategic level as well as with the workers. To me, that's the strength—that there's both. (WHO STOPS)

> A lot of what we spoke about openly was how do we develop trust, and that included being really open about things like making commitments … There was often an explicit understanding that we had to work in a collaborative way that involved trust and risk-taking and a new way of working. (Throughcare)

Credibility

Credibility is the combination of several qualities: authenticity, honesty, believability and reliability. A credible person is not necessarily one who readily acquiesces to every demand or shapes their position so as to avoid contradiction:

> It's very important to keep your credibility up. And credibility sometimes, perhaps, means doing things that some people don't like. So, getting runs on the board in terms of delivering on your strategic plan and delivering on your promises and commitments is very important. But I think even more important is the credibility of the organisation. Sometimes things get delayed or you may not be able to deliver—you've run out of funding or something—but, to me, for this organisation, it's the credibility that's … really important. And that means always sticking to your evidence base and never deviating from that … If it's not evidence based, we don't say it. And I think that's what credibility is about. (Change the Story)

A credible person acts with integrity, conviction and purpose, is able to back their position with evidence, but also accepts when they are wrong and adjusts their position accordingly. A credible person is realistic about the constraints imposed by their authorising/operating environment but also willing to test the boundaries. A credible person is not afraid to take proportionate risks, is willing to share decision-making and, having made an undertaking, follows through with their commitment. A credible person acts prudently and is willing to shift the goalposts but is also transparent about the prospects of success.

We have elected to portray credibility in terms of the qualities brought to the table by individuals. An individual actor possessing each of the qualities mentioned above can only be effective if they have executive sanction to use them:

> Yes, you've got to have that credibility and you've got to know what you're doing, for sure. And you can't be doing it on your own. You can't go out and do anything on your own; you really need that mandate and that strength from the organisation and from senior managers in the organisation ... But if you've got a ministerial mandate to do something, it really makes all the difference. It certainly does. (Whangarei Children's Team)

It is sometimes remarked that collaboration often occurs informally without the benefit of executive sanction or direction. Sometimes this occurs because the task of seeking approval to collaborate is too time-consuming and bureaucratically difficult. Sometimes, it is because collaboration partners do not have confidence that approval will be granted. And, if approval *is* granted, it is essential that collaboration partners at the coalface not be obliged to continually run the risk of having their decisions and commitments undermined or countermanded from above without due cause, because the cost to the credibility of the collaboration might fatally jeopardise hard-won goodwill:

> At a leadership level, it's giving your staff permission to share information and managing and then having trust and confidence that you will manage that risk. For some of our staff who unfortunately think their profession, whatever that might be, makes them more important and more at risk than others if they work collaboratively, they can be a barrier to doing the right thing for children. (Manaaki Tairawhiti Children's Team)

> I'd say there's another dimension that was critical to achieving [trusting relationships], and it was an individual within that constellation of relationships that showed the leadership and in whom people had the confidence that if they were saying that this is the potential and possibilities, they trusted that person to commit to it. (CAP directorate)

Credibility can be compromised or lost entirely if collaboration practitioners either do not possess the personal qualities outlined above or are inhibited from expressing those qualities because of constraints imposed by their authorising environment. It should be added that, in some contexts, credibility is also a function of the practitioner's knowledge of, empathy for and attachment to the circumstances of those whose lives stand to be affected by collaboration:

> Given the localised nature of things, [practitioners] need to have strong credibility and understanding of the local operating environment that they are leading out the work in. So, to that end, I'd say most of the time—not necessarily always—they need to be someone that's had their knees under various tables in the community for some time … I think the trick really goes back to having someone there that's got good local credibility and who knows who they need to be working with and influencing to get things happening in the right way. (Whangarei Children's Team)

Legitimacy

Legitimacy is the third leg of a three-legged stool on which the remaining legs represent trust and credibility. Without all three the stool cannot stand.

Demonstrating the legitimacy of a collaborative initiative is a complex matter. Among the broad questions that might be asked by collaboration partners are:

- What authority do we have to act in this space?
- What capacity do we bring to the collaboration?
- What is our track record with respect to the central issues of concern?
- Have all relevant stakeholders been consulted and their viewpoints considered?
- What is our standing with the diverse communities of interest with a stake in the issues?
- What issues of contention or contradiction might serve to impair our relationship with other collaboration partners and stakeholders?
- How does our history in this space and our capacity to act add value to the collaboration?

Again, it is important that authorisers act as enablers, not inhibitors, of collaborative action:

> I would say one of the key things [you] need to do early on is a bit of a stakeholder scan. So, who are the absolute key people, organisations, processes, that we have to engage to make it work? What is often a failure for these things is where key people are

left out … On the legitimacy front, making sure you've got the authorisers in mind. So, even if particular senior people in this process are not going to be engaged, at least knowing that they won't be an obstruction or, even better, are going to be actively supportive or provide the wherewithal to enable it to go ahead. (Throughcare)

It is clear from the interviews that establishing and demonstrating legitimacy were foremost in the thinking of those charged with the establishment of the collaborations we examined:

- For **Change the Story**, the involvement of Australia's National Research Organisation for Women's Safety (ANROWS) was integral to both the credibility and the legitimacy of the initiative, as was a comprehensive national consultation involving diverse stakeholders from all parts of the sector.

- The impetus for **Throughcare** came from the community sector, and a process of shared governance involving community sector and public sector partners ensured consistent communication with all relevant stakeholders.

- The approach to **CBEM** has been strongly grounded in the lived experience of people and communities that have been directly affected by natural disasters and who have experienced at first hand the successes and failures of past disaster recovery efforts.

- **WHO STOPS** and its subsidiary projects in Portland and Hamilton have derived significant legitimacy from the involvement of Deakin University's GOC and the academic researchers who have contributed their expertise to the task of building community awareness and a sense of local agency.

- **Children's Teams** in Rotorua, Gisborne and Whangarei, New Zealand, have worked hard to establish their legitimacy by reaching out to *iwi* and community leaders, and by ensuring that key positions are held by people who are capable and who have deep local connections to place and Māori culture.

Social licence

As discussed in Chapter 9, a concern for 'place' is a persistent theme in each of the cases examined. It is also a source of tension. In some instances, this entails an expectation that collaborative responses to problems will be tailored to the lived experience of the people and communities who require an intervention (Change the Story was somewhat different, but was nevertheless led, to a degree, by the interests and perspectives of stakeholders—as opposed to imposing a model from the top).

The notion of a social licence arises with expectations that the mode of intervention, and the relationships necessary to support a collaborative response, will have the confidence, trust and even permission of the communities in which it is operating. Because, whether or not those in charge of delivery live locally, their authorisers are usually 'out of place'. To the extent that collaborations are based on relationships and trust, and trust is offered conditionally, the licence exists in the exchange of trust implicit in collaborative action.

Linked to the notions of legitimacy and trust is the perceived need for collaborations to have the express or implied permission of communities of interest to engage in collaboration. These might be communities in the conventional sense of villages, towns or regions characterised by a shared identity and established social networks; they might also be 'interests' as manifest in civil society groupings, beneficiaries or users of services, institutions or even professional groupings (clinical practitioners, industry groupings and so on). Prima facie, it would seem obvious that for the concept of 'communities of interest' to be meaningful there would need to be avenues available for expressing and aggregating the views of a community, however it is defined.

The collaborations represented in the cases each exhibit both bottom-up and top-down approaches. Each is steered from below—either from the community or from a community of interest—while using top-down processes to moderate community views and shape a practicable path forward. In the case of the CAP, there is an evident tension between the local Children's Teams and governance group and the CAP directorate/ ministry in Wellington.

In New Zealand, particular emphasis is placed on the relationship between Crown entities and Māori/*iwi*. A high proportion of the population in each of these communities identifies as being of Māori descent: 37.5 per cent in Rotorua (StatsNZ 2013b), 48.9 per cent in Gisborne (StatsNZ 2013a) and 26.2 per cent in Whangarei (StatsNZ 2013c). Moreover, in each of these communities, Māori and Pacific Islander households figure disproportionately in the caseloads of agencies charged with the protection of children.

In these communities, public administration is still viewed through a postcolonial lens by Māori/*iwi* (Ruckstuhl et al. 2014) and, for this reason, the rollout of Children's Teams is seen by many in the Māori community as requiring an SLO. As recalled by a former Wellington-based official:

> One of the things that we've had fed back to us when we've moved further north is—this is particularly from *iwi*: 'Hang on a minute, this is another thing that the Crown and government are imposing on us without actually talking to us about it first.'

Final observations

The following broad observations are germane to issues of trust, credibility and legitimacy, although they also have wider ramifications for collaborative practice.

Consultation

Each of the collaborations in this study has commenced with a process of extensive consultation with a variety of internal and external stakeholders. Consultations have focused on both the framing of the problem to be addressed and the potential for a collaborative approach to address the problem. Consultation has occurred informally—for example, by providing ad hoc briefings for ministers, ministerial advisers and the executives of partner/affected organisations—and formally, in public forums with stakeholders and the wider community. To have a chance of success, collaboration needs to be built on acceptance and trust. And because collaboration usually involves a departure from BAU, it is essential to provide assurance to stakeholders—whether they are agency executives, frontline workers, interest organisations or end users. Consultation also affords opportunities to generate buy-in from stakeholders—a commitment to the aims of the collaboration and its modus operandi.

Evidence base

In each of the cases, a capacity to offer evidence in support of a collaborative approach has proved to be essential in winning support from partner organisations and from external stakeholders who might be concerned about any change to existing systems and processes (even where existing systems are demonstrably not working). This includes evidence about the nature and scale of the problem, the extent to which existing systems and programs have failed to demonstrate impact and whether collaborative approaches are impactful. While the first two are crucial to winning institutional and community support for collaboration, the last is essential to sustain the formal authorisation and social licence that enable collaboration to occur.

Expectations

Collaboration partners in each of the cases investigated for this study have struggled at times to temper the expectations of authorisers and communities of interest. As discussed in Chapter 2, collaborative approaches are often invoked when it has already been accepted that BAU is not working and there is no choice but to try something different. What this also means is that stakeholders of all types are impatient for positive results. Collaboration is not a quick fix, however; it requires a significant upfront investment of time in building relationships and trust, as well as the establishment of shared expectations and procedural norms. Authorisers, however, are often impatient for results and do not always appreciate that working collaboratively needs time and extensive groundwork or that definitive impact might not be immediately apparent (see Chapter 3).

Community empowerment

A recurring theme in each of the cases is about empowering and enabling communities of interest to assume a degree of intellectual and practical ownership of the aims and means of the collaboration. In relation to WHO STOPS, it is about creating an appetite for change and utilising a systems approach to identify intersections of interests where different actors can come together with some effect. In the case of Throughcare, it involves empowering offenders and their families to be involved in formulating their aspirations and options post release, as well as encouraging support workers to venture outside their programmatic silos. In the case of Change the Story, it took the form of engaging across sectoral and jurisdictional boundaries to lead a conversation in which people with quite different perspectives felt they had been 'heard'. With regard to the Children's Teams, it invoked the (imperfectly realised) ideal of 'nationally supported, locally led'; and, in the case of the CBEM community-led resilience initiative, it explicitly involves engaging local influencers and encouraging them to work together towards common goals.

Practice considerations

1. In what ways might it be expected that collaboration will yield results unobtainable by sticking with the status quo?

2. Do the partner organisations' executive or leadership understand the rationale and expected benefits of a collaborative approach?

3. Has a stakeholder scan been carried out that identifies the people, groups, communities and organisations/institutions with a stake in the aims and objects of the collaboration (including internal stakeholders)?

4. Has an assessment been made of the nature and history of each stakeholder's interest in the collaboration, and the nature of any strategic/reputational risks (or benefits) that might be attached to that interest?

5. Has a full and frank assessment been made of the partner organisations' own history of action—or inaction—with respect to the problems to be addressed by the collaboration?

6. Has a full and frank assessment been made of the partner organisations' reputation with the public generally, and with relevant stakeholders in particular?

7. Do the partner organisations' executive or leadership understand the importance of trust, credibility and legitimacy in the context of collaboration?

8. Are there people within partner organisations with the reputation, skills, knowledge, judgement and temperament to lead/participate in a collaborative initiative?

9. What aspects of the partner organisations' operational culture might act to inhibit the expression of the range of qualities required to earn trust, establish credibility and demonstrate legitimacy?

10. Is the organisation prepared to back those working at the collaboration front line by: a) giving unambiguous formal authority to act collaboratively, and b) giving collaboration leads the authority to obtain the consent of affected interests to do things differently (social licence)? The latter is especially relevant in circumstances in which the collaboration seeks to address complex problems that affect historically disempowered communities, including indigenous communities.

References

Arenas, Daniel, Pablo Sanchez, and Matthew Murphy. 2013. 'Different paths to collaboration between businesses and civil society and the role of third parties.' *Journal of Business Ethics* 115(4): 723–39. doi.org/10.1007/s10551-013-1829-5.

Austin, James E., and M. May Seitanidi. 2012. 'Collaborative value creation: A review of partnering between nonprofits and businesses—Part I. Value creation spectrum and collaboration stages.' *Nonprofit and Voluntary Sector Quarterly* 41(5): 726–58. doi.org/10.1177/0899764012450777.

Bardach, Eugene. 1998. *Getting Agencies to Work Together: The practice and theory of managerial craftsmanship*. Washington, DC: Brookings Institution Press.

Bowden, Alistair, and Malgorzata Ciesielska. 2016. 'Ecomuseums as cross-sector partnerships: Governance, strategy and leadership.' *Public Money & Management* 36(1): 23–30. doi.org/10.1080/09540962.2016.1103414.

Butcher, John R. 2018. '"Social licence to operate" and the human services: A pathway to smarter commissioning?' *Australian Journal of Public Administration* 78(1): 113–22. doi.org/10.1111/1467-8500.12340.

Casey, J. 2004. 'Third sector participation in the policy process: A framework for comparative analysis.' *Policy & Politics* 32(2): 241–57. doi.org/10.1332/030557304773558170.

Emerson, Kirk, Tina Nabatchi, and Stephen Balogh. 2012. 'An integrative framework for collaborative governance.' *Journal of Public Administration Research and Theory* 22(1): 1–29. doi.org/10.1093/jopart/mur011.

Galaskiewicz, Joseph, and Michelle Sinclair Colman. 2006. 'Collaboration between corporations and nonprofit organizations.' In *The Nonprofit Sector: A research handbook*, eds Walter W. Powell and Richard Steinberg, pp. 180–206. New Haven, CT: Yale University Press.

Goldsmith, Stephen, and William D. Eggers. 2005. *Governing by Network: The new shape of the public sector*. Washington, DC: Brookings Institution Press.

Googins, Bradley K., and Steven A. Rochlin. 2000. 'Creating the partnership society: Understanding the rhetoric and reality of cross-sectoral partnerships.' *Business and Society Review* 105(1): 127–44. doi.org/10.1111/0045-3609.00068.

Hartley, Jean, Eva Sørensen, and Jacob Torfing. 2013. 'Collaborative innovation: A viable alternative to market competition and organizational entrepreneurship.' *Public Administration Review* 73(6): 821–30. doi.org/10.1111/puar.12136.

Hilvert, Cheryl, and David Swindell. 2013. 'Collaborative service delivery: What every local government manager should know.' *State and Local Government Review* 45(4): 240–54. doi.org/10.1177/0160323X13513908.

McInerney, Paul-Brian. 2015. 'Walking a fine line: How organizations respond to the institutional pluralism of intersectoral collaboration.' *Social Currents* 2(3): 280–301. doi.org/10.1177/2329496515589849.

O'Leary, Rosemary, and C. Gerard. 2013. 'Collaborative governance and leadership: A 2012 survey of local government collaboration.' In *The Municipal Yearbook*, pp. 43–56. Washington, DC: International City/County Management Association.

Pell, Charlotte. 2016. 'Debate: Against collaboration.' *Public Money & Management* 36(1): 4–5. doi.org/10.1080/09540962.2016.1103410.

Ruckstuhl, Katharina, Michelle Thompson-Fawcett, and Hauauru Rae. 2014. 'Māori and mining: Indigenous perspectives on reconceptualising and contextualising the social licence to operate.' *Impact Assessment and Project Appraisal* 32(4): 304–14. doi.org/10.1080/14615517.2014.929782.

Schiller, Ruth S., and Michal Almog-Bar. 2013. 'Revisiting collaborations between nonprofits and businesses: An NPO-centric view and typology.' *Nonprofit and Voluntary Sector Quarterly* 42(5): 942–62. doi.org/10.1177/0899764012471753.

StatsNZ. 2013a. *2013 Census: QuickStats about Gisborne district*. Wellington: StatsNZ.

StatsNZ. 2013b. *2013 Census: QuickStats about Rotorua district*. Wellington: StatsNZ.

StatsNZ. 2013c. *2013 Census: QuickStats about Whangarei district*. Wellington: StatsNZ.

Wilson, Rob, Paul Jackson, and Martin Ferguson. 2016. 'Editorial: Science or alchemy in collaborative public service? Challenges and future directions for the management and organization of joined-up government.' *Public Money & Management* 36: 1–4. doi.org/10.1080/09540962.2016.1103408.

11

CONCLUSION: ARE WE COLLABORATING YET?

By their nature, wicked problems are complex and enduring while their impacts are significant and often ubiquitous. Almost by definition, the solutions to these problems are also complex and time-consuming and can be expensive, requiring focus, flexibility and prioritisation, specific experience and expertise, as well as dedicated resources. Often, these requirements cannot be met by one organisation, let alone one person, and a flexible admixture of different skills, capacities and experiences needs to be applied at the right time, in the right doses, by different organisations and within the right decision-making framework. Indeed, these problems are often best confronted with a collaborative response.

The purpose of this volume has been to identify the essential elements of effective collaborative practice to aid in the solution of wicked problems, based on findings from five case studies undertaken in the community services sector in Australia and New Zealand. In this chapter, we recap the major elements discussed and seek to bring together the essential ideas associated with achieving effective collaboration.

Typically, governments and organisations are structured to focus on specific areas of operation, service provision and/or problem-solving. These structures are usually well embedded and follow traditional models in terms of how they operate and who makes decisions about what is done and when. These structures become comfortable and habitual as we become used to hierarchical control structures and to working within a traditional organisational policy and practice framework. Additionally, decision-making and resource allocation frameworks are nested in formally identified spaces such as jurisdictions and/or industry areas. They are also enacted in the context of legislative and policy frameworks that seek to increase predictability and funnel decision-making into accepted pathways; managers expect to have control while responses to problems are expected to be within standardised conceptions of accepted practice. These primary operating spaces also impact on the operational environment and practice by signposting the legitimate modes of operation.

Government departments find it very difficult (if not impossible) to operate outside their jurisdictional remit, while non-governmental organisations (particularly the not-for-profit and community organisations on which we have focused in our cases) often shadow and service the jurisdictional framework within which government departments are obliged to operate. Additionally, innovation and risk-taking challenge government actors whose capacity to justify decision-making in accordance with precedent and policy authorisation is highly prized, especially given the propensity to assign blame for any mistakes made. Conversely, non-governmental actors often regard regulations, red tape, public service rules and risk-aversion as 'blockers' to outsiders wishing to attempt shared solutions to complex problems (Debus 2019).

Wicked problems often have the characteristics of being multi-jurisdictional and multi-programmatic; as such, they are complex and enduring because they do not conform or respond to the traditional structures of responsibility and authority within the purview of any one organisation or to the traditional policy and practice solutions that have worked elsewhere. Often, different organisations—government and private—need to pool their capacities to achieve positive outcomes. The pooling of capacity needs to occur at each stage of setting program or project objectives, development and design, resource allocation, decision-making as the program or project is implemented, and establishing the governance framework and formal reporting processes.

In this context, innovation, risk-taking and a flexible authorising environment are necessary to ensure the timely allocation of resources and structuring of the service delivery environment towards the solution of the particular wicked problem. Adding to this complexity, all of these attributes require a high level of trust between individuals and organisations.

However, genuine collaboration can be hard to identify and often organisations say they are collaborating when, in fact, they are pursuing some other form of joint effort. Indeed, they may use the appellation 'collaboration' out of ignorance about what genuine collaboration actually is.

Genuine and effective collaboration requires the coalescence of a number of attributes in leaders and decision-making structures that are often at odds with more traditional structures. As such, collaboration is often challenging, if not threatening, to traditional organisations and traditional managers as it relies less on hierarchical management structures and formal lines of command and more on a collective and genuine pursuit of the particular objective—even when that pursuit is best served by managers taking a back seat in preference to others better placed to make decisions and respond to problems.

As such, genuine collaboration often requires diffused, or distributed, leadership and flexibility, from both organisations and individuals, among whom roles are determined by knowledge and ability rather than positional authority. For collaboration to be successful, the authorising environment must be supportive of collaboration, not only in word, but also in deed.

Removing the barriers to effective collaboration

The existing business structures and processes within organisations can also impede effective collaboration. Traditional BAU can be damaging to collaboration. Indeed, the institutional and systemic barriers to collaboration that currently exist in government and organisations, together with the siloing of the public sector into segments and the shadowing of those structures by private organisations, present formidable barriers to collaboration both between organisations in the government sector and between government agencies and private sector organisations. These silos also create issues in collaboration regarding accountability.

Additionally, the rules-bound governance framework of BAU stifles both innovation and collaboration. Often, in practical terms, this means that collaborators find themselves working in environments where BAU no longer applies, where boundaries are malleable and there is little practical guidance, notwithstanding the fact that the scrutiny of performance remains intense. To work effectively in such circumstances requires the support of authorisers—organisational decision-makers who sit outside the collaborative process and whose positive sanction is necessary to uphold stakeholder confidence.

Indeed, authorisers of collaboration, while often not directly involved in collaborative action at the coalface, are nevertheless vital to its success. As such, it is critical for authorisers to understand their role in collaboration, to distribute authority to collaborators when needed and to help create processes and spaces in which collaboration can thrive.

In Chapter 2, we discussed the 'transgressive' nature of collaboration—by which we mean that when people are asked to 'go forth and collaborate' they are effectively being asked to be disruptive. Disruption can be unsettling and can sometimes have adverse consequences. However, it can also be positive and empowering and can lead to innovation. Authorisers need to be prepared to provide executive cover for their collaborative leads as they disrupt BAU while utilising risk management strategies to minimise potential harms.

Collaboration would be better supported if policymakers were willing to allow more risk-taking and help create an authorising environment that embraces experimentation and accepts the possibility of failure. This could be established by policymakers helping to create new adaptive models for collaborative governance. Dealing with complex problems requires innovation, which cannot occur in the absence of risk. Governments also cannot expect to pass on all the risk to nonstate actors.

The status quo frustrates collaboration by constraining the ability of organisations and workers to efficiently and effectively mobilise resources and assets to respond to complex problems and by creating bureaucratic, operational and organisational barriers for individuals, families and communities seeking assistance with complex problems. Reducing the emphasis on traditional governance structures and instilling a collaborative mindset in government organisations—one that allows individuals and collaborative endeavours to take risks and innovate—would reduce some of the barriers to collaboration embodied in traditional structures and modes of operation. Moreover, governments and organisations can do more than reduce barriers to collaboration; they can also take a more proactive role in encouraging, enabling and rewarding innovation.

Building patience and trust: A supportive authorising environment

In Chapter 3, we discussed the whole-of-system change to which some collaborative initiatives aspire. The wicked problems with which collaborations deal can be longstanding and entrenched and require long-term solutions and thus a long-term perspective from organisations and government. When working on entrenched wicked problems, where results are hard to measure, all stakeholders need patience and trust before results can be identified.

Because of the potentially disruptive nature of collaborative processes and the deployment of non-traditional operating modes, collaborators can be subjected to enhanced scrutiny. The problems collaborators face are also often longstanding and entrenched and, thus, a long-term solution is required. Despite this, collaborators can be pressured to demonstrate tangible impacts early in the collaborative process. Authorisers and collaborators need to share an understanding of the expectations of collaboration and authorisers should not be impatient for results, as impatience often masks unrealistic expectations.

The intangible impacts of collaboration are not always accorded the importance they deserve and are difficult to report on. Even when results are tangible, it can be difficult to attribute improvements to any one party when there are many actors working towards the same outcome. In collaboration, everyone needs to learn to share accountability. Authorisers need to understand that collaborations require intensive processes of relationship-building, establishing legitimacy and trust.

Collaborative intelligence

When seeking to articulate the attributes of effective collaboration, it is necessary to first identify the structural impediments to effective collaboration. As such, in Chapter 4, we described and discussed the attributes that are necessary for effective collaboration: collaborative practice; the behaviours, attitudes and values that support and sustain collaboration; and a supportive authorising environment, which creates the organisational spaces within which collaboration can occur. Thus, effective collaboration requires both organisational intelligence and collaborative intelligence (CQ). Organisational intelligence is the collective understanding of an organisation and the structures and permissions from leaders that need to be put in place to enable collaboration. CQ is the combination of skills and personal qualities required for effective collaboration.

Organisations with organisational intelligence will understand the relational nature of collaboration and the challenges of realising collaborative practice. They will have patience for collaboration and they will ensure the flexibility necessary to allow collaboration to grow.

The combination of CQ and a supportive authorising environment makes it possible for channels of trust and communication to be built between partners in collaboration, which, in turn, allow for broad agreement on the set of core issues and a shared understanding of the purpose of the collaboration, along with avenues for discussing the differences in perspective held by different stakeholder groups. Indeed, without both a supportive authorising environment and CQ, collaboration is unlikely to succeed.

Additionally, it is important to remember that collaborators must have the ability and confidence to challenge institutional rules and traditional practices when they are hindering the collaboration process. As discussed in Chapter 4, individuals involved in collaboration, and especially collaboration leaders, need a set of personal characteristics and capacities that extend beyond those that make up the traditional skill set of the public sector.

Formal and informal governance

In each of the cases, collaboration is subject to formal governance through a backbone group and/or a governance group consisting of partner organisations and, in some cases, organisations representing principal stakeholder interests. The primary purpose of formal governance is to provide an avenue for authorisation to collaborate and assurance that collaboration is occurring.

Although formal governance is indispensable, informal governance also serves important purposes. Whereas formal governance is usually exercised via agreed protocols or rules of engagement, and might be guided by terms of reference agreed among the parties and confirmed through an exchange of correspondence or an MOU, informal governance is more 'relational' than 'procedural'. Informal governance is concerned more with maintaining communications, listening to concerns, modelling behaviours and creating legitimacy. Both formal and informal governance were strongly in evidence in each of the five cases.

Design for collaboration

As indicated previously, examples of good collaboration are hard to find because, among other reasons, collaboration is not well understood and many multiparty activities are described as collaborations when they are not. This reality has implications for determining whether collaboration is the best response to a particular problem and ensuring that collaborations are structured to be fit for purpose.

Collaboration partners and stakeholders each bring their own, often distinct, institutional and administrative histories to the table, along with their own diverse perspectives and stakeholder interests that affect how the collaboration works. When designing collaboration, it is important to arrive at an understanding of the unique contributions offered by each collaboration partner and the ways in which the respective strengths of the partners can be leveraged to further the aims of the collaboration. In particular, the capacity to offer evidence in support of a collaborative approach is essential to win support for the collaboration from partner organisations and external stakeholders.

The strategies for collaboration need to be built from a comprehensive understanding of the problems themselves and the social, political and institutional ecologies in which they arise. It is important to have clarity about aims, strategy, process, communication and conduct, as well as a shared understanding of the collaboration's objectives, rationale, strategic direction and proposed actions—all based on a common language. Collaborative aims and actions should be co-designed and, where possible, informed by the lived experiences of the people and communities that are the focus of the collaboration. Every person engaged in collaboration has the potential to act as a 'collaboration champion', and the 'soft diplomacy' they bring to bear—sharing good news and celebrating achievements— can be an important factor in generating and sustaining community engagement.

We also identified that it is important to confirm whether collaboration is the best strategy to address the issue at hand. This requires a clear understanding of the social, geographical and historical characteristics of the particular issue. Although all collaborations might operate with a similar rationale, are obliged to address a similar set of practical and strategic problems and employ a similar suite of operational and governance disciplines, each collaboration is contextually unique. As such, collaboration is not a readily deployable organisational model or template; rather, it is a way of thinking and behaving.

Given the complexity of the problems requiring resolution and the unique context of each collaboration, it would be unwise for any government or organisation to unilaterally mandate a prescriptive model for collaboration. Instead, we must build each collaboration separately.

Importantly, genuine communication and constructive engagement are critical inputs into collaboration design. Indeed, in the cases examined for this study, collaboration leaders consistently exhibited an ability to engage in respectful conversations with a wide range of stakeholders about the purpose of collaboration and this, in turn, informed the design process.

Collaborative governance

In Chapter 6, we discussed the importance of authorisation and assurance and the communication channels that are required between the collaboration and the organisation. It is essential to establish strong management pathways to enable formal authority to cascade down to the collaboration and assurance to flow up to executive management. This requires open communication channels and trust between the formal authority and the collaboration. Additionally, it requires a leadership style different to that traditionally seen in hierarchical, rules-based organisations.

Collaborative leadership

Leadership is the bedrock of successful collaboration and, in Chapter 7, we discussed the nature of leadership in a collaborative environment. Collaboration is not a linear process but is complex, changeable and dependent on the sometimes unpredictable dynamics of interorganisational and even interpersonal relationships. As such, collaborative leadership needs to be sensitive to context and capable of frequent recalibration and adjustment should the need arise.

Collaborative leadership is not the mandate or prerogative of any single partner or individual. Leadership is not a 'role' or a 'position'. Rather, in the context of collaboration, leadership might be considered a set of qualities and behaviours exhibited at multiple levels by individual participants. In some cases, collaborations will attract people who already possess the qualities needed to establish and sustain collaborative action: the ability and willingness to listen, the capacity to understand diverse perspectives and communicate ideas, the ability to develop and sustain interpersonal and interorganisational relationships, the willingness to work with people to arrive at a common understanding of a problem and a common language around which to frame possible solutions and the moral courage and drive to achieve change. Not everyone will possess these qualities in equal measure, but they *can* be developed, encouraged and supported.

Place-based solutions

In Chapter 9, we discussed place-based solutions to wicked problems. Place-based approaches—often associated with the collective impact framework—present a unique response to problems rather than a one-size-fits-all response and are grounded in the lived experiences of the individuals and communities the collaboration seeks to serve. Our research reinforces the potential for collaborative action to enable bespoke responses to problems that are informed by, and responsive to, the characteristics of place and the specific circumstances of the people who inhabit those places.

To make this possible, it is necessary for all collaboration partners—especially those from within the government agencies that often provide resources and host the collaborative structure—to genuinely engage affected communities of interest and harness local insight. Understandably, this can be more difficult than it first appears owing to the fact that public servants are obliged to work within their agency's policy framework. For this reason, it is essential for authorisers to encourage collaboration leaders to 'curate' collaborative spaces in which knowledge and ideas can be shared, collaboration aims and strategies can be formulated and innovative local solutions can be developed and tested.

Building skills

According to many of the people we interviewed for our study, the skill sets and behaviours traditionally valued and incentivised by public sector organisations are not always well suited to meeting the challenges of collaborative action. Although the capacity for collaborative action might be lacking in organisations, it cannot be assumed to be naturally present in communities. It might be necessary, therefore, to invest in capacity building in both organisations and communities in order to fully harness local insight, identify and better align local capability, and in so doing empower communities of interest to clearly articulate their needs and preferred solutions, and normalise respectful conversations about difficult or sensitive issues and participating in collaboration design.

Collaborations need to earn the trust of stakeholders and thereby establish credibility and legitimacy. It is hard enough for individual agencies or organisations to win the trust of stakeholders—especially in policy spaces characterised by a history of unfulfilled expectations, policy failures and abrupt changes in direction. Winning trust can be even more difficult in multiparty settings in which collaboration partners bring their own 'baggage' to the table.

Collaborations are fundamentally about relationships between people rather than between organisations and collaborative purpose is about fidelity to collaboration aims rather than blind compliance with rules and operational norms. Of course, this often flies in the face of convention, especially in public sector organisations in which compliance with operational and procedural norms is sacrosanct. For this reason, organisations need to do more than pay lip-service to collaboration; they also need to proactively develop the human capital necessary for collaborative endeavour and ensure that collaborative capability is valued, encouraged and supported.

A final word

Although 'collaboration' has become something of a mantra in some policy domains, it is not a quick fix or a panacea for all problems. Collaboration is not easy; if it were, examples of effective collaborations would be easier to find. There are barriers to collaborative action, including institutional rigidity, incompatible organisational values and operating systems, stakeholder resistance and cost (among others).

Cost is a factor worthy of careful consideration. Collaboration is not free or cheap and should not be regarded as an opportunity to do more with less. The desire for economy and efficiency is a powerful driver of decision-making in all sectors, particularly in those beset by resource scarcity. And indeed, collaboration might be a vehicle for realising a more efficient and effective deployment of resources. But collaborative action does not come out of thin air. Each of the stages of collaboration entails financial and opportunity costs as well as operational and reputational risks.

Genuine collaboration requires a significant investment of time and money in each of its stages. Moreover, organisational resolve and executive commitment are needed to authorise and empower those individuals charged with the task of making collaboration 'happen'. Accountability for success does not reside exclusively with those sitting around the collaboration table; it also rests with executive managers— the authorisers—who sit outside the collaboration itself, but who are responsible for organisational outcomes.

Some executive-level managers might think that the costs are too high given the levels of uncertainty and complexity that attach to collaborative action—and in some cases their reticence is well founded. Having said that, it is also essential to factor into decision-making the potential financial and opportunity costs—as well as the political and reputational risks—of *not* collaborating. Allowing wicked problems to persist in the face of evidence that prevailing programmatic treatments are not working also entails a range of economic, political and social costs. Rather than asking 'Is collaboration affordable?', reframe the question as 'Can we afford to not collaborate?'.

Collaboration is not for the faint of heart and it is not trite to suggest that collaboration is all about 'heart' in the best sense of the word. The many people to whom we spoke—each with experience at the front line of collaborative practice—exhibited intellectual commitment, passion and personal dedication to their collaborative endeavour. They also shared feelings of frustration and occasional despair concerning some of the difficulties they encountered in framing a collaboration narrative and sustaining collaborative action. Importantly, no-one told us that collaboration was not worth trying, whatever the circumstances.

As we have observed elsewhere in this book, many collaborations fail, for a variety of reasons, including inadequate planning and problem specification, inconsistent executive support, unrealistic expectations, insufficient or inappropriate stakeholder engagement, a failure to implement measures to ensure continuity in the face of personnel changes or external factors such as changes in policy, a change of leadership or a change of government. The fact is, if people are given clear, unambiguous authority to collaborate and are allowed to thoughtfully curate secondary operating spaces in which multiparty collaboration can occur, most will embrace the challenge with goodwill and rise to the occasion.

Collaboration is the way of the future, but it is an art that has yet to be fully mastered. It is our sincere hope that this book will assist towards that end.

References

Ansell, Chris and Alison Gash. 2012. 'Stewards, mediators, and catalysts: Toward a model of collaborative leadership.' *The Innovation Journal* 17(1): 2–21.

Debus, Peter. 2019. 'How do public servants deal with the outside world: Is there any truth to the stories we tell ourselves?' *The Mandarin*, 31 October. Available from: www.themandarin.com.au/119366-how-do-public-servants-deal-with-the-outside-world-is-there-any-truth-to-the-stories-we-tell-ourselves/.

APPENDIX 1: PRACTICE CONSIDERATIONS

In this appendix, we collate the 'practice considerations' presented at the end of Chapters 2 to 10. Our purpose is to present in one place our suggestions about how practitioners might go about systematically untying the Gordian knot called *collaboration*.

Chapter 2: A new business as usual

1. Is there a collaborative mindset in your organisation? Does collaboration figure as an organising theme of your organisation's way of working, and does collaboration occur in practice?

2. Are people within your organisation free to engage collaboratively across programmatic, organisational or sectoral boundaries?

3. What opportunities exist in your organisation for employees to add to their collaboration skill set?

4. Does your organisation have any collaboration 'protocols' to guide and regulate collaborative processes?

5. What aspects of your organisation's/sector's BAU potentially acts to constrain or inhibit collaboration?

6. What would have to happen to allow for change to occur?

7. Is it presently possible in your organisation for people to 'lead from below'—to exercise creativity and initiative in ways that are conducive to the revision of current practices or the adoption of new ones?

8. Are there people who occupy positions of influence within your organisation who might be prepared to champion or lead a process involving the review of, and reflection on, those aspects of BAU that are not conducive to collaboration?

9. Can you identify people in your organisation, or in your partner organisations, who might be enlisted as 'collaboration champions'?

Chapter 3: Designing impactful collaboration

1. Establish a baseline against which the impact of collaboration will be assessed. Ask questions such as: a) What is the nature of the problem(s); b) What factors contribute to the persistence of the problem(s); c) What is the nature of the desired change(s); d) How will collaboration contribute to the change agenda; and e) What will a positive impact look like?

2. Identify relevant sources of baseline data as well as any gaps in information. Where there are gaps, investigate whether other indicators or surrogate measures might be used. Identify institutions or people with relevant knowledge and expertise to peer review existing data and advise on cost-effective means for the ongoing collection, interpretation and reporting of data.

3. Engage with relevant data custodians in each of the partner organisations to identify any issues or problems—and solutions. These might include privacy considerations, the de-identification of data, statutory restrictions, the interoperability of data platforms and so on.

4. Is it possible to enlist the assistance or participation of independent researchers or research organisations with demonstrated expertise in the problems being addressed? What sources of external validation are available to affirm the collaborative approach and strategic aims?

5. Identify and evaluate the applicability of all available and relevant tools for the measurement of impact. Investigate resources such as the Social Impact Toolbox developed by the University of Technology Sydney in partnership with Community Sector Banking[1] or Platform C—a platform created to offer support, learning and connections for people looking to achieve large-scale impact through collaboration.[2]

---

1 See www.socialimpacttoolbox.com.
2 See platformc.org.

6. Devise an impact framework for sign-off by authorisers. Have direct and indirect measures of collaboration impact been peer reviewed by people with relevant expertise? Have all relevant internal and external stakeholders been consulted? Have the feasibility and sustainability of data collection been assessed?

7. As part of the impact framework, consider how the impact of collaboration will be reported. Ensure that any reporting of collaboration impact is subject to governance processes agreed by authorisers.

8. Spell out the 'path to impact' for authorisers and stakeholders. Keep in mind that collaborations take time to mature and it might be difficult to directly attribute impact to collaboration.

9. What interim indicators might be used to validate the collaboration? How might collaboration be a driver of cultural change, changed behaviour or practice or changes in operational and/or public policy?

Chapter 4: Collaborative intelligence and organisational intelligence

1. Does your organisation have honest and full discussions regarding the nature of and challenges associated with successful collaboration, including in relation to whether or not it would genuinely support a collaborative process?

2. Does it recognise and discuss the idea of CQ, including to identify where the traditional governance structures may restrict the opportunity for effective collaboration?

3. Does your organisation have a written resource describing collaborative processes and the challenges and potential mitigations needed to communicate effectively?

4. Does your organisation value, encourage and reward attitudes, behaviours and practices that are consistent with CQ, including in relation to its performance management processes and activities?

5. Can you identify those aspects of your organisation's culture or business practices that either: a) inhibit the expression of CQ, or b) recognise and foster CQ?

6. Does your organisation value and offer incentives for measured risk-taking and forging relationships with internal and external stakeholders?

7. Are there potential CQ exemplars in your organisation who might be enlisted to act as CQ 'champions'?

8. Do the recruitment practices and reward frameworks of your organisation support and reinforce personal qualities and attributes that are consistent with CQ?

9. What steps would you need to take to devise a 'CQ strategy' for your collaboration, and how might you capture the impact CQ has on collaboration success?

Chapter 5: Designing the collaboration and its operational framework

1. Set out the case for *and* against collaboration, taking into account the fact that collaboration is not the answer to *every* problem. Would another form of working together be more appropriate to the task at hand? Is there a shared vision about the task to be undertaken or about the problem that needs to be addressed?

2. Reflect on how historical factors, the intersection of policy spaces, organisational culture and stakeholder relationships contribute to the problem/task; and identify what needs to change and assess the potential barriers to change.

3. Identify all relevant stakeholders and potential collaboration partners: who is onside and who needs to be persuaded? Appraise the trustworthiness and credibility of key agencies, institutions and actors from the perspective of major stakeholders. Consider how any trust/credibility deficits might be addressed as well as how established trust/credibility might be leveraged in support of collaboration aims.

4. Carry out a strengths, weaknesses, opportunities and threats (SWOT) analysis of the key systems, behaviours, processes, institutions and actors that need to change to address the problem or carry out the task.

5. Assess the amount of executive-level backing for a collaborative approach. Assess the potential for a 'zippered' approach that entails peer-to-peer interactions with partner organisations (taking care to

spell out the risks of a 'button' approach). Identify potential champions and influencers inside and outside all partner organisations and devise a strategy to mobilise their support for collaboration.

6. Assess whether partner organisations are 'collaboration ready'. What aspects of their organisational culture present barriers to collaboration? What aspects of their culture enhance the prospects of collaboration? Is there an organisational commitment to 'moving the dial' where impediments exist? Do partner organisations have a track record of innovation?

7. Assess authorisers' appetite for risk: Do partner organisations understand the risks associated with collaboration? Do they embrace uncertainty? And are they prepared to accept and learn from failure?

8. Assess the level of decision-making authority brought to the table by collaboration partners. Do participants have the knowledge, skill and authority to participate in decision-making? What resources are available to build the collaborative capacity of collaboration leaders and other participants? Consider engaging expert brokerage/facilitation in the formative stages.

9. Construct a governance framework that will provide: a) clarity about the respective roles and responsibilities of collaboration partners, and b) the assurance necessary for authorisers in partner organisations to embrace the kind of risk associated with collaboration.

10. Think about how impact might be demonstrated over the course of the collaboration, including indirect indicators (for example, evidence of more effective multiparty working) and direct indicators (evidence of improved outcomes). Enlist the assistance of people and institutions with relevant expertise in the formulation of appropriate indicators.

11. Formulate realistic timelines/targets for each stage of the collaboration—wherever possible, taking account of learnings from other collaborations—and, using the governance framework, ensure that authorisers and stakeholders know what to expect over the short, medium and longer terms.

12. Develop a communication/consultation strategy and associated protocols to guide engagement with internal stakeholders (that is, within partner organisations) and external stakeholders (that is, individuals, groups and communities likely to be affected by the collaboration) around the rationale, purpose and proposed strategies for collaboration. Ensure consistent, transparent messaging. Actively manage stakeholder expectations.

Chapter 6: Authorisation, governance and assurance

1. Distributed leadership, decentred authority and collective accountability are the three pillars of effective collaboration. Assess the degree to which these principles are consistent with the mission, values and operating culture of each partner organisation. Identify potential impediments (for example, inconsistent understandings about what these principles mean in practice) or constraints (for example, the statutory framework within which partner organisations are obliged to operate) and possible solutions.

2. Undertake a comprehensive risk assessment that addresses:

   • the risks (reputational, industrial, operational, legal or political) that might arise as a consequence of entering into a collaborative arrangement

   • the risks that might arise as a result of not collaborating (for example, continuation or worsening of existing problems)

   • the levels of trust prevailing between partner organisations and within organisations (for example, between business units or program areas affected by the proposed collaboration)

   • the legacy of past relationships between partners, especially where there is a history of mistrust or conflict

   • any policy gaps or misalignment of priorities and approaches that have contributed to the problems the collaboration is intended to address

   • the respective risk appetite of partner organisations and any differences in their respective risk management frameworks that might affect collaborative action.

   It is essential that all collaboration partners contribute to the exercise in an open and forthright manner, even if the conclusions drawn from the assessment make for uncomfortable reading.

3. Prepare an analysis of the advantages and disadvantages of competing governance models, including (but not limited to) participant governance, lead organisation governance or the establishment of a networked administration organisation (or some combination of the three).

4. To the extent that the proposed collaboration will exist in a secondary operating space, consider the implications for each of the partners with a special emphasis on the delegation of authority for decision-making and the provision of assurance.

5. Identify any skills, knowledge or information gaps that might in some way affect the capacity of partner organisations to engage in the collaborative endeavour and propose strategies to address these. Specify how preferred strategies will be resourced and implemented. Identify any existing internal capability within partner organisations that can be deployed to address the problem and/or indicate whether external expertise will be required and how it might be sourced.

6. Specify how and where decision-making will occur with respect to the collaboration and the level of authority and delegation capable of being exercised by the representatives of partner organisations. Set out clear protocols stipulating the manner in which the governance/ backbone group advises authorisers about decisions taken and/or requests approval from authorisers for recommended actions. These protocols need to be able to identify points of disagreement between partner organisations, timely communication of approval and/or pathways for the timely resolution of disagreements.

7. Set out the expectations that will apply to each partner organisation and to delegates participating in any governance/backbone group. These might include expectations about financial contributions, the provision of operational support (for example, operating premises, payroll, financial management, human resource management, information technology, and so on) and 'behavioural' expectations (for example, ethical conduct, conflict resolution, internal and external communications and sharing of information and knowledge).

8. Consider the need to codify the governance framework for the proposed collaboration in the form of a written instrument, such as a contract, head agreement or MOU. Also consider whether to set out the same expectations and processes in a 'mission statement' for the purposes of providing assurance to a wider range of stakeholders.

Chapter 7: Leading collaboration

1. Consider who might be best to exercise leadership roles within the collaboration. Ensure that you are selecting potential collaboration leaders based on collaboration competencies rather than on rank, position or formal responsibilities.

2. Give careful consideration to the leadership model you think is most appropriate to this collaboration. Give careful consideration to potential power imbalances between collaboration partners and key stakeholders. Carefully assess any sensitivities that might arise and how these might be ameliorated by sharing or distributing leadership roles within the collaboration partnership.

3. Benchmark your proposed collaboration leadership against other, comparable initiatives. Speak to the leaders of other collaborations to find out what works and what does not. Use available, relevant self-assessment tools such as the Collaboration Health Assessment Tool developed by the Centre for Social Impact.[3]

4. Take stock of the skills mix within the collaboration, including any gaps in key collaboration leadership competencies. Identify strategies to address those gaps and to leverage the strengths of partners. Identify sources of support or training within partner organisations or externally, including specialist consultants or facilitators. Identify potential mentors within partner and stakeholder organisations who might work individually or collectively with the collaboration team.

5. Formulate a leadership plan that takes into account any developmental needs of key partners such as the:

    a. competencies required to support boundary-spanning activities

    b. competencies required for each phase of collaboration.

6. Formulate a strategy for the purpose of socialising the collaboration among authorisers, partners and stakeholders, and for addressing and resolving any differences that might arise.

7. Ensure that authorisers understand the dynamics of collaboration leadership and the nature and desirability of shared accountability within a leadership group. Keep authorisers apprised of any issues that arise and the manner in which any disagreement about the aims, goals, strategies or means will be resolved.

---

3   To access the Collaboration Health Assessment Tool, go to: www.csi.edu.au/chat/about/.

8. Develop a business continuity and succession plan in anticipation of possible changes in key personnel to ensure that the collaboration stays on track.

Chapter 8: Engagement

1. Identify all organisational, community and individual relationships that are to any degree important to the collaboration. Try to characterise the nature of those relationships—for example, are they constructive or adversarial? Comprehensively map the 'ecosystem' in which the collaboration needs to operate.

2. Who are the internal and external stakeholders who need to be 'brought into the tent'? Remember, stakeholders can be organisations, individuals or communities of interest. Within organisations, what functional or business lines need to be on side?

3. Think hard about the core messages of the collaboration; test assumptions and consider all sources of evidence that support or challenge the collaboration's central value proposition.

4. Work hard to have respectful conversations. Think carefully about what respectful conversations sound like. Identify sources of available knowledge and/or expertise that might be used to inform or guide an effective and consistent communication strategy.

5. Identify potential sources of middle-management resistance. Which core business functions within partner organisations are key to the operational success of the collaboration? For example, key players in communications, marketing, branding, legal, finance or human relations might need to be brought on board with the aims of the consultation. What strategies are available to gain the cooperation and/or support of these key gatekeepers?

6. Who are the potential collaboration champions in partner organisations? What avenues are available to enlist their support? Are they sufficiently well placed and well regarded, both in their organisations and externally? What opportunities exist to bring them into conversations with internal and external stakeholders?

7. Are there external influencers who might be enlisted to help promote the aims of the collaboration and build support among a wide range of stakeholders? These might include community leaders, leaders in civil society or business and others with a positive public profile and the capacity to reach multiple stakeholder audiences.

8. Consider the potential benefits of using an expert third-party facilitator to assist with the tasks of communication and building trust. This might be a private consultant or someone from an academic institution who has a professional interest in the objects of the collaboration, or it might be someone drawn from a community sector/civil society organisation who has standing within the relevant communities of interest.

9. It is important that any person acting in a facilitation role is seen to be impartial. Moreover, the facilitator must be capable of earning the respect of participants and stakeholders as well as being able to respond constructively to any disagreements or conflicts that might arise.

10. If engaging a consultant to perform this role, it will be necessary to confirm the availability of funds for the purpose (and, in this regard, it might be necessary to equitably share the costs between collaboration partners to ensure equal ownership of the process). It is also advisable for collaboration partners to come to a consensus view about the brief provided to the facilitator and to ensure the brief is authorised by the executive of each partner organisation.

Chapter 9: Enabling place-based solutions

1. Carefully consider all of the potential characteristics of place that might have some bearing on: a) the prevalence and severity of the social problems the collaboration seeks to address; and b) the engagement of diverse local stakeholders in articulating the aims and objectives of the collaboration.

2. Factors that might have some bearing include: a) geographic factors such as distance and community infrastructure; and b) socioeconomic factors such as levels of economic participation, educational attainment, social cohesion and social exclusion.

3. Identify potential sources of relevant knowledge and expertise both within and external to the community that might be brought to bear on: a) appropriately framing the problem/s to be addressed; b) facilitating the establishment of the collaboration; c) identifying and communicating the range of feasible options; and d) articulating potential indicators of impact.

4. Identify and wherever possible coopt influencers from within the community whose involvement or endorsement has the potential to confer informal authority and legitimacy on social-purpose collaboration and facilitate access to sections of the community that might otherwise be hard to reach.

5. Develop a communication strategy that will speak to the range of audiences that have an interest in the purposes of the collaboration, taking into account issues such as access to digital media, levels of literacy and the proportion of the population from non–English-speaking backgrounds.

6. Prior to the commencement of the collaboration, seek clarity from authorisers/partners about the authority of frontline collaboration partners to exercise decision-making and shape the collaboration in such a way as to meet the needs of place and earn the trust and cooperation of community stakeholders.

Chapter 10: Earning trust, credibility and legitimacy

1. In what ways might it be expected that collaboration will yield results unobtainable by sticking with the status quo?

2. Do the partner organisations' executive or leadership understand the rationale and expected benefits of a collaborative approach?

3. Has a stakeholder scan been carried out that identifies the people, groups, communities and organisations/institutions with a stake in the aims and objects of the collaboration (including internal stakeholders)?

4. Has an assessment been made of the nature and history of each stakeholder's interest in the collaboration, and the nature of any strategic/reputational risks (or benefits) that might be attached to that interest?

5. Has a full and frank assessment been made of the partner organisations' own history of action—or inaction—with respect to the problems to be addressed by the collaboration?

6. Has a full and frank assessment been made of the partner organisations' reputation with the public generally, and with relevant stakeholders in particular?

7. Do the partner organisations' executive or leadership understand the importance of trust, credibility and legitimacy in the context of collaboration?

8. Are there people within partner organisations with the reputation, skills, knowledge, judgement and temperament to lead/participate in a collaborative initiative?

9. What aspects of the partner organisations' operational culture might act to inhibit the expression of the range of qualities required to earn trust, establish credibility and demonstrate legitimacy?

10. Is the organisation prepared to back those working at the collaboration front line by: a) giving unambiguous formal authority to act collaboratively, and b) giving collaboration leads the authority to obtain the consent of affected interests to do things differently (social licence)? The latter is especially relevant in circumstances in which the collaboration seeks to address complex problems that affect historically disempowered communities, including indigenous communities.

www.ingramcontent.com/pod-product-compliance
Lightning Source LLC
Chambersburg PA
CBHW050811270326
41926CB00052B/4629